Critical Essays on Steinbeck's The Grapes of Wrath

Critical Essays on Steinbeck's
The Grapes of Wrath

John Ditsky

G. K. Hall & Co. • Boston, Massachusetts

Library of Congress Cataloging-in-Publication Data

Critical essays on Steinbeck's The grapes of wrath / [edited by] John
Ditsky.
    p. cm. — (Critical essays on American literature)
    Includes index.
    ISBN 0-8161-8887-4 (alk. paper)
    1. Steinbeck, John, 1902-1968. Grapes of wrath. I. Ditsky,
John. II. Series.
PS3537.T3234G847 1989
813'.52—dc19   88-24736
                                                          CIP

This publication is printed on permanent/durable acid-free paper
MANUFACTURED IN THE UNITED STATES OF AMERICA

CRITICAL ESSAYS ON
AMERICAN LITERATURE

This series seeks to anthologize the most important criticism on a wide variety of topics and writers in American literature. Our readers will find in various volumes not only a generous selection of reprinted essays and reviews, but also original essays, bibliographies, manuscript sections, and other relevant materials.

This collection of reviews and essays traces the critical reputation of John Steinbeck's *The Grapes of Wrath*, offering a sizable gathering of reviews and a broad selection of more recent scholarship. Also included is a section on the historical circumstances of the Dust Bowl years.

Among the noted early reviewers are Malcolm Cowley, Philip Rahv, Stanley Kunitz, and Louis Kronenberger. The essays of Jackson J. Benson, Peter Lisca, Christopher L. Salter, Warren French, and volume editor John Ditsky are reprinted, and commissioned specifically for publication in this volume are the essays of Roy Simmonds, Carroll Britch and Cliff Lewis, Louis Owens, and Mimi Reisel Gladstein.

We are confident that this book will make a permanent and significant contribution to American literary study.

JAMES NAGEL, GENERAL EDITOR

Northeastern University

CONTENTS

INTRODUCTION   1
        John Ditsky

Reviews

    Hungry Caravan   23
        Louis Kronenberger

    But . . . Not . . . Ferdinand   25
        Burton Rascoe

    American Tragedy   27
        Malcolm Cowley

    A Must Book   29
        Earle Birney

    [Review of *The Grapes of Wrath*]   30
        Philip Rahv

    [Review of *The Grapes of Wrath*]   32
        James N. Vaughan

    In the Great Tradition   33
        Charles Angoff

    Wine Out of These Grapes   35
        Stanley Kunitz

    Mostly of *The Grapes of Wrath*   36
        Art Kuhl

    Careers at Crossroads [Excerpt]   42
        Wilbur L. Schramm

Graphics

    The Dust Bowl 1936   47
    The '30s Migration West   48
    U.S. Route 66: The Mother Road   49
    Arvin Camp: The Haven   50
        Don Morris

Articles and Essays

The Background to the Composition of *The Grapes of Wrath*   51
    Jackson J. Benson

The Reception of *The Grapes of Wrath* in Britain:
A Chronological Survey of Contemporary Reviews   74
    Roy Simmonds

The Dynamics of Community in *The Grapes of Wrath*   87
    Peter Lisca

Growth of the Family in *The Grapes of Wrath*   97
    Carroll Britch and Cliff Lewis

The Culpable Joads: Desentimentalizing *The Grapes of Wrath*   108
    Louis Owens

The Ending of *The Grapes of Wrath:* A Further
Commentary   116
    John Ditsky

From Heroine to Supporting Player: The Diminution
of Ma Joad   124
    Mimi Reisel Gladstein

John Steinbeck's *The Grapes of Wrath* as a Primer for
Cultural Geography   138
    Christopher L. Salter

John Steinbeck and Modernism (A Speculation on
His Contribution to the Development of the
Twentieth-Century American Sensibility)   152
    Warren French

INDEX   163

INTRODUCTION

Written roughly one-third of the way through his career, John Steinbeck's *The Grapes of Wrath* (1939) is certainly his best-known volume of fiction as well as, for most readers, his finest achievement as an author. Not only does it consistently appear on lists drawn up of "necessary" American literary works, but it is surely the single book by which its writer has made his greatest claim on the popular as well as the professional literary imagination of this era; indeed, those who speak to praise Steinbeck — as well as those who intend to condemn or dismiss him — often do so on the basis of a recollection of this single ambitious volume, one that nevertheless is generally accepted as a masterwork. It is therefore fitting that, in this period of the fiftieth anniversary of the first publication of *The Grapes of Wrath*, a new survey of nearly half a century of written response to the novel should be undertaken, and such a survey is the objective of this introduction.[1]

As a reading of the novel's early reviews will show, publication of *The Grapes of Wrath* was a much-heralded event that drew considerable attention from the press, and not just from professional reviewers. Steinbeck's reputation as a writer to watch had been established with such earlier books as *Tortilla Flat* (1935), *In Dubious Battle* (1936), and *Of Mice and Men* (1937); and the celebrated short stories that had been appearing in major magazines for years had been gathered in *The Long Valley* (1938). Appearing as they had in the midst of the Great Depression, these books created a climate for Steinbeck's first "big" book that included expectations and presuppositions that *The Grapes of Wrath* could only confirm, though not in each instance on the basis of objective considerations of this single title. In short, in the heated political and socioeconomic atmosphere of the thirties, Steinbeck's book would necessarily have been given an examination in terms of how well it reflected and reacted to its times and its subject matter — its documentary interest, in other words. Though the reviews collected in this and previous such volumes[2] often rise above the pettier sorts of scrutiny that now often strikes us as wrongheaded as well as dated, they contain ample evidence to the effect that a great many readers and reviewers were preoccupied with the accuracy (or its

1

claimed lack thereof) with which Steinbeck had depicted his Okies and their plight. This sort of focus involves not only Steinbeck's apparent sympathy for his migrants and the political implications — usually presumed, since Steinbeck had no political axe to grind, having no faith in political solutions that came in the form of "-isms" — of that sympathy, but also the crudeness and vulgarity, so-called, of their actions and their speech. The question of Steinbeck's artistry was often largely overlooked.

This "documentary" interest mentioned above was naturally paramount in importance to Steinbeck's friends and associates of the thirties, many of whom were actively involved with efforts to improve the migrants' welfare and some of whom are still around; these individuals are often naturally impatient with the sometimes loftier concerns of academic Steinbeck specialists, and the many productive meetings that have taken place between the two camps have also something of the wary truce about them. Yet the first generation of Steinbeck's literary critics themselves had erred in trying to lump the writer in with the literary naturalists of an earlier era, instead of taking him on his own terms without assuming that every time a character formulated an idea, that character's voice was necessarily identical with that of the writer himself. Steinbeck was no more a naturalist than he was a Marxist, but he used key characters to locate magnetic poles of ideal oppositioning. The reader is left to project the next stage in the evolution of humankind posited by the events of his books.

Before launching into that survey of criticism of *The Grapes of Wrath*, then, I think it instructive to consider a key and often-cited early instance of serious Steinbeck criticism at its best, albeit a somewhat flawed best. In his essay "The Boys in the Back Room" (1940–41),[3] Edmund Wilson decides that Steinbeck's real interests are in "biological realism," and that therefore the inadequacies of Steinbeck's philosophy are to blame for his artistic shortcomings, such as what Wilson perceives to be a failure to create convincingly individualized characters. Wilson describes Steinbeck's "tendency to present human life in animal terms," and claims that the writer "almost always in his fiction is dealing either with the lower animals or with humans so rudimentary that they are almost on the animal level. . . ." But even without the hindsight of almost half a century, one can argue that Wilson, of all people, fails to see the acceptance of the animal in human nature as a precondition for evolution upward on the moral scale or, in other words, that humankind might be a dramatic balancing of the animal aggregate and the choice-making individual. Failing to consider the possibility that there might be a difference between the voices of Tom Joad, Jim Casy, Ma Joad, the narrator of the "intercalary" chapters, or John Steinbeck himself, Edmund Wilson places *The Grapes of Wrath* into a bin called "propaganda novel," where it refuses to be confined.

The scholar undertaking such a survey as the present one must necessarily rely upon the most thorough Steinbeck bibliography around: Tetsumaro Hayashi's two-volume *A New Steinbeck Bibliography*,[4] which lists writing about all of Steinbeck's work in print through 1981. (The reader must be on guard, however, for a number of typographical errors.) Inclusion should also be made of the *PMLA* annual bibliography, which lists Steinbeck criticism published in each given year, and also the bound annual *American Literary Scholarship*, which not only notes each year's contributions to Steinbeck studies but also summarizes and evaluates them. Excellent summaries of important Steinbeck criticism are provided by Warren French in the Steinbeck section of *Sixteen Modern American Authors*. The interested reader and/or scholar is also directed to the pages of the *Steinbeck Quarterly* (currently actually published twice a year), the journal of the International John Steinbeck Society; *SQ* publishes critical articles, reviews, and lists of publications and events of interest to Steinbeckians, as the journal calls its readers. It is especially helpful as a source of knowledge about Steinbeckiana emanating from places other than North America, Steinbeck's foreign reputation always having been a high one.[5]

As to Steinbeck's domestic reputation, that quite naturally peaked after the publication of *The Grapes of Wrath*, in spite of what might be termed the book's original notoriety. When the fuss about the book's journalistic fidelity to events as they actually were began to die down, it left John Steinbeck a celebrity whose life would never be the same. There was a second result of Steinbeck's enormous fame, of course (and to many of his critics the first is a negative factor in the second): each succeeding title after *The Grapes of Wrath* would be compared with its achievement and found, to some degree or other, lacking. Even Steinbeck's later popular successes, such as *East of Eden* and *Travels with Charley*, were dismissed by most of the critics who had admired *Grapes*.

Steinbeck's familiarity with the California migrant-worker problem was well-known by the time *The Grapes of Wrath* appeared; he had written a series of essays on the situation for a California newspaper in 1936, and these had been published in pamphlet form as *Their Blood Is Strong* in 1938. Mention is made of these accounts in the publisher's promotional booklet the Viking Press issued on the book's initial appearance; entitled *John Steinbeck: Personal and Biographical Notes*, it was written by Lewis Gannett (later to assemble the first Viking *Portable Steinbeck*), and prepares the prospective reviewer for Steinbeck's "biggest and richest and ripest, his toughest book and his tenderest, *The Grapes of Wrath*." Though Gannett's summation smacks of jacket-blurb writing, his short work is interesting as an index of the state of Steinbeck's reputation in 1939 — before the novel appeared. After it had, it was included in Harry Thornton Moore's critical survey *The Novels of John Steinbeck*, the first book-length treatment of the author and also the first extended consideration of the new novel. Though Moore naturally uses extensive plot summary in approaching the recent publication, his assessment is objective throughout; he judges the book's worth initially in terms of its "photographic" qualities, but also notes that Steinbeck has attempted something artistically more complex: an epic dimension that works especially well in the interchapters. Margaret Marshall, writing in the *Nation*, attacks Steinbeck's artistry as an example of an unformed, "wilderness" sensibility, while V. F. Calverton took the opposite view, hailing Steinbeck's achievement in the realistic depiction of characters and circumstances in the most positive of terms.[6]

By 1940 Steinbeck's novel began to get the most serious attention it plainly deserved, but not from Lyle H. Boren of Oklahoma, who made a blistering attack upon the book as a "dirty, lying, filthy" besmirchment of the name of the fair state of Oklahoma, and this from the floor of the U.S. House of Representatives. Less ludicrously, indeed more accurately, Percy H. Boynton, in *America in Contemporary Fiction*, stresses the fact that in *Grapes*, Steinbeck had discovered his true theme, the unity of mankind in a universal soul. Samuel Levenson's "The Compassion of John Steinbeck" effectively removes *The Grapes of Wrath* from consideration as a Marxist call for revolutionary solutions, noting as he does the author's apparent reliance upon "love" as the source of the answer to America's crisis. At a time when the last book reviews were still finding their way into print, Steinbeck's novel was already beginning to be understood in some critical depth.[7]

Early in 1941 one of the most significant of the early articles about *Grapes* was published: Frederic I. Carpenter's "The Philosophical Joads." Carpenter's concern with the American dream led him to praise Steinbeck's discernment of the tension between the dream and its betrayal, and shows how Steinbeck's Joads represent an interweaving of important "skeins" of American thought — the ideas of Whitman, Emerson, Dewey, and William James — to produce "a new kind of Christianity — not otherworldly and passive, but earthly and active." Yet in the same year Edmund Wilson's classic attack on Steinbeck (previously cited) was published, and in her *The Novel and Society* N. Elizabeth Monroe sniffed her disdain for the characters Steinbeck dared to ask his readers to care about. Finally, though he insists on calling the novel "proletarian," Joseph Warren Beach accords *The Grapes of Wrath* tentative ranking with the accepted classics of world literature.[8]

Such literary assessments as Beach's are given succinct coverage by Warren French in *Sixteen Modern American Authors* (506–9). French also mentions Alfred Kazin's chapter on Steinbeck in *On Native Grounds*, citing Kazin's balanced view that Steinbeck had managed to create, in *Grapes*, a kind of realism that avoided the extremes endemic to the thirties. Maxwell Geismar, on the other hand, found himself growing increasingly weary of Steinbeck's artistic escapism, as he saw it, toward the needs of the moment. Carey McWilliams, author of the era's classic

Factories in the Fields, defended the novel against the charge that its description of the Okies' plight was inaccurate. Other useful articles published during the war years, when scholarship generally declined owing to the pressures of realistic distraction and the shortage of paper, include Barker Fairley's pioneering excursion into John Steinbeck's mode of expression, his use of a refined vernacular; and Lincoln R. Gibbs's "John Steinbeck: Moralist," which perhaps put the last stake into the heart of objections to Steinbeck's "indecency" of language, and did so, naturally, on grounds of fidelity to realistic presentational needs. Conversely, Floyd Stovall, in *American Idealism*, largely agrees with Frederic Carpenter's assessment of Steinbeck's ideological roots, but seems to be bothered by the writer's acceptance of the "*is*ness" of things. While Martin Shockley finishes the discussion of the Okies begun by Carey McWilliams at the Oklahoma end of U.S. 66, J. Donald Adams, in *The Shape of Books to Come*, appears to be following in Edmund Wilson's narrow path. B. R. McElderry, Jr., wrote "*The Grapes of Wrath*: In the Light of Modern Critical Theory" in 1944, and in it vigorously defends the novel against the charge that its "sentimentality" precludes consideration of its greatness. Harry Slochower's *No Voice Is Wholly Lost* (1945) rounds out the war years by reasserting Steinbeck's theme of the group's reformation against the common enemy. Finally, by 1943 Steinbeck's longtime editor Pascal Covici had produced the first edition of *The Portable Steinbeck* for Viking—only the second title in the series—with an introduction (non-critical, and essentially an expansion of his earlier monograph) by Lewis Gannett; the volume included excerpts from *The Grapes of Wrath*.[9]

In 1946 James Gray issued *On Second Thought*, the Steinbeck section of which treats the author of *The Grapes of Wrath* as, essentially, a regionalist in whose works the tough and the tender aspects can be seen to clash. W. M. Frohock's "John Steinbeck's Men of Wrath" asserts that the quality of anger is what gives strength to a novel such as *Grapes*; this angry quality is largely missing from the later works Frohock surveys in his 1950 volume *The Novel of Violence in America*. Edwin Berry Burgum's "The Sensibility of John Steinbeck" appeared in *Science and Society* that year (published as part of a book the following year); Burgum argues that Steinbeck's writing is often marred by a "brutality" that only in *Grapes* is redeemed by a "new optimism" that arises out of his characters' educational experience. Finally, Woodburn O. Ross traces the similarities—and differences—of Steinbeck's thinking and that of Auguste Comte, discussing *Grapes* along with the other Steinbeck writings then available.[10]

Nineteen forty-seven saw the publication of an important essay on *Grapes* alone: Chester E. Eisinger's "Jeffersonian Agrarianism in *The Grapes of Wrath*." Eisinger demonstrates how deeply Jefferson's ideas that persons derive their integrity from their relationship with the land permeate Steinbeck's novel, but then observes that agrarianism is, nonetheless, "an anachronism in the midst of the machine-made culture of twentieth-century America." Leo Gurko's survey of the literature of the American thirties, *The Angry Decade*, finds that *Grapes* typifies the era's twin themes of social consciousness and flight from unbearable reality. In "John Steinbeck, Californian," Freeman Champney argues that Steinbeck's strengths and weaknesses alike can be traced to his origins, but acknowledges that *Grapes* overcomes the latter in being "a big book, a great book." Donald Weeks's "Steinbeck Against Steinbeck" blames Steinbeck's inadequate absorption of the ideas of his marine-biologist friend Edward F. Ricketts for the weakness of his thinking. Another article by Woodburn Ross, "John Steinbeck: Naturalism's Priest," claims that Steinbeck has constructed a curious religion of the acceptance of nature as it is — "holy," as *Grapes*'s Jim Casy put it — while also embracing scientific inquiry into that nature. In 1948 Frederick Bracher praised this latter aspect of Steinbeck's thinking in his "Steinbeck and the Biological View of Man," asserting that Steinbeck's writing weakens when it forsakes the scientific for the mystical. In 1949 Blake Nevius showed how Steinbeck creates characters freed of the inhibitions of imposed values. Increasingly, critics during the late forties were looking for the sources of Steinbeck's system of thought and belief — and assuming that finding one was finding all.[11]

The first decade of criticism of *The Grapes of Wrath* ended, and the new decade of the fifties began, with something like a period of apathy toward Steinbeck's major achievement. Michael F. Moloney echoes Woodburn Ross's paralleling of Steinbeck and Comte — and includes some others — in his *Catholic World* piece in 1950. Alexander Cowie briefly praises *Grapes* a year later for its innovative technical features. George F. Whicher indicts Steinbeck for "cleverness" in his chapter on the writer in *The Literature of the American People*, while Frederick Hoffman asserts the often-made charge of sentimentality against Steinbeck's works after *In Dubious Battle*. Bernard Bowron rather famously shackles the novel with the appellation " 'wagons west' romance" in the *Colorado Quarterly*, a journal that a year later announced the arrival of Warren French upon the Steinbeck scene (see his essay in this volume) with a skillfully argued attack upon Bowron's dismissal of the novel as a variation on a popular-entertainment theme. By the mid-fifties, however, Steinbeck studies, especially those devoted to his most famous work, had entered doldrums that would never find themselves repeated.[12]

In 1956 Charles Child Walcutt's *American Literary Naturalism: A Divided Stream* analyzes Steinbeck's concern with matters of form; Walcutt notes that Steinbeck never lets himself be bound by the patterning of naturalistic theory, whether or not the critic realizes that the novelist may not have been a naturalist at all. Things really began to pick up in 1957 with the publication of the Tedlock and Wicker critical anthology (see note 2), which included some materials on *Grapes* and some writing by Steinbeck himself. George Bluestone analyzed the novel in discussing the process by which the novel was turned into a motion picture in his volume *Novels into Film*. Peter Lisca's "*The Grapes of Wrath* as Fiction," which appeared in *PMLA*, satisfies its stated purpose of treating the novel as a serious literary accomplishment rather than as some sort of proletarian document. Lisca concludes that because of its carefully crafted thematic unity, Steinbeck "was able to create a well-made and emotionally compelling novel out of materials which in most other hands have resulted in sentimental propaganda." Lisca expanded his remarks for his pioneering critical study of the bulk of Steinbeck's career output, *The Wide World of John Steinbeck*, published in 1958.[13]

Lisca's book-length study, the first to give professional literary-critical attention to Steinbeck's oeuvre to date, would have been enough reason to celebrate the importance of 1958 in Steinbeck studies, but it was not the only major contribution of that year. George De Schweinitz contributed a note to an ongoing debate in the pages of *College English* over the "Christian" values of *Grapes*, a debate begun by a key article by Martin S. Shockley in 1956 and replied to by Eric W. Carlson about a year afterward. R. W. B. Lewis used a related approach to discuss "The Picaresque Saint," as he referred to Tom Joad in discussing what he saw as Steinbeck's overall failures at character delineation. A brief but concise note on a subject much written about, "On the Ending of *The Grapes of Wrath*" was published by Theodore Pollock in *Modern Fiction Studies*. Lastly, Frank H. Jackson approached the novel from the standpoint of "Economics in Literature" in the *Duquesne Review*.[14]

With 1959 came Walter Fuller Taylor's "*The Grapes of Wrath* Reconsidered," which argued that heretofore Steinbeck's critics had been imposing their own readings upon the work instead of assessing it in its own terms; hence, a gap had grown up between the book's substance and the standard responses to it, a gap that the criticism of the future would have to address. Yet the tendency to try to fit a writer into some "stream" or other is an ongoing one, and in 1961 Edwin T. Bowden (in *The Dungeon of the Heart*) found the main theme of *Grapes* to be that traditional American one of the problem of isolation. In 1961 as well, the second important original volume of criticism of Steinbeck appeared: Warren French's *John Steinbeck*, in Twayne's United States Authors Series. French's chapter on *Grapes*, "The Education of the Heart" indicates by its very title the theme he sees as major. French's essay is lucid and—as his later writing proves—well able to adjust to developments in the critic's viewpoint.[15]

In the following year, 1962, another series title appeared, F. W. Watt's *John Steinbeck*. While this volume is considerably slimmer than French's and has little time to make an impression, its usefulness for the student writer is far above that of the "notes" and "study guide" items that are not worth mentioning here. *College English* continued to plumb the biblical depths of *Grapes* by printing pieces by Gerald Cannon, H. Kelly

Crockett, and Charles T. Dougherty in its December 1962 issue, with a response from T. F. Dunn following half a year later. (There is also a short item dating from this year by Enno Klammer on the novel's parallels with Exodus.) A chapter in Edwin M. Moseley's volume (on Christ figures in the modern novel) is devoted to Steinbeck's depiction of the "increased strength" the people "achieve through Casy's martyrdom." And Arthur Mizener, who had by this time lost all patience with Steinbeck and his works — all of them — asked, tendentiously enough, "Does a Moral Vision of the Thirties Deserve a Nobel Prize?" in the *New York Times Book Review* on the occasion of that award. Mizener, never a man to soften his language, indicted Steinbeck as a writer who, "in his best books, watered down by tenth-rate philosophizing" his "real but limited talent." Seldom have a prize-winning author's public achievements so differed from the assessments of many of his critics than on the occasion of Steinbeck's reception of the Nobel Prize in 1962; he could do nothing right, it seemed, and to critics like Mizener it had become a "melancholy task" to reread him.[16]

Walter Allen wrote a characteristically balanced appraisal of *Grapes* for his 1963 survey of major fiction in modern Britain and the U.S. Like F. W. Watt's coverage, Allen's is primarily a consolidation of what has gone before. Another book that appeared in this same year, Joseph Fontenrose's *John Steinbeck: An Introduction and Interpretation*, was part of another rigid-format series, in this case Holt, Rinehart and Winston's "American Authors and Critics" list. Fontenrose, professionally a classicist, is especially good at noting the pervasive presence of themes and motifs from classic texts in *Grapes*. Conversely, Robert J. Griffin and William A. Freedman provided a specialized treatment of machine/animal motifs in *Grapes* in the same year. J. Paul Hunter defended the novel against those who were beginning to write off Steinbeck's significance entirely by showing how its themes come to an artistically hopeful final focus. Lastly, Warren French's *A Companion to "The Grapes of Wrath"* appeared in the same year, the first collection of original reviews and essays (see note 2) dealing exclusively with this single but acknowledgedly singular effort. French's collection brought a new perspective to the study of a book that all too suddenly appeared to have turned a quarter of a century old.[17]

Criticism of *The Grapes of Wrath* entered its second quarter-century with the publication of Robert Detweiler's essay "Christ and the Christ Figure in American Fiction," which brought together the insights offered by previous articles on the subject. Another specialized view was provided by Walter Rundell, Jr., in his "*The Grapes of Wrath*: Steinbeck's Image of the West," also in 1964. James Woodress's "John Steinbeck: Hostage to Fortune" considers the Nobel Prize winner's career as falling into three "phases," the success of *Grapes* being a crucial factor in this evolution and, as Woodress saw it, decline. A year later *Modern Fiction Studies* published a special Steinbeck issue that included Jules Chametzky's ambivalent reconsideration of Steinbeck's choice of endings for the novel, appropriately entitled "The Ambivalent Endings of *The Grapes of Wrath*"; James W. Tuttleton's survey of Soviet reaction to the publication of *The Grapes of Wrath*; and Peter Lisca's blaming of Steinbeck's "decline" after the war on his abandonment of the biological view of man that animates earlier books like *Grapes*. In 1966 W. J. Stuckey contributed the novel view that *Grapes* was but a variation on the traditional theme that work provides value — and solutions. Warren French's *The Social Novel at the End of an Era* neatly fits *Grapes* into the context of its times. Though *Grapes* criticism was becoming increasingly specialized in nature, some writers were still approaching the work as if for the very first time. In 1967 the son of Pascal Covici, Steinbeck's editor and confidant, wrote a chapter for another volume edited by Warren French. In "John Steinbeck and the Language of Awareness," Pascal Covici, Jr., argued that the strengths of Steinbeck's volumes such as *Grapes* lay in their presentation of his characters' struggle for consciousness of their true conditions (echoing French, of course). Paul McCarthy contributed an article on "House and Shelter as Symbol" in the novel.[18]

The thirtieth anniversary of the novel's appearance in print led to the reconsideration piece "The Radical Humanism of John Steinbeck" by Daniel Aaron in *Saturday Review*. Finer tuning was provided, also in 1968, by Chris Browning's "Grape Symbolism in *The Grapes of Wrath*" in *Discourse*. Tetsumaro Hayashi, a Japanese-American Shakespeare scholar whose avid interest helped lead to the foundation of the Steinbeck Society, wrote on "The Function of the Joad Clan in *The Grapes of Wrath*" for *Modern Review*. Leonard A. Slade, Jr., returned once again to the subject of biblical allusions, a vein of study beginning to show signs of running out. Perhaps the year's biggest event, however, was the appearance of the Crowell Casebook on the novel edited by Agnes McNeill Donohue (see note 2). This enormously useful collection is a landmark in the specialized study of Steinbeck's most attended-to single work. The following year Bryant N. Wyatt surveyed Steinbeck's "protest novels" under the rubric "experimentation as technique." Also in 1969 an important critical volume was written by Lester J. Marks. Entitled *Thematic Design in the Novels of John Steinbeck*, Marks's study echoed Covici and French in pointing to *Grapes*'s characters' arrival at new perceptions, chief among them the one that "the physical unity of all things" can provide "faith in a vast spiritual unity." Marks's book was also the first to attempt an overview of the entire career of the recently deceased novelist.[19]

The 1970s began with something of a second wind being given to *Grapes* criticism. Mary Washington Clarke issued yet another short note on the ending of the novel as a bridging of the "generation gap." Arnold F. Delisle devoted an entire article to the function of the turtle chapter (3) alone. Richard B. Hauck included Jim Casy in yet another survey of Christ figures in modern writing. Jack Nimitz discussed *Grapes* from the standpoint of that then-current buzz-word, "ecology." Collin G. Matton gave brief consideration to the importance of water imagery to the book's conclusion. As might be expected, the pages devoted to *Grapes* in Richard O'Connor's biography for younger readers are of little critical value. Finally, but most important, John Clark Pratt published a monograph on Steinbeck as part of a "Contemporary Writers in Christian Perspective" series. His discussion of *Grapes* is interwoven throughout his essay, but his cogent and open-minded argument praises the novel overall, and points to the final chapter's "syncretic allegory" as a lucid expression of "the paradox that Steinbeck is trying to delineate."[20]

The year 1971 proved no less busy for the workers in what Warren French calls Steinbeck's vineyard. J. Wilkes Berry contributed a short piece on the theme of endurance, while James P. Degnan included his 1970 Corvallis, Oregon, paper on Steinbeck's antagonism toward California's large landowners in a collection of that conference's proceedings. Robert B. Downs returned to the novel's fidelity to documentary fact in a chapter in his *Famous American Books*. And in a section devoted to *Grapes*, Leonard Lutwack included Steinbeck in his critical volume on "heroic fiction." In this year as well, Pascal Covici, Jr., compiled a revised *Portable Steinbeck* that, though it tended to place new emphasis on the later works, nonetheless included some seven selections from *The Grapes of Wrath*. Another series title, James Gray's issue for the University of Minnesota Pamphlets on American Writers, treats *Grapes*'s centrality in Steinbeck's canon as owing to its being an "admirably modeled work of art having impressive size and just proportion, movement, balance, symmetry, and power," though he faults the book's ending scene for "excessive strain."[21]

Sam Bluefarb, a year later, treated the Joad family in terms of the "escape" motif, while Peter Lisca discussed "the dynamics of community" in the novel in a piece included here. Lisca's festschrift item was followed by his own edition of the novel itself (see note 2), completely reset and accompanied by critical articles to form an invaluable addition to the Viking Critical Library series. Two of the articles printed for the first time in this collection were delivered at the University of Connecticut's conference on *Grapes* in 1969: that of Pascal Covici, Jr., which emphasized the importance of work in the thinking of Steinbeck and his characters as well; and that of John R. Reed, who defends the novel against those who do not agree that its artistry transforms its rude materials into a spiritually satisfying achievement. Betty Perez, in a chapter appearing for the first time in the Lisca collection, discusses the symbolism of house and home in a deliberately different way than does Paul McCarthy in the aforementioned article. Rather belatedly, Sol Zollman treated the book's polemical dimension in an article in a Canadian literary/political journal. Comparing Steinbeck and Lawrence, Reloy Garcia's monograph attempts to explain Steinbeck's post-*Grapes* decline as a writer. Robert Murray Davis's

general collection of Steinbeck essays for Prentice-Hall's Twentieth Century Views series also appeared in 1972.[22]

Few new articles on *Grapes* appeared during 1973, but it is worth
mentioning A. Carl Bredahl's brief consideration of the "drinking metaphor" (and the liquids involved) in the novel in *Steinbeck Quarterly*,
certainly a novel topic. W. Richard Fossey looked at the novel as "the end
of the western dream," since the state from which the Joads migrated was
the last one to be opened for settlement. Amusingly, Kathleen Farr Elliott
apparently solved the mysterious appearance in *Grapes* of the legend
"IITYWYBAD." I contributed yet another discussion of the book's ending
to *Agora* (included in this volume), adumbrating my later theory that
Steinbeck structures certain key scenes as a dramatist might. Mary Ellen
Caldwell gave us, in the same year, a fresh look at the functioning of the
intercalary chapters, especially the famous chapter 15 "truck stop" incident. During this year as well, Richard Astro published the fullest book-
length account written of the interrelationship of Steinbeck and Edward
F. Ricketts both as men and as sources of ideas. Although Astro has
retreated somewhat since on the subject of the novelist's indebtedness to
the marine biologist, his book still makes for patently seminal reading.
Like French, DeMott, myself, and others, Lawrence William Jones
continued giving new attention to Steinbeck's notions of narrative
technique—as "fabulist"—in a monograph written for the Steinbeck
Society's monograph series, though *Grapes* is cited as a poor model for this
approach.[23]

The new focus on Steinbeck's formal structures was continued during
1974 with Howard Levant's book-length consideration of Steinbeck's total
book-length output from a strictly formalist standpoint. Levant rigidly
characterizes the book's final quarter as "a hollowed rhetoric, a manipu-
lated affirmation, a soft twist of insistent sentiment." Despite its salient
preconceptions, Levant's treatise subjects Steinbeck's works to their most
rigorous examinations ever, and *Grapes* largely withstands its own assault.
A fascinating illustrated discussion of the likely influence on the novelist
of Farm Security Administration–sponsored photographers, especially
Dorothea Lange, was contributed by D. G. Kehl to the photography
journal *Image*. Because it radically rejects the appropriateness of the
"turtle" motif, Stuart L. Burns's piece on the ending is worth considering.
And the indefatigable Warren French added a chapter to Tetsumaro
Hayashi's *Study Guide* to the major Steinbeck works.[24]

Nineteen seventy-five proved to be yet another banner year for studies
of *The Grapes of Wrath*, though at times it must have seemed hard to tell
exactly what it said on the banner. Duane R. Carr gave a short Blakean
reading to the volume, while Martha Heasley Cox used the unpublished
journals (currently being edited by Robert DeMott) Steinbeck kept during
the writing of *Grapes* to establish how carefully Steinbeck planned for his

final tableau. A 1974 "Steinbeck and the Sea" Conference paper by historian William Appleman Williams, "Steinbeck in Perspective," takes a cold-eyed look at the writer as a mirror of thirties America—weaknesses and all. Warren French considered the aftermath of the novel's publication for *Steinbeck Quarterly* and also treated it in rewriting his Twayne volume: *Grapes* was, he decided, "neither riddle nor tragedy—it is an epic comedy of the triumph of the 'holy spirit.' " French's second critique showed a remarkable capacity for critical growth, and it accordingly outshines such 1975 comparative studies as Linda Ray Pratt's pairing of Steinbeck and Agee—arguing that Steinbeck transmuted historical reality into myth by fiat—and Stanley Trachtenberg's pairing of Steinbeck and Nathanael West—claiming that Steinbeck's holding to the possibility of social progress cost him dearly with the critics of the thirties. A short but pioneering study of Steinbeck's female characters, including those in *Grapes*, was contributed by Sandra Beatty. Finally, a chapter in Nelson Valjean's biographical account of Steinbeck's "California years" deals with the writing of *Grapes*, but it is noncritical in nature and is in any event superseded by the Jackson J. Benson chapter included here.[25]

In 1976 Benson, then at work on the authorized biography of Steinbeck, issued some of his findings on the background to the writing of the novel. Horst Groene, giving special focus to the character of Al instead of Tom, discussed Steinbeck's positioning between the poles of agrarianism and technological advancement in an article in *Southern Review*, while Lewis Moore Hopfe returned to the apparently inexhaustible vein of biblical symbolism in the novel. A title that tells nearly all is Floyd C. Watkins's "Flat Wine from *The Grapes of Wrath*" in another festschrift volume. Sylvia Jenkins Cook, in her *From Tobacco Road to Route 66: The Southern Poor White in Fiction*, showed how Steinbeck transformed the poor-white stereotype (while not, strictly speaking, writing about it) by depoliticizing it. Yet another volume of conference proceedings, this one cued to the American Bicentennial year, included both Kenneth D. Swan's discussion of *Grapes* as an index to the values Steinbeck searched for in his country, and Warren French's provocative thesis (included here) that most of the novels following *Grapes* represent "a complete swing of the pendulum from his foreshadowing of Post-Modernism to his embracing of a Pre-Modernist, Victorian compromise with traditional establishments. . . ." But the year's major contribution was British critic Roy S. Simmonds's (see his essay in this volume) *Steinbeck's Literary Achievement*. Simmonds's judicious assessment of Steinbeck's standing was both concisely expressed and also free of many of the standing assumptions that weaken some American criticism.[26]

The next two years witnessed the start of a brief falling-off of critical focus on *The Grapes of Wrath*. James D. Brasch shows good reason to look beyond Jim Casy's initials to an even greater kinship with the author of Ecclesiastes. Martha Heasley Cox continued to exploit her knowledge of the *Grapes* journals for a First International Steinbeck Congress (Kyushu University, Fukuoka, Japan) paper on the real and fictional governmental camps Steinbeck knew. Miles Donald discussed the book in his survey *The American Novel in the Twentieth Century*. Finally, Peter Lisca, like Warren French before him, rewrote his original full-length volume of criticism of all of Steinbeck's fiction, calling it *John Steinbeck: Nature and Myth*. While Lisca's new presentation is as strong as ever in support of the novel's greatness, the focus of the new volume necessarily requires pinning that greatness to the exploitation of biblical motifs; however, Lisca's summary of the main themes and devices used in the book is also a model of concision.[27]

The next couple of years, 1979–80, were moderately active ones so far as criticism of *Grapes* went. My recapitulation of the novel's first forty years for *Southern Humanities Review* (actually commissioned for a series of *The New Republic* retrospectives) tied the book's enduring power to the great American "road" theme, while calling for new directions in criticism. Mimi Reisel Gladstein, in Hayashi's *Steinbeck's Women*, continued the study of what she calls the "indestructible woman" in Steinbeck that would later culminate in the article on Ma Joad included here, as well as in a book that represents a revision of an earlier thesis. Thomas Kiernan's biography of the writer appeared in 1979, but its chapters on the period of the creation of *Grapes* are not of any particular critical value, and in any event they have been wholly superseded by the account given in Jackson J. Benson's massive biography (1984), essentially present in this collection. From the following year, Paul McCarthy's series title for Frederick Ungar is of interest; its *Grapes* chapter faults the novel whenever "allegorical emphasis . . . dilutes the realism." As if things were going back to their beginnings, this year's studies also included Patrick B. Mullen's consideration of the novel's folkloric aspects. And John Vassilowitch, Jr., manages to squeeze a bit of mileage out of an anachronism in the truck-stop chapter.[28]

Four varied and useful articles on *The Grapes of Wrath* appeared in 1981. Mimi Gladstein strengthened her coverage of Ma Joad by comparing her to Hemingway's Pilar (in *For Whom the Bell Tolls*) in *Steinbeck Quarterly*. Reloy Garcia viewed the novel as the story of a failed quest for an El Dorado that instead became the story of a growth of consciousness in some of the characters. Third is Christopher L. Salter's contribution to a symposium of geographers; this piece's unique approach warranted its inclusion in this volume. And last is Paul McCarthy's article on the presentation of the rural family in depression writing.[29]

The fifth decade of criticism of *The Grapes of Wrath* hit full stride in 1982, and the pieces published that year nicely index the critical concerns of the eighties. Sylvia Cook, writing in the *Steinbeck Quarterly*, took a long look back at the political climate of the thirties and concluded that Steinbeck had achieved a result more artful than any of the committedly proletarian writers of the period. Helen Lojek called Jim Casy a "Politico of the New Jerusalem," arguing that the former preacher fits into the American tradition of adapting religious uses to primarily secular ends. Warren Motley used the standpoint of the eighties to point out the centrality of the progression from patriarchy to matriarchy in the novel. Robert Con Davis, in the introduction to his Prentice-Hall collection of essays (see note 2), makes a balanced appraisal of the major criticism of the novel to date, pointing to the shift from interest in the work's documentary qualities to a concern for its artistic structure, eventually arriving at a realization that the book belongs in the broad tradition of American romantic literature rather than elsewhere. Davis also prints for the first time an essay by Joan Hedrick, whose feminist complaint is that Steinbeck failed to deal realistically with the "myth of the earth mother," and thereby failed to write "a truer, more political, and more humanistic book." Apparently a wave of concerns flowing out of the Modern Language Association conventions of the prior decade had at last washed over *The Grapes of Wrath* by 1982, leaving it none the worse off for its ordeal.[30]

In 1983 F. Odun Balogun compared Steinbeck's work to that of James T. Ngugi (*Petals of Blood*) from the standpoint of supposedly shared proletarian origins and sympathies. Joyce Compton Brown contributed a tidbit to *Explicator*, while Patrick W. Shaw discussed the stages of Tom Joad's consciousness-raising (in psychological terms) in *Steinbeck Quarterly*. A volume by Brian St. Pierre on Steinbeck's "California Years" focuses sharply on the novel's biographical underpinnings. Another study with a regional basis is Stoddard Martin's *California Writers: Jack London, John Steinbeck, The Tough Guys*—uneven but lively. Also in 1983 Mary Allen's *Animals in American Literature* considers the expedient use, generally by killing, to which Steinbeck's characters put the animals in their lives. The following year, 1984, apparently evidenced a falling-off of article-length interest in *The Grapes of Wrath*, almost as if there were little more to say about it. Yet this was also the year of Jackson J. Benson's massive biography, already cited for the background to the novel largely included here. An article by Richard S. Pressman has recently—and most usefully—discussed the way the novel acquires dramatic tension as a result of conflicting tugs toward biological and political solutions. And recent book chapters devoted to Steinbeck continue to develop older notions in greater depth: David Wyatt surveys the Eden myth in Steinbeck's works; and Carol Shloss faults the writer for not sharing Dorothea Lange's honest photographer's approach to her subject, his adopting a disguise while among the migrants constituting "surveillance" that amounts to "usury." Book-length studies of Steinbeck continued to emerge, however, and in 1985 Louis Owens's *John Steinbeck's Re-vision of America* clearly consolidated all that had gone before. *Grapes*, he stated, is "the most thorough evaluation and rejection of the American myth offered by any American writer"; at the same time, the book "both condemns the illusion of Eden in

the West and offers a way out of the wasteland created by that illusion."
Finally, there is John H. Timmerman confessing in 1986 that "A thorough
bibliography of articles and book chapters on the novel would cover pages
[!]," and again trying to break down the many approaches to the novel in a
systematic way; his conclusion might as well serve as this compiler's own:
"In terms of thematic complexity and artistic skill, however, the work
stands also as one of the masterpieces of American literature." Amen.[31]

It is safe to say that whereas for many years at least half of all critical
articles on Steinbeck concerned *The Grapes of Wrath* wholly or in
substantial part, that is no longer the case. As the new pieces commissioned for this volume will show, however, the case is hardly that there is
nothing much left to say about *Grapes*, but rather that more detailed
examinations of the earlier works are being made, while the later ones are
at last beginning to receive their fair share of attention. The new pieces,
then, indicate the kinds of things yet remaining to be done. Jackson J.
Benson has assembled some of his previous articles in order to flesh out the
fullest and most accurate account to date of how John Steinbeck came to
write his most famous work. Warren French contributes a provocative
analysis of Steinbeck's career-peaking in *Grapes* in terms of modernism.
The chapters by Louis Owens and by Cliff Lewis and Carroll Britch
demonstrate, in their revisionist ways, how much has previously been
taken for granted in the ways we look at the Joads and their function in the
novel's development. Roy S. Simmonds complements the early reviews
reprinted in this and other volumes (see note 2) by helpfully surveying
original British response to the publication of *The Grapes of Wrath*. From
the unique perspective of the cultural geographer, Christopher L. Salter's
reprinted essay shows the kind of insight into the novel another field of
study can provide, and vice versa. Mimi Reisel Gladstein adroitly uses her
familiarity with the film version of *Grapes* to comment on the character of
Ma Joad as Steinbeck meant her to be. My article on the novel's ending is
included as an example of this miniature genre. And finally, Peter Lisca's
festschrift chapter on the "dynamics of community" in *Grapes* is reprinted
as a demonstration of this major Steinbeck critic's customary lucidity.
Clearly, so far as criticism of *The Grapes of Wrath* is concerned as the
novel attains its fiftieth birthday, the Joads are still in motion, and their
vehicle with them.

This book is dedicated to my normally patient wife, Sue, who put up
with its editor's fretting about it for a couple of years or more, and to my
daughter Kate. I am grateful, too, for almost twenty years of encouragement from the Steinbeck Society's Tetsumaro Hayashi, who has seen to it
that my attention never wandered from Steinbeck studies for long. Special
thanks are due to those whose suggestions made a hard task enormously
easier (if not easy): Warren French, Robert DeMott, Preston C. Beyer, Roy

S. Simmonds, and Jackson J. Benson. When I undertook to assemble this volume I did not know I would be able to count so heavily on the services of the women in my university's Word Processing Centre: Veronica Edwards, Lucia Brown, and Nancy Gurnett. I thank them from the bottom of a grateful heart, for they regularly made a readable manuscript out of scissors-and-paste assemblages. Finally, my greatest thanks are reserved for Department Research Associate Colleen Cassano, who, in spite of the many persistent demands on her and her time, was able to suggest more improvements — and correct more annoying errors and inconsistencies — than will ever be realized. For her legendary equanimity, my deepest gratitude.

JOHN DITSKY

University of Windsor

Notes

1. Appearing not long after the publication of the book itself, the movie *The Grapes of Wrath* has established itself over the years as something of a film classic, though John Ford's values were in many respects not those of John Steinbeck (see the essay by Mimi Gladstein included here). But the film per se is beyond the scope of this volume, and critiques primarily of it will not appear in this survey. Nor will — for reasons of relative inaccessibility — criticism published outside North America and Europe. Lastly, it seems pointless to include explication that does not truly explain anything — such as the many identifications of the novel's final tableau with supposed models in Maupassant or elsewhere. The survey presupposes, of course, reader familiarity with *The Grapes of Wrath*.

2. Previous such volumes including selections of both early reviews and later essays include: E. W. Tedlock and C. V. Wicker, eds., *Steinbeck and His Critics: A Record of Twenty-Five Years* (Albuquerque: University of New Mexico Press, 1957), hereafter referred to in the annotation as T&W; Warren French, ed., *A Companion to "The Grapes of Wrath"* (New York: Viking Press, 1963), hereafter cited as French; Agnes McNeill Donohue, ed., *A Casebook on "The Grapes of Wrath"* (New York: Thomas Y. Crowell, 1968), hereafter cited as Donohue; Peter Lisca, ed., *John Steinbeck, "The Grapes of Wrath": Text and Criticism* (New York: Viking Press, 1972), hereafter cited as Lisca; and Robert Con Davis, ed., *Twentieth Century Interpretations of "The Grapes of Wrath"* (Englewood Cliffs, N.J.: Prentice-Hall, 1982), hereafter cited as Davis. Other titles by these editor-critics will be given full identifying annotation separately. The reader who seeks out these useful volumes will note that certain pieces have been reprinted in them at least twice; it was the intention behind this book, however, to make available materials not nearly so conveniently accessible, and to commission new criticism reflecting recent changes in the way *The Grapes of Wrath* is perceived.

3. Edmund Wilson, "The Boys in the Back Room," originally published as a series in the *New Republic* in 1940 (San Francisco: Colt Press, 1941); collected in *Classics and Commercials* (New York: Farrar, Straus and Giroux, 1950), 19–56; Steinbeck section (5), 35–45 (Donohue, 151–58).

4. Tetsumaro Hayashi, ed., *A New Steinbeck Bibliography (1929–1971)* (Metuchen, N.J.: Scarecrow Press, 1973), and *A New Steinbeck Bibliography (1971–1981)* (Metuchen, N.J.: Scarecrow Press, 1983). There is some overlapping of coverage — and consequent duplication of entries — between the two volumes, and their systems of entry enumeration are not complementary.

5. *ALS's* Steinbeck annotations have had a number of editors over the years. Warren French, "John Steinbeck," in *Sixteen Modern American Authors: A Survey of Research and Criticism*, ed. Jackson R. Bryer, 499–527 (Durham, N.C.: Duke University Press, 1974). (An updated revision is slated for late-1989 release.) The Steinbeck Society and *Steinbeck Quarterly* are headquartered at Ball State University, Muncie IN 47306.

6. John Steinbeck, *Their Blood Is Strong* (San Francisco: Samuel J. Lubin Society, 1938); Lewis Gannett, *John Steinbeck: Personal and Biographical Notes* (New York: Viking Press, 1939); Harry Thornton Moore, *The Novels of John Steinbeck: A First Critical Study* (Chicago: Normandie House, 1939), 53–72; Margaret Marshall, "Writers in the Wilderness," *Nation* 149 (25 November 1939): 576–79; V. F. Calverton, "Steinbeck, Hemingway, and Faulkner," *Modern Quarterly* 11 (Fall 1939): 36–44.

7. Lyle H. Boren, "*The Grapes of Wrath*," *Congressional Record* 86 (1940): 139–40 (Donahue, 27–29); Percy H. Boynton, *America in Contemporary Fiction* (Chicago: University of Chicago Press, 1940), 241–57; Samuel Levenson, "The Compassion of John Steinbeck," *Canadian Forum* 20 (September 1940): 185–86.

8. Frederic I. Carpenter, "The Philosophical Joads," *College English* 2 (December 1941): 315–25 (Donohue, 80–89; T&W, 241–49; Lisca, 708–19), N. Elizabeth Monroe, *The Novel and Society* (Chapel Hill: University of North Carolina Press, 1941), 17–18; Joseph Warren Beach, "John Steinbeck: Art and Propaganda," in *American Fiction, 1920–1940* (New York: Macmillan, 1941), 327–47 (T&W, 250–65).

9. Alfred Kazin, "John Steinbeck," in *On Native Grounds* (New York: Reynal and Hitchcock, 1942), 393–99; Maxwell Geismar, "John Steinbeck: Of Wrath or Joy," in *Writers in Crisis: The American Novel, 1925–1940* (Boston: Houghton Mifflin, 1942), 239–41, 263–70 (Donohue, 134–42); Carey McWilliams, "California Pastoral," *Antioch Review* 2 (March 1942): 103–21 (Donohue, 32–51; Lisca, 657–79); Barker Fairley, "John Steinbeck and the Coming Literature," *Sewanee Review* 50 (April 1942): 145–61; Lincoln R. Gibbs, "John Steinbeck, Moralist," *Antioch Review* 2 (June 1942): 172–84 (T&W, 92–103); Floyd Stovall, "*The Grapes of Wrath*," *American Idealism* (Norman: University of Oklahoma Press, 1943), 159–66; Martin Shockley, "The Reception of *The Grapes of Wrath* in Oklahoma," *American Literature* 15 (January 1944): 351–61 (French, 117–31; Donahue, 52–62); J. Donald Adams, "John Steinbeck—Main Street and the Dust Bowl," in *The Shape of Books to Come* (New York: Viking Press, 1944), 131–43; B. R. McElderry, Jr., "*The Grapes of Wrath*: In the Light of Modern Critical Theory," *College English* 5 (March 1944): 308–13 (French, 199–208; Donohue, 126–33); Harry Slochower, "*The Grapes of Wrath*," in *No Voice Is Wholly Lost* (New York: Creative Age Press, 1945), 299–306; Pascal Covici, ed., *The Portable Steinbeck*, intro. Lewis Gannett (New York: Viking Press, 1943; rev. 1946; rev. 1958).

10. James Gray, *On Second Thought* (Minneapolis: University of Minnesota Press, 1946), 133–40; W. M. Frohock, "John Steinbeck's Men of Wrath," *Southwest Review* 31 (Spring 1946): 144–52; W. M. Frohock, *The Novel of Violence in America* (Dallas: Southern Methodist University Press, 1950), 129–33; Edwin Berry Burgum, "The Sensibility of John Steinbeck," *Science and Society* 10 (Spring 1946): 132–47 (T&W, 104–18); Edwin Berry Burgum, "*The Grapes of Wrath*," in *The Novel and the World's Dilemma* (New York: Oxford University Press, 1947), 283–88; Woodburn O. Ross, "John Steinbeck: Earth and Stars," in *The University of Missouri Studies in Honor of A. H. R. Fairchild* 179–97 (Columbia: University of Missouri Press, 1946) (T&W, 167–82).

11. Chester E. Eisinger, "Jeffersonian Agrarianism in *The Grapes of Wrath*," *University of Kansas City Review* 14 (Winter 1947): 149–54 (Lisca, 720–28); Leo Gurko, "The Joads in California," in *The Angry Decade* (New York: Dodd, Mead, 1947), 201–21 (Donohue, 63–67 [excerpt]); Freeman Champney, "John Steinbeck, Californian," *Antioch Review* 7 (September 1947): 345–62 (T&W, 135–51; Robert Murray Davis, ed., *Steinbeck: A Collection of Critical Essays* [Englewood Cliffs, N.J.: Prentice-Hall, 1972], 18–35); Donald Weeks, "Steinbeck Against Steinbeck," *Pacific Spectator* 1 (Autumn 1947): 447–57; Woodburn O. Ross, "John Steinbeck: Naturalism's Priest," *College English* 10 (May 1949): 432–38 (T&W,

206-15); Frederick Bracher, "Steinbeck and the Biological View of Man," *Pacific Spectator* 2 (Winter 1948): 14-29 (T&W, 183-96); Blake Nevius, "Steinbeck: One Aspect," *Pacific Spectator* 3 (Summer 1949): 302-10 (T&W, 197-205).

12. Michael F. Moloney, "Half-Faiths in Modern Fiction," *Catholic World* 171 (August 1950): 349-50; Alexander Cowie, *The Rise of the American Novel* (New York: American Book Company, 1951), 754; George F. Whicher, "Proletarian Leanings," in *The Literature of the American People*, ed. Arthur Hobson Quinn, 958-61 (New York: Appleton-Century Crofts, 1951); Frederick J. Hoffman, *The Modern Novel in America* (Chicago: Henry Regnery, 1951), 160-68; Bernard Bowron, *"The Grapes of Wrath*: A 'Wagons West' Romance," *Colorado Quarterly* 3 (Summer 1954): 84-91 (French, 208-16); Warren French, "Another Look at *The Grapes of Wrath*," *Colorado Quarterly* 3 (Winter 1955): 337-43 (French, 217-24).

13. Charles Child Walcutt, "Later Trends in Form: Steinbeck, Hemingway, Dos Passos," in *American Literary Naturalism: A Divided Stream* (Minneapolis: University of Minnesota Press, 1956), 258-59, 263, 268-69 (Donohue, 162-65); George Bluestone, *"The Grapes of Wrath*," in *Novels into Film* (Baltimore: Johns Hopkins Press, 1957), 147-69 (French, 165-89; Robert Murray Davis, ed., *Steinbeck: A Collection of Critical Essays* [Englewood Cliffs, N.J.: Prentice-Hall, 1972], 102-21); Peter Lisca, *"The Grapes of Wrath* as Fiction," *PMLA* 72 (1957): 296-309 (Donohue, 166-81; Lisca, 729-47; Robert Murray Davis, ed., *Steinbeck: A Collection of Critical Essays* [Englewood Cliffs, N.J.: Prentice-Hall, 1972], 75-101); Peter Lisca, *The Wide World of John Steinbeck* (New Brunswick, N.J.: Rutgers University Press, 1958), 144-77.

14. Martin S. Shockley, "Christian Symbolism in *The Grapes of Wrath*," *College English* 18 (November 1956): 87-90 (Donohue, 90-95; T&W, 266-71); Eric W. Carlson, "Symbolism in *The Grapes of Wrath*," *College English* 19 (January 1958): 172-75 (Donohue, 96-102; Lisca, 748-56); George De Schweinitz, "Steinbeck and Christianity," *College English* 19 (May 1958): 369 (Donohue, 103-4); R. W. B. Lewis, "The Picaresque Saint," in *The Picaresque Saint: Representative Figures in Contemporary Fiction* (New York: Lippincott, 1958), 181-86 (Davis, 144-49); Theodore Pollock, "On the Ending of *The Grapes of Wrath*," *Modern Fiction Studies* 4 (Summer 1958): 177-78 (Donohue, 182-84; French, 224-26); Frank H. Jackson, "Economics in Literature," *Duquesne Review* 3 (Spring 1958): 80-85.

15. Walter Fuller Taylor, *"The Grapes of Wrath* Reconsidered," *Mississippi Quarterly* 12 (Summer 1959): 136-44 (Donohue, 185-94; Lisca, 757-68); Edwin T. Bowden, "The Commonplace and the Grotesque," in *The Dungeon of the Heart* (New York: Macmillan, 1961), 138-49 (Donohue, 195-203); Warren French, "The Education of the Heart," in *John Steinbeck* (New York: Twayne Publishers, 1961), 95-112.

16. F. W. Watt, *John Steinbeck* (Edinburgh: Oliver and Boyd, 1962; New York: Grove Press, 1962), 62-75; Gerald Cannon, "The Pauline Apostleship of Tom Joad," *College English* 24 (December 1962): 222-24 (Donohue, 118-22); H. Kelly Crockett, "The Bible and *The Grapes of Wrath*," *College English* 24 (December 1962): 193-99 (Donohue, 105-14); Charles T. Dougherty, "The Christ Figure in *The Grapes of Wrath*," *College English* 24 (December 1962): 224-26 (Donohue, 115-17); Thomas F. Dunn, "The Bible and *The Grapes of Wrath*," *College English* 24 (April 1963): 566-67 (Donohue, 123-25); Enno Klammer, *"The Grapes of Wrath*: A Modern Exodus Account," *Cresset* 25 (February 1962): 8-11; Edwin M. Moseley, "Christ as the Brother of Man," in *Pseudonyms of Christ in the Modern Novel* (Pittsburgh: University of Pittsburgh Press, 1962), 163-75 (Donohue, 209-18); Arthur Mizener, "Does a Moral Vision of the Thirties Deserve a Nobel Prize?," *New York Times Book Review* (9 December 1962), 4, 43-45 (Donohue 267-72).

17. Walter Allen, *"The Grapes of Wrath*," in *Tradition and Dream: The English and American Novel From the Twenties and Our Time* (London: Phoenix House, 1963), 161-66; also in *The Modern Novel in Britain and the United States* (New York: Dutton, 1964), 161-66; Joseph Fontenrose, *"The Grapes of Wrath*," in *John Steinbeck: An Introduction and Interpretation* (New York: Holt, Rinehart and Winston, 1963), 67-83; Robert J. Griffin and

William A. Freedman, "Machines and Animals: Pervasive Motifs in *The Grapes of Wrath*," *Journal of English and Germanic Philology* 62 (April 1963): 569–80 (Donohue, 219–31; Lisca, 769–83); J. Paul Hunter, "Steinbeck's Wine of Affirmation in *The Grapes of Wrath*," in *Essays in Modern American Literature*, ed. Richard E. Langford, 76–89 (De Land, Fla.: Stetson University Press, 1963) (Lisca, 801–13; Davis, 36–47).

18. Robert Detweiler, "Christ and the Christ Figure in American Fiction," *Christian Scholar* 47 (Summer 1964): 111–24; Walter Rundell, Jr., "*The Grapes of Wrath*: Steinbeck's Image of the West," *American West* 1 (Spring 1964): 4–17, 79; James Woodress, "John Steinbeck: Hostage to Fortune," *South Atlantic Quarterly* 63 (Summer 1964): 385–97 (Donohue, 278–90); Jules Chametzky, "The Ambivalent Endings of *The Grapes of Wrath*," *Modern Fiction Studies* 11 (Spring 1965): 34–44 (Donohue, 232–44); James W. Tuttleton, "Steinbeck in Russia: The Rhetoric of Praise and Blame," *Modern Fiction Studies* 11 (Spring 1965): 79–89 (Donohue, 245–56); Peter Lisca, "Steinbeck's Image of Man and His Decline as a Writer," *Modern Fiction Studies* 11 (Spring 1965): 3–10; W. J. Stuckey, *The Pulitzer Prize Novels: A Critical Backward Look* (Norman: University of Oklahoma Press, 1966), 118; Warren French, *The Social Novel at the End of an Era* (Carbondale and Edwardsville: Southern Illinois University Press, 1966), 42–86; Pascal Covici, Jr., "John Steinbeck and the Language of Awareness," in *The Thirties: Fiction, Poetry, Drama*, ed. Warren French, 47–54 (De Land, Fla.: Everett Edwards, 1967); Paul McCarthy, "House and Shelter as Symbol in *The Grapes of Wrath*," *South Dakota Review* 5 (Winter 1967–68): 48–67.

19. Daniel Aaron, "The Radical Humanism of John Steinbeck: *The Grapes of Wrath* Thirty Years Later," *Saturday Review* 51 (28 September 1968): 26–27, 55–56; Chris Browning, "Grape Symbolism in *The Grapes of Wrath*," *Discourse* 11 (1968): 129–40; Tetsumaro Hayashi, "The Function of the Joad Clan in *The Grapes of Wrath*," *Modern Review* 20 (March 1968): 158–59, 161–62; Leonard A. Slade, Jr., "The Use of Biblical Allusions in *The Grapes of Wrath*," *College Language Association Journal* 11 (1968): 241–47; Bryant N. Wyatt, "Experimentation as Technique: The Protest Novels of John Steinbeck," *Discourse* 12 (1969): 143–53; Lester J. Marks, *Thematic Design in the Novels of John Steinbeck* (The Hague: Mouton, 1969), 66–82.

20. Mary Washington Clarke, "Bridging the Generation Gap: The Ending of Steinbeck's *The Grapes of Wrath*," (Houston) *Forum* 8 (Summer 1970): 16–17; Arnold F. Delisle, "Style and Idea in Steinbeck's 'The Turtle,'" *Style* 4 (Spring 1970): 135–54; Richard B. Hauck, "The Comic Christ and the Modern Reader," *College English* 31 (1970): 498–506; Jack Nimitz, "Ecology in *The Grapes of Wrath*," *Hartford Studies in Literature* 2 (1970): 165–68; Collin G. Matton, "Water Imagery and the Conclusion to *The Grapes of Wrath*," *NEMLA Newsletter* 2 (May 1970): 44–47; Richard O'Connor, *John Steinbeck* (New York: McGraw-Hill, 1970), 60–71; John Clark Pratt, *John Steinbeck: A Critical Essay* (Grand Rapids, Mich.: William B. Eerdmans, 1970).

21. J. Wilkes Berry, "Enduring Life in *The Grapes of Wrath*," *CEA Critic* 33 (1971): 18–19; James P. Degnan, "In Definite Battle: Steinbeck and California's Land Monopolists," in *Steinbeck: The Man and His Work*, ed. Richard Astro and Tetsumaro Hayashi, 65–74 (Corvallis: Oregon State University Press, 1971); Robert B. Downs, "Okies and Arkies," in *Famous American Books* (New York: McGraw-Hill, 1971), 311–19; Leonard Lutwack, "*The Grapes of Wrath* as Heroic Fiction," in *Heroic Fiction: The Epic Tradition and American Novels of the 20th Century* (Carbondale: Southern Illinois University Press, 1971), 47–63 (Davis, 63–75); *The Portable Steinbeck*, rev. ed., intro. Pascal Covici, Jr. (New York: Viking Press, 1971); James Gray, *John Steinbeck* (Minneapolis: University of Minnesota Press, 1971).

22. Sam Bluefarb, "The Joads: Flight into the Social Soul," in *The Escape Motif in the American Novel: Mark Twain to Richard Wright* (Columbus: Ohio State University Press, 1972), 95–112; Peter Lisca, "The Dynamics of Community in *The Grapes of Wrath*," in *From Irving to Steinbeck: Studies in American Literature in Honor of Harry R. Warfel*, ed. Motley Deakin and Peter Lisca, 129–40 (Gainesville: University of Florida Press, 1972); Pascal Covici, Jr., "Work and the Timeliness of *The Grapes of Wrath*" (Lisca, 814–24); John R.

Reed, "*The Grapes of Wrath* and the Esthetics of Indigence" (Lisca, 825–39); Betty Perez, "House and Home: Thematic Symbols in *The Grapes of Wrath*" (Lisca, 840–53); Sol Zollman, "John Steinbeck's Political Outlook in *The Grapes of Wrath*," *Literature and Ideology* 13 (1972): 9–20; Reloy Garcia, *Steinbeck and D. H. Lawrence: Fictive Voices and the Ethical Imperative* (Muncie, Ind.: Steinbeck Monograph Series [No. 2], 1972), 11, 23, 26–33; Robert Murray Davis, ed., *Steinbeck: A Collection of Critical Essays* (Englewood Cliffs, N.J.: Prentice-Hall, 1972).

23. A. Carl Bredahl, Jr., "The Drinking Metaphor in *The Grapes of Wrath*," *Steinbeck Quarterly* 6 (Fall 1973): 95–98; W. Richard Fossey, "The End of the Western Dream: *The Grapes of Wrath* and Oklahoma," *Cimarron Review* 22 (1973): 25–34; Kathleen Farr Elliott, "Steinbeck's 'IITYWYBAD,' " *Steinbeck Quarterly* 6 (Spring 1973): 53–54; John Ditsky, "The Ending of *The Grapes of Wrath*," *Agora* 2 (Fall 1973): 41–50; Mary Ellen Caldwell, "A New Consideration of the Intercalary Chapters in *The Grapes of Wrath*," *Markham Review* 3 (May 1973): 115–19 (Davis, 105–14); Richard Astro, *John Steinbeck and Edward F. Ricketts: The Shaping of a Novelist* (Minneapolis: University of Minnesota Press, 1973); Lawrence William Jones, in *John Steinbeck as Fabulist*, ed. Marston LaFrance, 17–18. (Muncie, Ind.: Steinbeck Monograph Series [No. 3], 1973).

24. Howard Levant, *The Novels of John Steinbeck: A Critical Study* (Columbia: University of Missouri Press, 1974), 93–129; D. G. Kehl, "Steinbeck's 'String of Pictures' in *The Grapes of Wrath*," *Image* 17 no. 1 (March 1974): 1–10; Stuart L. Burns, "The Turtle or the Gopher: Another Look at the Ending of *The Grapes of Wrath*," *Western American Literature* 9 (May 1974): 53–57 (Davis, 100–104); Warren French, "Steinbeck's *The Grapes of Wrath* (1939)," in *A Study Guide to Steinbeck: A Handbook to His Major Works*, ed. Teysumaro Hayashi, 29–46 (Metuchen, N.J.: Scarecrow Press, 1974).

25. Duane R. Carr, "Steinbeck's Blakean Vision in *The Grapes of Wrath*," *Steinbeck Quarterly* 8 (Summer–Fall 1975): 67–73; Martha Heasley Cox, "The Conclusion of *The Grapes of Wrath*: Steinbeck's Conception and Execution," *San Jose Studies*, 1 (November 1975): 73–81; William Appleman Williams, "Steinbeck in Perspective," in *Steinbeck and The Sea*, ed. Richard Astro and Joel W. Hedgpeth, 39–44 (Corvallis: Oregon State University Sea Grant College Program, 1975); Warren French, "After *The Grapes of Wrath*," *Steinbeck Quarterly* 8 (Summer–Fall 1975): 73–78; Warren French, *John Steinbeck* (Boston: Twayne, 1975), 92–102; Linda Ray Pratt, "Imagining Existence: Form and History in Steinbeck and Agee," *Southern Review* 11 (January 1975): 84–98; Stanley Trachtenberg, "West's *Locust*: Laughing at the Laugh," *Michigan Quarterly Review* 14 (1975): 187–98; Sandra Beatty, "A Study of Female Characterization in Steinbeck's Fiction," *Steinbeck Quarterly* 8 (Spring 1975): 50–56 (also in *Steinbeck's Women: Essays in Criticism*, ed. Tetsumaro Hayashi, 7–16 [Muncie, Ind.: Steinbeck Monograph Series (No. 9), 1979]; Nelson Valjean, *John Steinbeck: The Errant Knight* (San Francisco: Chronicle Books, 1975), 161–68.

26. Jackson J. Benson, " 'To Tom, Who Lived It': John Steinbeck and the Man from Weedpatch," *Journal of Modern Literature* 5 (April 1976): 151–94; Horst Groene, "Agrarianism and Technology in Steinbeck's *The Grapes of Wrath*," *Southern Review* 9 (1976): 27–31 (Davis, 128–33); Lewis Moore Hopfe, "Genesis Imagery in Steinbeck," *Cresset* 39 (May 1976): 6–9; Floyd C. Watkins, "Flat Wine from *The Grapes of Wrath*," in *The Humanist in His World: Essays in Honor of Fielding*, ed. Barbara Bitter and Frederick Sanders, 57–69 (Greenwood, S.C.: Attic, 1976), also in Floyd C. Watkins, *In Time and Place: Some Origins of American Fiction* (Athens: University of Georgia Press, 1977), 19–29; Sylvia Jenkins Cook, *From Tobacco Road to Route 66: The Southern Poor White in Fiction* (Chapel Hill: University of North Carolina Press, 1976), 153–83; Kenneth D. Swan, "John Steinbeck: In Search of America," in *Steinbeck's Prophetic Vision of America*, ed. Tetsumaro Hayashi and Kenneth D. Swan, 12–27 (Upland, Ind.: Taylor University for the John Steinbeck Society of America, 1976); Warren French, "John Steinbeck and Modernism," in *Steinbeck's Prophetic Vision*, 35–55; Roy S. Simmonds, *Steinbeck's Literary Achievement* (Muncie, Ind.: Steinbeck Monograph Series [No. 6], 1976), 5–6, 14–15, 22, 27.

27. James D. Brasch, "*The Grapes of Wrath* and Old Testament Skepticism," *San Jose Studies* 3 (May 1977): 16–27; Martha Heasley Cox, "Fact into Fiction in *The Grapes of Wrath*: The Weedpatch and Arvin Camps," in *John Steinbeck: East and West*, ed. Tetsumaro Hayashi, 12–21 (Muncie, Ind.: Steinbeck Monograph Series [No. 8], 1978); Miles Donald, "The Traditional Novel," in *The American Novel in the Twentieth Century* (New York: Barnes and Noble, 1978), 59–72; Peter Lisca, "*The Grapes of Wrath*: An Achievement of Genius," in *John Steinbeck: Nature and Myth* (New York: Thomas Y. Crowell, 1978), 87–110 (Davis, 48–62).

28. John Ditsky, "*The Grapes of Wrath*: A Reconsideration," *Southern Humanities Review* 13 (Summer 1979): 215–20; Mimi Reisel Gladstein, "Female Characters in Steinbeck: Minor Characters of Major Importance?", in *Steinbeck's Women: Essays in Criticism*, ed. Tetsumaro Hayashi, 17–25 (Muncie, Ind.: Steinbeck Monograph Series [No. 9], 1979); Mimi Reisel Gladstein, *The Indestructible Woman in Faulkner, Hemingway, and Steinbeck* (Ann Arbor: UMI Research Press, 1986), 75–100; Thomas Kiernan, *The Intricate Music: A Biography of John Steinbeck* (Boston: Little, Brown, 1979), 223–47; Paul McCarthy, *John Steinbeck* (New York: Frederick Ungar, 1980), 65–86; Patrick B. Mullen, "American Folklife and *The Grapes of Wrath*," *Journal of American Culture*, 1 (1978): 742–53; John Vassilowitch, Jr., "Bing Crosby and *The Grapes of Wrath*," *Steinbeck Quarterly* 13 (Summer–Fall 1980): 97–98.

29. Mimi Reisel Gladstein, "Ma Joad and Pilar: Significantly Similar," *Steinbeck Quarterly* 14 (Summer–Fall 1981): 93–104; Reloy Garcia, "The Rocky Road to Eldorado: The Journey Motif in John Steinbeck's *The Grapes of Wrath*," *Steinbeck Quarterly* 14 (Summer–Fall 1981): 83–93; Christopher L. Salter, "John Steinbeck's *The Grapes of Wrath* as a Primer for Cultural Geography," in *Humanistic Geography and Literature: Essays on the Experience of Place*, ed. Douglas C. D. Pocock, 142–58 (London: Croom Helm, 1981); Paul McCarthy, "The Joads and Other Rural Families in Depression Fiction," *South Dakota Review* 19 (Autumn 1981): 51–68.

30. Sylvia Cook, "Steinbeck, the People, and the Party," *Steinbeck Quarterly* 15 (Winter–Spring 1982): 11–23; Helen Lojek, "Jim Casy: Politico of the New Jerusalem," *Steinbeck Quarterly* 15 (Winter–Spring 1982): 30–37; Warren Motley, "From Patriarchy to Matriarchy: Ma Joad's Role in *The Grapes of Wrath*," *American Literature* 54 (October 1982): 397–412; Robert Con Davis, "Introduction," *Twentieth Century Interpretations of "The Grapes of Wrath"* (Davis, 1–11); Joan Hedrick, "Mother Earth and Earth Mother: The Recasting of Myth in Steinbeck's *The Grapes of Wrath*" (Davis, 134–43).

31. F. Odun Balogun, "Naturalist Proletarian Prose Epics: *Petals of Blood* and *Grapes of Wrath*," *Journal of English* 11 (September 1983): 88–106; Joyce Compton Brown, "Steinbeck's *The Grapes of Wrath*," *Explicator* 41 (Summer 1983): 49–51; Patrick W. Shaw, "Tom's Other Trip: Psycho-Physical Questing in *The Grapes of Wrath*," *Steinbeck Quarterly* 16 (Winter–Spring 1983): 17–25; Brian St. Pierre, *John Steinbeck: The California Years* (San Francisco: Chronicle Books, 1983), 69–104; Stoddard Martin, *California Writers: Jack London, John Steinbeck, The Tough Guys* (New York: Macmillan, 1983), 67–122; Mary Allen, "The Cycle of Death: John Steinbeck," in *Animals in American Literature* (Urbana: University of Illinois Press, 1983), 115–34; Jackson J. Benson, *The True Adventures of John Steinbeck, Writer* (New York: Viking Press, 1984); Richard S. Pressman, " 'Them's Horses — We're Men': Social Tendency and Counter-Tendency in *The Grapes of Wrath*," *Steinbeck Quarterly* 19 (Summer–Fall 1986): 71–79; David Wyatt, *The Fall into Eden: Landscape and Imagination in California* (New York: Cambridge University Press, 1986), 124–57, esp. 147–51; Carol Shloss, "John Steinbeck and Dorothea Lange: The Surveillance of Dissent," in *In Visible Light: Photography and the American Writer, 1840–1940* (New York: Oxford University Press, 1987), 200–31, 283–85; Louis Owens, *John Steinbeck's Re-Vision of America* (Athens: University of Georgia Press, 1985), 128–40; John H. Timmerman, *John Steinbeck's Fiction: The Aesthetics of the Road Not Taken* (Norman: University of Oklahoma Press, 1986), 102–32.

Reviews

Hungry Caravan
Louis Kronenberger*

This is in many ways the most moving and disturbing social novel of our time. What is wrong with it, what is weak in it, what robs it of the stature it clearly attempts, are matters that must be presently be pointed out; but not at once. First it should be pointed out that *The Grapes of Wrath* comes at a needed time in a powerful way. It comes, perhaps, as *The Drapier's Letters* or *Uncle Tom's Cabin* or some of the social novels of Zola came. It burns with no pure gemlike flame, but with hot and immediate fire. It is, from any point of view, Steinbeck's best novel, but it does not make one wonder whether, on the basis of it, Steinbeck is now a better novelist than Hemingway or Farrell or Dos Passos; it does not invoke comparisons; it simply makes one feel that Steinbeck is, in some way all his own, a force.

The publishers refer to the book as "perhaps the greatest single creative work that this country has produced." This is a foolish and extravagant statement, but unlike most publishers' statements, it seems the result of honest enthusiasm, and one may hope that the common reader will respond to the book with an enthusiasm of the same sort. And perhaps he will, for *The Grapes of Wrath* has, overwhelmingly, those two qualities most vital to a work of social protest: great indignation and great compassion. Its theme is large and tragic and, on the whole, is largely and tragically felt. No novel of our day has been written out of a more genuine humanity, and none, I think, is better calculated to awaken the humanity of others.

Throughout the Southwest hundreds of thousands of small farmers and share-croppers have been driven, by the banks and the big landowners, from their farms — to move westward, with their families, in a dusty caravan of jalopies, to California. To California, because handbills lure them there with promises of work. But the real purpose of the handbills is to flood the California market with such a surplus of workers that the price of labor sinks to almost nothing. Hungry men, by accepting

*Reprinted with permission from the *Nation* 148 (15 April 1939): 440–41. Copyright 1939 The Nation Company, Inc.

lower wages, oust ill-paid men from their jobs; then, in desperation, the ousted men snatch the jobs back at wages even lower. The result is a horde of the starving and homeless, living in filth in roadside camps, forever wandering, all thought of security ended.

In the fate of one such family—the Joads of Oklahoma—John Steinbeck has told the fate of all. Their fate is the theme of an angry and aroused propagandist, but the Joads themselves are the product of a lively novelist. A racy, picturesque, somewhat eccentric tribe, with certain resemblances to Erskine Caldwell's Georgia exhibits, the Joads—mean, merry, shameless Grandpa; brooding, conscience-stricken Uncle John; strong, tough, understanding Ma; Al, a squirt thinking only of women and cars; Tom, who has been in prison for killing a man in a brawl—the Joads, with their salty, slanting speech, their frank and boisterous opinions, their unrepressed, irrepressible appetites, would, in a stable world, be the stuff of rich folk-comedy. But suddenly uprooted and harassed, they are creatures forced to fight for their very existence. During the first half of Steinbeck's long book the Joads, both as people and as symbols, have tremendous vitality. Steinbeck's account of this one family leaving home and journeying forth in a rickety makeshift truck is like some night-lighted, rude Homeric chronicle of a great migration. It has a vigor, as of half-childlike, half-heroic adventuring, that almost blots out the sense of its desperate origins and painful forebodings.

But after the Joads reach California, something—a kind of inner life—disappears from the book. The economic outrage, the human tragedy are made brutally clear. The chronicle of the Joads remains vivid; the nature of their fate becomes ever more infuriating. As a tract, the book goes on piling up its indictment, conducting the reader on a sort of grand tour of exploitation and destitution. And all this has, emotionally at least, a very strong effect. But somehow the book ceases to grow, to maintain direction. It is truly enough a story of nomads; but from that it does not follow that the proletarian novel must fall into the loose pattern of the picaresque novel. Artistically speaking, the second half of *The Grapes of Wrath*, though it still has content and suspense, lacks form and intensity. The people simply go on and on, with Steinbeck left improvising and amplifying until—with a touch of new and final horror—he abruptly halts.

The Grapes of Wrath is a superb tract because it exposes something terrible and true with enormous vigor. It is a superb tract, moreover, by virtue of being thoroughly animated fiction, by virtue of living scenes and living characters (like Ma), not by virtue of discursive homilies and dead characters (like the socialistic preacher). One comes away moved, indignant, protesting, pitying. But one comes away dissatisfied, too, aware that *The Grapes of Wrath* is too unevenly weighted, too uneconomically proportioned, the work of a writer who is still self-indulgent, still undisciplined, still not altogether aware of the difference in value of various human emotions. The picturesqueness of the Joads, for example, is fine wherever it makes them live more abundantly, but false when simply laid on for effect. Steinbeck's sentimentalism is good in bringing him close to the lives of his people, but bad when it blurs his insight. Again, the chapters in which Steinbeck halts the story to editorialize about American life are sometimes useful, but oftener pretentious and flatulent.

But one does not take leave of a book like this in a captious spirit. One salutes it as a fiery document of protest and compassion, as a story that had to be told, as a book that must be read. It is, I think, one of those books—there are not very many—which really do some good.

But . . . Not . . . Ferdinand   Burton Rascoe*

Many years hence, maybe a new bunch of Baconians (who think Shakespeare wasn't Shakespeare) will rise up with learned theses to prove that John Steinbeck was not John Steinbeck, but was, in fact, Charlie McCarthy.

They will have much to go on. If the Bard of Avon can be called "myriad-minded" and accused of being two other fellows on the available evidence, then Steinbeck's chances of being known as Steinbeck are certainly slim; for, even if you wouldn't want to call the man "myriad-minded" (maybe you wouldn't want to call anybody that), you have to admit that not one of his books, except in the superficie of idiosyncratic cadence, remotely resembles any of his other books. He is not a school, as Hemingway is.

An author is usually known by the stuff behind which he is stymied. You write a story which goes over well and an unimaginative editor wants you to write the same story over and over again. He gets mad if you have another idea and tells you the public (he means himself) wants more of the same.

The compliant writer, in the face of a large check and in the much more repellent face of a process server in a matter in which the landlord would like to have his rent, usually tries to remember what he wrote that the editor thought was so hot and try to do it over again, with just enough of a new slant to make it sound like another story.

But not (Ferdinand) Steinbeck.

He is always different.

I know of no top-notch other writer in my time, including Cabell, Dreiser, Anderson, Jeffers, and Robinson, who had so many bad breaks at the start of his career as Steinbeck. For a long period, every time he had a

*Reprinted with permission from *Newsweek* 13 (17 April 1939):46. Copyright 1939 Newsweek, Inc., all rights reserved.

new book coming out, the publishing house folded up ten minutes after the book was off the press. Thus he got no publicity, no advertising, little distribution of his wares. He earned less in royalties than he earned as a hod carrier in the construction of Madison Square Garden.

His first big success was *Tortilla Flat*, which went begging for months among the publishers until Ben Abramson of the Argus Book Shop, Chicago, told Pat Covici of Covici-Friede that Steinbeck was a good investment. Pat was delighted with the manuscript Ben turned over to him, saw *Tortilla Flat* become a best seller, published *In Dubious Battle* (which also got high praise and became a best seller), *Of Mice and Men* (which was a great success both as a novel and as a play), *The Red Pony* (issued in a limited, high-priced edition), and *The Long Valley* (also issued in a limited, high-priced edition). And then Covici-Friede was foced to the wall and Pat, an able editor-publisher, went over to Viking Press, taking Steinbeck with him.

Viking Press has just issued Steinbeck's *Grapes of Wrath* ($2.75). Reports are that advance orders for the book are more than treble the advance orders on all the other Steinbeck books put together. It is a book of 619 pages, which is to say, about 195,000 words or about twice the length of both *Tortilla Flat* and of *Of Mice and Men*.

It is about tenant farmers in Oklahoma, who got pushed off their land by the wicked landlords and struck out in a jalopy for California, where they thought you didn't have to work but could just live on oranges picked from somebody else's trees. They found out different. The book has beautiful and, even magnificent, passages in it; but it is not well organized; I can't quite see what the book is about, except that there are "no frontiers left and no place to go."

The title is from Julia Ward Howe's "Battle Hymn of the Republic" with its line "He is tramping out the vintage where the grapes of wrath are stored." In chapter 23, he explains what he means by the title, in an impassioned essay about the California vineyards, which, he says, have fallen into the hands of the banks: "The decay spreads over the state, and the sweet smell is a great sorrow in the land. Men who can graft trees and make the seed fertile and big can find no way to let the hungry people eat their produce. . . . The works of the roots of the vines, of the trees, must be destroyed to keep up the price, and this is the saddest, bitterest thing of all. Carloads of oranges dumped on the ground . . . etc." (Secretary Wallace, please take note: Steinbeck is predicting a revolution from the vicious circle that has grown up around crop destruction for price maintenance.)

American Tragedy

Malcolm Cowley*

While keeping our eyes on the cataclysms in Europe and Asia, we have lost sight of a tragedy nearer home. A hundred thousand rural households have been uprooted from the soil, robbed of their possessions — though by strictly legal methods — and turned out on the highways. Friendless, homeless and therefore voteless, with fewer rights than medieval serfs, they have wandered in search of a few days' work at miserable wages — not in Spain or the Yangtze Valley, but among the vineyards and orchards of California, in a setting too commonplace for a color story in the Sunday papers. Their migrations have been described only in a long poem and a novel. The poem is "Land of the Free," by Archibald MacLeish, published last year with terrifying photographs by the Resettlement Administration. The novel, which has just appeared, is John Steinbeck's longest and angriest and most impressive work.

The Grapes of Wrath begins with Tom Joad's homecoming. After being released from the Oklahoma State Penitentiary, where he has served four years of a seven-year sentence for homicide, he sets out for his father's little farm in the bottom lands near Sallisaw. He reaches the house to find that it is empty, the windows broken, the well filled in and even the dooryard planted with cotton. Muley Graves, a neighbor, comes past in the dusk and tells him what has happened. It is a scene that I can't forget: the men sitting back on their haunches, drawing figures with a stick in the dust; a half-starved cat watching from the doorstep; and around them the silence of a mile-long cottonfield. Muley says that all the tenant farmers have been evicted from their land — "tractored off" is the term he uses. Groups of twenty and thirty farms are being thrown together and the whole area cultivated by one man with a caterpillar tractor. Most of the families are moving to California, on the rumor that work can be found there. Tom's people are staying temporarily with his Uncle John, eight miles away, but they will soon be leaving. Of this whole farming community, no one is left but stubborn Muley Graves, hiding from the sheriff's men, haunting empty houses and "jus' wanderin' aroun'," he says, "like an ol' graveyard ghos'."

Next morning Tom rejoins his family — just in time, for the uncle too has been ordered to leave his farm. The whole family of twelve is starting for California. Their last day at home is another fine scene in which you realize, little by little, that not only a family but a whole culture is being uprooted — a primitive culture, it is true, but complete in its fashion, with its history, its legends of Indian fighting, its songs and jokes, its religious practices, its habits of work and courtship; even the killing of two hogs is a ritual.

*Reprinted with permission from the *New Republic* 98 (3 May 1939): 382–83.

With the hogs salted down and packed in the broken-down truck among the bedclothes, the Joads start westward on U.S. Highway 66. They are part of an endless caravan—trucks, trailers, battered sedans, touring cars rescued from the junkyard, all of them overloaded with children and household plunder, all wheezing, pounding and screeching toward California. There are deaths on the road—Gramps is the first to go—but there is not much time for mourning. A greater tragedy than death is a burned-out bearing, repaired after efforts that Steinbeck describes as if he were singing the exploits of heroes at the siege of Troy. Then, after a last wild ride through the desert—Tom driving, Rose of Sharon and her husband making love and Gramma dying under the same tarpaulin—the Joads cross the pass at Tehachapi and see before them the promised land, the grainfields golden in the morning.

The second half of the novel, dealing with their adventures in the Valley of California, is still good but somewhat less impressive. Until that moment the Joads have been moving steadily toward their goal. Now they discover that it is not their goal after all; they must still move on, but no longer in one direction—they are harried by vigilantes, recruited as peach pickers, driven out again by a strike; they don't know where to go. Instead of being just people, as they were at home, they hear themselves called Okies—"and that means you're scum," they tell each other bewilderedly. "Don't mean nothing itself, it's the way they say it." The story begins to suffer a little from their bewilderment and lack of direction.

At this point one begins to notice other faults. Interspersed among the chapters that tell what happened to the Joads, there have been other chapters dealing with the general plight of the migrants. The first half-dozen of these interludes have not only broadened the scope of the novel but have been effective in themselves, sorrowful, bitter, intensely moving. But after the Joads reach California, the interludes are spoken in a shriller voice. The author now has a thesis—that the migrants will unite and overthrow their oppressors—and he wants to argue, as if he weren't quite sure of it himself. His thesis is also embodied in one of the characters: Jim Casy, a preacher who loses his faith but unfortunately for the reader can't stop preaching. In the second half of the novel, Casy becomes a Christ-like labor leader and is killed by vigilantes. The book ends with an episode that is a mixture of allegory and melodrama. Rose of Sharon, after her baby is born dead, saves a man from starvation by suckling him at her breast—as if to symbolize the fruitfulness of these people and the bond that unites them in misfortune.

Yet one soon forgets the faults of the story. What one remembers most of all is Steinbeck's sympathy for the migrants—not pity, for that would mean he was putting himself above them; not love, for that would blind him to their faults, but rather a deep fellow feeling. It makes him notice everything that sets them apart from the rest of the world and sets one migrant apart from all the others. In the Joad family, everyone from

Grampa— "Full a' piss an' vinegar," as he says of himself — down to the two brats, Ruthie and Winfield, is a distinct and living person. And the story is living too — it has the force of the headlong anger that drives ahead from the first chapter to the last, as if the whole six hundred pages were written without stopping. The author and the reader are swept along together. I can't agree with those critics who say that *The Grapes of Wrath* is the greatest novel of the last ten years; for example, it doesn't rank with the best of Hemingway or Dos Passos. But it belongs very high in the category of the great angry books like *Uncle Tom's Cabin* that have roused a people to fight against intolerable wrongs.

A Must Book

Earle Birney*

This is a MUST book. It is not the novel by which Steinbeck steps from the fashionable second-raters to the front ranks of living American fictionists. It is not only a work of concentrated observation, folk humor, and dramatic imagination playing over the whole American continent. It is, more importantly, what Milton would call a "deed" — the act of a man out of the pity and wrath of his heart.

It is a rebellious protest, tempered but by no means obscured by art, against the gradual murder of a half-million southwest farmers by the human instruments of an inhuman and outworn economy. When the land their grandfathers had wrested from the prairie grass is taken from them by drought and the banking system, and pooled for tractor cultivation, they pile their goods and kids in pathetic jallopies and struggle west to California, lured by lying promises of work and land. They arrive, as the big California ranchers had planned, in such myriads and in such extremes of need that they are forced to work for no more than what will keep them half-alive. When the picking is over, and while unsold fruit is destroyed, they are hounded into the highways and left to starve, unprotected by law, unaided by humanity. "And children dying of pellagra must die because profit cannot be taken from an orange."

The book is not free from Steinbeck's old faults. In the ending especially there is theatricality; pain and cruelty are sometimes sensationalized in the manner of Faulkner and Hemingway. There are overtones of mysticism and sentimental individualism which occasionally confuse the dominant social philosophy. The feel of dirt in the farmer's fingers seems at times more important than tractors. The central character, Ma Joad, is too infallibly heroic and sybilline, the preacher too shadowy for his important role. The crudities of American folk-speech are perhaps exag-

*Reprinted with permission from the *Canadian Forum* 19 (June 1939): 94–95.

gerated. Middle-class Toronto, speaking through the word-drunk Mr. Bridle, has already denounced the book, in consequence, as "the most unblushing parade of naturalistic indecency so far Nordized since the war," "more elemental than the worst of Dos Passos," etc.

But the sweep of the book's vision and the controlled passion of its style will carry away all but the most hardened prudes. In one short sentence, Steinbeck can catch the whole human tragedy of an abandoned farmhouse: "The wild cats crept in from the fields at night, but they did not mew at the doorsteps any more."

This is no "proletarian novel." It is rather the only thing a class-conscious artist can write so long as the working people of the earth — of our Canadian prairies too — suffer and die like this under their economic overlords. Steinbeck has no pseudo-Marxist hero from the *Daily Worker* office organizing the farmers along with their bosses into "Leagues for Peace and Democracy." These proletarians of the soil are in the bitter process of learning for themselves in their own terms what wage-labor and capital mean, of creating for themselves fire-hardened leaders and cadres for the coming revolution.

That the end will be revolution is implicit from the title onwards. Self-interest dictates that the Haves will not concede; self-preservation and the ultimately superior power of numbers means that the masses will win, so long as they retain the will to "turn their fear to wrath." The inevitable fruit of the system are the bitter grapes of wrath, and there will one day be a tramping out of the vintage. The book will not, as Clifton Fadiman hopes, "effect something like a revolution in the minds . . . of overcomfortable people," as he assumes *Les Misérables* and *Uncle Tom's Cabin* did. *Les Misérables* did not prevent the Paris Commune nor *Uncle Tom's Cabin* the Civil War. Steinbeck is not so much warning the rich, whom he sees cannot help themselves, as arousing the poor, who can, to courage, endurance, organization, revolt.

[Review of *The Grapes of Wrath*]   Philip Rahv[*]

. . . Since one expected more from Miss Herbst [*Rope of Gold*], a reaction of disappointment was in order. On the other hand from Mr. John Steinbeck — whose inspired pulp-story, *Of Mice and Men*, swept the nation like a plague — one expected nothing. It is therefore gratifying to report that in *The Grapes of Wrath* he appears in a more sympathetic light than in his previous work, not excluding *In Dubious Battle*. This writer, it can

*Reprinted from the *Partisan Review* 6 (Spring 1939): 111–12 by permission of the Philip Rahv estate.

now be seen, is really fired with a passionate faith in the common man. He is the hierophant of the innocent and the injured; and his new book, though it by no means deserves the ecstatic salutations it has received in the press, is an authentic and formidable example of the novel of social protest.

The book is at the same time a detailed exposure of dreadful economic conditions and a long declaration of love to the masses. It is an epic of misery—a prodigious, relentless, and often excruciating account of agrarian suffering. Once introduced to the Joads, a large family of tenant farmers in Oklahoma, we don't lose sight of them through 619 pages of the most minute and literal description of their misfortunes. Living in the dustbowl area, the Joads are evicted by the banks that convert their land to large-scale cotton farming, and together with thousands of other ruined farmers they start on the long auto-trek to California. But all that awaits them is the fate of migratory workers, notoriously the most depressed stratum of the farm population. Mr. Steinbeck spares us not a single scene, not a single sensation, that could help to implicate us emotionally. And he is so much in earnest that a number of times he interrupts his story in order to grapple directly with his thesis. Thus several chapters are devoted to outright political preaching from the standpoint of a kind of homespun revolutionary populism.

But the novel is far too didactic and long-winded. In addition to the defects that are peculiar to his own manner, Mr. Steinbeck has assembled in this one book all the familiar faults of the "proletarian" literary mode. There are the usual idealized portraits and the customary conversions, psychologically false and schematic as ever, to militant principles. Moreover, the technical cleverness displayed in *Of Mice and Men* is lacking in this novel, which should be credited with valid political observation and sincere feeling, but which fails on the test of craftsmanship. Its unconscionable length is out of all proportion to its substance; the "ornery" dialect spoken by its farmers impresses one as being less a form of human speech than a facile convention of the local-color schools; and as to problems of characterization, Mr. Steinbeck does not so much create character as he apes it. For aping, too, can be turned into a means of "re-creating" life. It would appear from this and similar novels that on a sufficiently elementary level, and so long as a uniform scheme of behavior—however simple—is imposed upon characters, all a fiction writer requires to make his people seem real is the patience to follow them everywhere, the perseverance to copy down everything they say and everything they do.

[Review of *The Grapes of Wrath*]   James N. Vaughan*

Five generations of Joads somehow lived and somehow died on American soil before "grampa," then a young man, settled in Oklahoma. Grampa wrested his new land from the Indians. In the evening of the first Oklahoma generation the exhausted earth was converted into a dead and ashy dust. Long before this, catastrophe had befallen, the Joads through mortgage foreclosure had lost title on their forty acres. As tenant farmers of the dust bowl they sought vainly with primitive equipment to compel the dessicated earth to provide both for themselves and for the institutional owner of the land desirous of its "margin of profit." The Joads (and a quarter of a million others who were similarly circumstanced) were eventually "tractored" off the land. With pathetic credulity they accepted the idea, propagated by lying handbills widely circulated in Oklahoma, that work was plentiful in California. The family therefore having exchanged all it possessed for a dilapidated jalopy and a few dollars departed from its dreary homestead to search for a secure future 2,000 miles away.

Security is what the Joads sought. In Oklahoma, though practically destitute, they had achieved a stable rooted circumscribed existence which was prized principally because of its security. To the anxieties and tensions emergent from the undefined, whether of location or of expectations, they had been strangers. They could be accounted happy. When driven from their land three generations of them were living together and the fourth (destined to be stillborn) was in the dark womb of its mother. The story of the disastrous move to the west is a story of death, desertion and hunger. It is the story of the terrors of a people, the organic earthy principles of whose existence has been destroyed for reasons of which they had but the dimmest understanding. His tale of pain, starvation, wretchedness and death, Mr. Steinbeck relates with tenderness and even with detachment so far as the mere story is concerned. If his realism is at times vulgar to a revolting degree, it must be admitted that it offends in this respect on so few occasions that it may be passed over without further mention.

Besides being a novel, *Grapes of Wrath* is a monograph on rural sociology, a manual of practical wisdom in time of enormous stress, an assault on individualism, an essay on behalf of a rather vague form of pantheism and a bitter, ironical attack on that emotional evangelistic religion which seems to thrive in the more impoverished rural districts of this vast country.

The structure of general ideas found in the book is for the most part elaborated by a very effective device consisting of interruptions in the story of the Joads for short excursions into the implications of that story. The

*Reprinted with permission from *Commonweal* 30 (28 July 1939): 341–42. Copyright Commonweal Foundation.

argument is this: Here are representatives of the seventh American generation of solid people who are driven to destitution and death by the forces of "capitalism." In the day of their distress no help is extended to them. On the contrary they are regarded with fear and loathing by possessors of property. The loathing which they inspire in the Californians on whom they descend arises from fear that they constitute a threat to property. Ownership of property freezes a person into an "I" which is incapable of joining with others to constitute a "we." Notwithstanding the force and terror devices used by the Californians (by property holders) for keeping these migrant starvelings in their place (in a cowed condition) some day they will band together to take by violence what will not now be peacefully surrendered, viz., some of the owners' superfluity of goods, and unneeded acreage. The inevitability of the day of violence is expressly asserted. Meantime to arm themselves for the coming struggle, the downtrodden must be spiritually prepared. This preparation will involve the creation of a collectivistic mentality which will prize the cause of the "people" and will view the perils and death of individuals as well as the rights of individuals as of minor significance.

Some fundamental ideas are overlooked by Mr. Steinbeck. In the first place the relief of the conditions he describes does not require violence — as our experience of the last six years has shown. In the next place the doctrine that the spirit of the beehive must supersede a society of persons who are unique, independent and responsible is the absolute negation of the American way of life viewed in its ideal evolution. Moreover, the spread between the truly horrible conditions here faithfully depicted and the deduction in favor of collectivism is really boundless. Again alternatives in the life of the spirit are not even explored when an author contents himself with juxtaposing the acrobatical Christianity typified in the earlier life and doings of his preacher Casy and the wholly vague kind of pantheism which is expounded by Casy in his post-exodus manifestations.

The impact of this book is very powerful. Whoever reads it will find he has gained a better total grasp on the need in this country for rectification of any and all conditions which now or hereafter may correspond in any degree with the terrible plight of the dust bowl tenant farmers.

In the Great Tradition

Charles Angoff*

There should be rejoicing in that part of Hell where the souls of great American imaginative writers while away their time, for at long last a worthy successor to them has appeared in their former terrestrial abode.

*Reprinted from *North American Review* 247 (Summer 1939): 387–89 by permission of the University of Northern Iowa.

With his latest novel Mr. Steinbeck at once joins the company of Hawthorne, Melville, Crane, and Norris, and easily leaps to the forefront of all his contemporaries. The book has all the earmarks of something momentous, monumental, and memorable: universal compassion, a sensuousness so honestly and recklessly tender that even the Fathers of the Church would probably have called it spiritual; and a moral anger against the entire scheme of things that only the highest art possesses. The book also has the proper faults: robust looseness and lack of narrative definitiveness — faults such as can be found in the Bible, *Moby-Dick*, *Don Quixote*, and *Jude the Obscure*. The greatest artists almost never conform to the rules of their art as set down by those who do not practice it. The critics of Bach's time upbraided him severely for not writing fugues as perfect as those of Georg Philipp Telemann.

Apparently nothing much happens in Mr. Steinbeck's tale. A poor white family, the Joads, evicted from their home in the Middle West by the banks, pile into an old automobile and head West toward the land where oranges grow, seeking work of any kind, finding it occasionally at about five cents an hour, but most of the time hounded by police, and in the end get stuck in thick California mud, which looks no more like oranges than Kansas mud. Nothing much happens, but before one has gone a hundred pages into the book, one finds oneself in a whole world of stress and strain, love and hate, charity and cruelty, cowardice and the most sublime heroism.

The dreadful, almost incredible poverty of contemporary American Life, which the New Deal has been trying to combat, beats mercilessly against the Joad family, who can't understand why they should be so hungry in a land so rich.

"The people come with nets to fish for potatoes in the river, and the guards hold them back, they come in rattling cars to get the dumped oranges, but the kerosene is sprayed. And they stand still and watch the potatoes float by, listen to the screaming pigs being killed in a ditch and covered with quicklime, watch the mountains of oranges slop down to a putrefying ooze; and in the eyes of the people there is the failure; and in the eyes of the hungry there is a growing wrath. In the souls of the people the grapes of wrath are filling and growing heavy, growing heavy for the vintage."

But the people, with the patience of Christ, keep on going, helping one another to the last bite of bread and the last drop of milk. As Ma Joad, one of the most notable characters in American fiction, says, "I'm learnin' one thing good. Learnin' it all a time, ever' day. If yo're in trouble or hurt or need — go to the poor people. They're the only ones that'll help — the only ones."

So the Joads exchange help with their fellow wanderers, and they give sustenance and sympathy to one another in the family, especially to those among them whom an indifferent world has treated harshly and stupidly:

son Tom, who served a term in jail; Uncle John, whose wife died because he couldn't afford medical care for her; Preacher Jim Casy, who finally saw the folly of his sermonizing; and daughter Rose of Sharon, whose unemployed husband left her in the middle of her pregnancy.

Ma Joad watches over all of them and dozens of others. She has particular fear for the men lest they collapse inwardly, and she rejoices when she notices rage in their faces, for she knows that "the break would never come as long as fear could turn to wrath." Her final act of magnificence comes at the very end of the book, in a barn, where she has taken her shivering daughter who had just delivered herself a dead child. Both notice a man not far away, dying of starvation.

> "Ma's eyes passed Rose of Sharon's eyes, and then came back to them. And the two women looked deep into each other. The girl's breath came short and gasping.
> "She said, 'Yes.'
> "Ma smiled. 'I knowed you would. I knowed!' "
> Ma and Pa and Uncle John and the younger Joads leave the barn.
> "Rose of Sharon sat still in the whispering barn. Then she hoisted her tired body and drew the comfort about her. She moved slowly to the corner and stood looking down at the wasted face, into the wide, frightened eyes."

Rose of Sharon offers him one of her breasts. " 'You got to,' she said." And thus he was saved from a stable rat's grave.

Some of the literary Episcopalians have already complained about such passages, wholly oblivious to the eternal heartbreak in them, as their predecessors complained about similar passages in the works of Flaubert, Zola, and Hardy. Steinbeck need not worry. His book offers more praise to God than a dozen Cathedrals of St. John the Divine.

Wine Out of These Grapes   Stanley Kunitz*

A book is published by one of our best novelists. It is greeted enthusiastically by critics as one of the most important books of our time. The American people like the book so much that it becomes one of the fastest-selling titles in American publishing history. That book, of course, is *The Grapes of Wrath*, by John Steinbeck, and we are glad to note that, according to our monthly tabulation of "current library favorites," it is the most popular title in our public libraries today. But there are some libraries where the book is not available despite the public demand for it. The Buffalo (N.Y.) Public Library has barred it because "vulgar words are

*Reprinted with permission from *Wilson Library Bulletin* 14 (October 1939): 165. Copyright The H. W. Wilson Company.

employed by characters in the book." (There are vulgar words in Shakespeare and the Bible and *Tom Jones* and *Tristram Shandy* too, and for all we know maybe Buffalo bars them as well.) The public library in Kansas City has been ordered by the Board of Education to remove all copies of Steinbeck's "obscene" book from its shelves. The book is also banned in Kern County, California, where much of the action of the book takes place, and it is reported that the Associated Farmers (which is not a farmers' organization) hopes to forbid circulation of the book thruout the whole state. Librarians who have been told that they "ought to be ashamed to handle such a filthy book" may properly answer that of course we are ashamed, terribly ashamed, but not of the book. What we are ashamed of is that it could be written about our country, that it *had* to be written, that the conditions, the abuses, that it describes actually exist. *Factories in the Field*, a factual study by Carey McWilliams, ought to convince any skeptic that Steinbeck used more than nightmarish imagination in depicting the plight of the migratory farm workers. If the rumblings in Washington are any indication, "something is going to be done about it." You cannot muzzle a good book. You cannot keep the truth from being told.

Mostly of *The Grapes of Wrath*   Art Kuhl*

He isn't treading the wine press alone, not John Steinbeck. Ninetenths of the critical coterie of the United States is treading right along with him, and the net result is that *The Grapes of Wrath* is being loudly trumpeted as the great American novel. Of course that would make Steinbeck the greatest of our novelists, and that's a distinction of no little weight, one that should be deliberated upon before it's bestowed—just in case there should be some little question about it, you understand.

Take me, for example. I think *The Grapes of Wrath* isn't even a truly great novel. It's interesting and well written, better by far than the usual best seller, but it stops this side of greatness.

In that opinion, I have, I know, little support from the secular critics, Burton Rascoe excepted, but a little thing like my being in the minority doesn't necessarily invalidate the opinion, does it?

You see, I really believe that Steinbeck is a master of prose. More than any other man who is writing English today, he understands the language. Not only does he have an almost infallible feeling for the right word— that's still somewhat common in this day of many writers—but he has a rhythmic sense, and the typewriter has almost killed rhythm in English

*Reprinted with permission from *Catholic World* 150 (November 1939): 160–65.

prose. Saroyan has that same sense and uses it to good effect; Faulkner, in his more lucid passages, and particularly in the stories he tells as from the mind of a child, has it; Hemingway in "The Snows of [Kilimanjaro]" had that and little else. But Steinbeck is far and away better than any of them at the inner pulsation that makes good prose almost the equivalent of poetry. He has the same control of pace that marks Georges Bernanos as a master architect of language; in fact certain chapters of *The Grapes of Wrath* march in perfect step with Bernanos's bitter *Diary of My Times*. Each man is, in the best sense of the term, a stylist.

It is strange really that so little has been written about this characteristic of rhythmic control as a hallmark of the greater writer. Everyone admits the high persuasive values of meter or rhythm in poetry, but few seem to realize that prose makes use of those same values. The quality and quantity of syllables, the length of sentences, the stress that is gained through this or that word order, the connotative values that speed or stem the flow of thought — these are tools of the prose artist, and they are essentially tools of rhythm. It is rather generally admitted that the present generation's failure to read the Bible has fractured certain qualities in our prose; few critics, however, seem to realize that the loss has been one of rhythm. The verses of the Bible are great, literarily speaking, for many reasons, but one of the chief of these is that the verses do not merely walk; they move in dance tempos to the pulse of varying beat. Too much of our writing today is without that tempo and without the simple clarity of construction that is the surest means of attaining it.

But Steinbeck has the secret of rhythm. Even his longer passages of description will stand the test of being read aloud, and there is no test more severe. In the very cadences of his sentences and his paragraphs Steinbeck achieves his purpose; in *The Grapes of Wrath* it is the purpose of blasting.

Beyond that he has a sure ear for dialogue. He seems to know the people of whom he writes, to know them so well that he always makes them speak precisely their own language. This was superbly evident in *Of Mice and Men*. Lennie's halting, repetitious, simple speech *was* Lennie; you could hear the very quality of his voice in the words that he spoke. George's rough speech *was* George, even when he was using the crude poetry that described their ranch-to-be and the rabbits they would raise and the way they wouldn't have to take orders from anybody. Perhaps the greatest tribute to the realistic dialogue of that novel was the fact that Steinbeck could transcribe it almost literally for the stage. The speeches of his characters could be taken whole, put before the canvas scenery, and made to sound terribly, hauntingly real; in fact they brought the very scenery to life. That means that Steinbeck has reached one of the summits in the novelist's art: he has become a dramatist of conversation. Dialogue that conveys an idea and moves a story forward is not too difficult to write, though it presents its own problems; dialogue that fulfills that double purpose and then goes further to become strongly characteristic, revelatory of the speaker even when the author includes no asides and no explanations, is a product of high art. Steinbeck writes just such dialogue.

I have said that the gift was superbly evident in *Of Mice and Men*, implying that it is not so evident in *The Grapes of Wrath*; that is perhaps incorrect. I was acutely conscious of the mastery in that first novel; it made me stop and consider and marvel. *The Grapes of Wrath*, on the other hand, has dialogue that is less obtrusive; it is perhaps better precisely because one doesn't realize consciously that it is better — or even that it is at all good. The Joads speak naturally; at least (it is just as good) their speech sounds natural to the reader. Even profanity, which spots the book, comes somehow to be an accepted part of that speech; you may be pained to see it used so frequently, but you are no more surprised by it than you are by the habitual swearing of a riveter.

So much then is on the credit side for *The Grapes of Wrath* and Steinbeck. But the novel tilts at a rather surprising angle, for it has lost one of the literary legs on which Steinbeck seemed to stand most firmly. In *Tortilla Flat* he drew his characters with surprising fluency; Danny and his friends were completely real and completely characterized; even the minor characters were defty drawn and set apart. In *Of Mice and Men* the same thing was true. The people of that book were real people; they did not melt into mere stereotypes; they stood as characters wholly integrated. But *The Grapes of Wrath* has too little of the fine-point etching, the careful individualization that gave those two novels their primary appeal.

It is not a case of Steinbeck's having lost completely his power of realizing a character. Casy, the ex-preacher; Ma, the bulwark of the Joads; Tom, the hothead out on parole; Grandpa, the obscene old patriarch of the family — these are characters that are fully conceived. But something seems to happen to Steinbeck's powers as the novel wears on; that is one of the reasons for my own belief that the book is too long — too long, not for the reading, but for the writing. In the shorter compass of his earlier books Steinbeck burned steadily, and his characters were always authentically executed. In this, his first long work, he has a chance to dissipate his efforts, to spread out and be more leisurely; near the end of the road he seems to lose his breath.

Thus the first chapters of the novel have admirable minor characters like the truck driver who helps Tom along the road and the rebel who will not leave the land. But as the novel wears on, these men, of course, disappear and no one ever comes to take their places. Everyone, even the major characters, begins to be part of a chorus that is singing Steinbeck's message; characterization goes by the board. As a result the people who were not developed early are not developed at all; Pa remains constantly nebulous, never quite coming clear.

What is even more tragic is the fact that the very characters that were strongly developed drop out along the way. Casy, who is something of a reprobate but an interesting one, disappears after he is arrested in Hooverville and makes no further appearance except for a brief and not very characteristic bow before he is killed off. Even Tom, who seemed to be intended to carry the main weight of the story, is gone before the story ends, and for a long time he lies hidden in a culvert, completely outside the action of the story.

Of course I may be entirely wrong in this supposition, but I believe that Steinbeck had a definite purpose in performing this conjuring act upon his characters. "Life itself," he said, "isn't run after the fashion of a play. The heroes and heroines don't linger about until the curtain goes down at the end of the third act; they're just as likely to wander off along about the middle of the second or even the very beginning of the first. I'll have my characters do that too. For really it isn't just these people about whom I'm writing that are important; their story is important, but they aren't, not as individuals." So in *The Grapes of Wrath* he lets a character drop out of sight whenever it pleases him, and to a degree he succeeds in fastening attention upon his story rather than upon his actors.

Now Steinbeck is undoubtedly right about the wandering tendency of life's heroes and heroines; for the most part we live rather consistently on anticlimaxes. We're always leaving the room just before the body of the murdered man rolls across the lintel and Mrs. Jones screams that she's been robbed. And perhaps Steinbeck is right in believing that it is his story, not his characters, that is important. But he seems to have forgotten that if he is right, he had no business writing the novel that he did, not if he expected it to be taken seriously as a great novel.

In fact it seems to be questionable whether he should even pretend to be writing a novel when he writes with that express philosophy. For characterization, the description and even the definition of man, is the very heart of the novel; the person is as important to the novel as he is to the Christian scheme of salvation; the only timeless quality in the matter of any writing is the character, the nature, of man.

When Steinbeck forgot that, he fell victim to corn. Corn is a very descriptive if somewhat ambiguous word from the lexicon of modern swing music; to a swing addict it means any sweet music, any music in which the appeal is strictly sentimental, in which the melody is too lush and too obvious. Corny literature is writing in which the same element of the obvious predominates.

The extreme is the cigar-store novel in which the hero is strong and unbelievably handsome and good, the heroine is meltingly sweet and virtuous, and the villain is too, too heartless and cruel; the fault is a lack of consistent characterization, a failure to see man as he really is, a composite not to be stripped too quickly to a single quality. Such a novel attempts to speak of incarnate good, incarnate evil. Short of the extreme but still on the corny side is the propaganda literature in which characters become types, mere sketchy representatives, not of virtue or evil, but of forces and masses. And Steinbeck has to a degree yielded to just such corn. He has tried to write a novel in which the really important elements are nameless things without faces; he has tried to write about the banks and starvation and a thing that we call the system. To a degree he has succeeded, but in the process he has forgotten the proper end of a novel. He has laid himself open to that somewhat threadbare question: It's propaganda, but is it art?

Certainly he makes no attempt at all to hide the fact that he is writing propaganda. And in writing it he has hit upon a scheme that might well have saved his book entirely from the usual propaganda pitfalls, especially the pitfall of "types." He has gone back to a device of the old picaresque novelists. It used to be the custom, because novels were frowned upon as frivolous and because the stories were so frequently tinged with indecency, to attempt a rescue by appending to each chapter a small portion of moralizing. This moral tail was appended to please the high-minded and to placate the censors; it was something of an essay added to the body of the narrative. Of course most readers skipped the moralizing and read only the story.

Steinbeck has used the same technique, but with an entirely different purpose. At intervals throughout the book he has inserted chapters that are diatribes on the economic system, the background of the story that he is writing. These chapters have no direct connection with the story in the sense that they do not directly move the action of that story forward. But they interpret; they place this single narrative in the broad frame of chaos, balancing the single story against the story of a people, accenting this as typical of a great migrating class.

The result is that the actual narrative is somewhat rescued from the usual blurring that stereotypes propaganda art. Steinbeck really could have written a story that was as individual as the people who move through life, for this technique could have enabled him to focus on his story. He could have written a novel that would have been as effective as the short story that I believe in part inspired *The Grapes of Wrath*. That short story appears, as I recall it, in the 1936 O'Brien collection, and it is the story of a little girl, one of a family of down-and-out transients in California, who wanted shoes. The author there annotated his story by interpolating direct quotations from an objective sociological study of this migrant class in California. The result was overpowering, just as Steinbeck's novel so often is. But the short story remained consistently good art; it let the interpolations take care of the propaganda and contented itself with dramatic reporting. Steinbeck instead has wobbled.

That he has wobbled may be credited to a stress and conflict within him. Evidently he was powerfully tempted to submit entirely to the newest focal point of left wingers — the "we-ness" of life. Emphasizing the Communistic denatured substitute for the Mystical Body of Christ — The Brotherhood of Man without consideration of the Fatherhood of God — the leftists are now intent upon proclaiming the merger of man-mind: It is not the I, it is the we that counts; we must submerge the individual in the totality. It's the same old blarney that the Third International has been using for such a long time, but now it is being given a hypodermic and sent back into the game by the artists of the proletariat.

Steinbeck is enough of an artist to resist the temptation to a degree at least. He is wise enough to see that if the individual becomes completely unimportant, if it is only the mass that counts, then man is less than man and novel writing is stupid or even impossible. If no single person really counts for anything, then the novelist doesn't count for anything, and he had best stop writing. If only the fundamental likenesses of man are important and the equally fundamental disparities are to be overlooked, then it is still possible to compile an encyclopedia, but there isn't any sense in trying to write literature.

He does not see, I believe, that this state is itself an indictment of the philosophy that he almost adopts, Communism. The dehumanizing nature of Communism is in few places more evident than it is here.

But Steinbeck does manage to avoid being led into the actual detailed statement of a solution to the problem that he proposes. He does not so much as attempt to indicate the name of the solution. Failure to shy clear of that pitfall has too often wrecked a good art form in the past. *Waiting for Lefty*, for example, the Communist play "classic," falls short because of its dramatically insecure last few speeches. Entirely apart from the fact that Communism is no solution sociologically, having an actor shout its name is no solution dramatically; in fact is simply stupid. Steinbeck at no point pins himself down as Odets did. Broadly speaking, the Steinbeck novel is merely inherent protest; it is not and does not pretend to be constructive beyond mention of the we.

For that reason the too frequent Catholic denunciations of the book as plain Red palaver are certainly unjustified. Protest against the iniquities of tenant farming or sharecropping, against Cain-modeled refusal to give a fellow man a decent break, against unemployment and its funereal parade of evils — such protest is Catholic and catholic, not Communist alone.

But for the same reason, too, Steinbeck plays hob with his own dramatic sense in at least two intervals. Because he cannot resort to description of his intended solution, he goes into symbolism, and he is not too good at the handling of symbols. Early in the book he devotes a chapter to a plodding turtle, his own way of affirming deep conviction in the ultimate invincibility of the class. Two things are wrong with the chapter: Its writing is, as usual, highly picturesque, and the rhythms of the prose are authentic, but the chapter is for all that tedious; it is as if someone were to describe in detail the process of rending a daisy petal from petal; the reader is strongly tempted to mutter "So what?" Second — and this is perhaps more important — the allegory is too plainly trite. We pay off for imaginations that are bright and new-coined.

That second accusation holds even more true in the final use of symbolism, the concluding pages of the novel. There a young woman whose baby has died at birth gives suck to a starving old man. In the plainer language of Hollywood, that is so much hokum. One is surprised that the Steinbeck imagination would stoop to go through so low a door.

For when all is said — and not all has been, not by a long shot — Steinbeck is really one of our finest imaginative writers today. *The Grapes of Wrath* is sometimes vulgar and a bit dirty at the edges, a rather surprising fact in view of the care that went into the writing of *Of Mice and Men*. Even *Tortilla Flat*, which dealt with an amoral group of *paisanos*, stayed, except in one instance, on the near side of the railroad tracks. Usually resort to the merely dirty indicates a lag in flights of fancy, but in view of earlier work that accusation can hardly be brought against Steinbeck. Perhaps it is best to forgive his occasional lapses; he really doesn't need pornography to make his books sell, and he may come back to straighter roads in the days ahead.

He may in fact come to be what he has been called, America's great novelist. He is not yet great today.

Careers at Crossroads [Excerpt]   Wilbur L. Schramm*

The third book was opened eagerly because it is by the most promising young novelist in America. What Thomas Wolfe was in 1930, John Steinbeck has been for the last several years. Lacking Wolfe's endless memory for subjective details, Wolfe's occasional lightning flashes, still he had almost from the beginning qualities Wolfe never attained: objectivity, solidity, and above all, the ability to lose himself in something greater than himself, the ability to connect his wires to a voltage greater than his own. In Steinbeck's case this is the problem of the common man. For several years now he has been producing warm, powerful portraits of common men, each book showing some advance over the one preceding, each book showing great power moving toward maturity. *In Dubious Battle*, stories like "Chrysanthemums" and "The Red Pony," and *Of Mice and Men* were landmarks that led his readers to expect soon the great novel. *The Grapes of Wrath* will justify their hopes.

It is the story of the Okies, the Oklahoma farmers driven from their land by dust and depression and centralizing economics, driven to seek vainly for asylum in California. The central characters are the Joads, Grandpa and Grandma, Uncle John, Ma and Pa, Tom and Rose of Sharon, Al and the kids. They are so alive that they almost step out of the pages of the book, and when lusty old Grandpa is left in an unmarked grave beside the road because the undertaker wants forty dollars to bury him, the

*Reprinted with permission from *Virginia Quarterly Review* 15 (Autumn 1939): 630–32.

reader feels a sense of personal loss. This ability John Steinbeck has: to breathe life into his characters and to tear at our hearts with their problems and their struggles. Whereas Dos Passos' social books are built on hate for an economic system, *The Grapes of Wrath* is built on a love for the people bound to that system. It is a significant difference.

The Joads are related to the whole exodus by means of impersonal chapters, a sort of poetic history, which form an interesting parallel to Dos Passos' News Reels although they occupy far more space than Dos Passos ever gave his device. For this reader they occupy a little too much space; he would be happier if the book leaned a bit more heavily on the Joads' own story. He would be happier if the material were never overdramatized. But these are small cavils. *The Grapes of Wrath* is a book with big shoulders. No American book of our time is more moving; no book is a better indication of what the proletarian novel can be. A comparison with Dickens is inevitable, and yet Steinbeck is not like Dickens except in his fierce sympathy and in the moving quality of his writing. He is not another Dickens or anyone else; he is himself, a force in his own right.

And he is still the most promising novelist in America. The only change in his status is that *The Grapes of Wrath* has given rich fruition to that promise, richer hope of what is to come. There is no sign yet that Steinbeck is at the height of his powers. No other young novelist has such a magnificent arsenal of weapons. The only question now is: How high can Steinbeck go?

Graphics

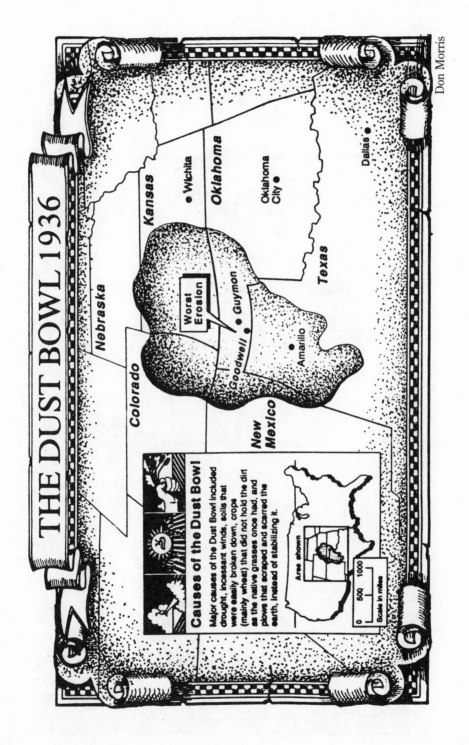

THE DUST BOWL 1936

Nebraska

Kansas

Colorado

• Wichita

Oklahoma

Oklahoma
City •

Worst
Erosion

• Guymon

Goodwell •

• Amarillo

Texas

Dallas •

New
Mexico

Causes of the Dust Bowl

Major causes of the Dust Bowl included drought, incessant winds, soils that were easily broken down, crops (mainly wheat) that did not hold the dirt as the native grasses once had, and plows that scraped and scarred the earth, instead of stabilizing it.

Area shown

Scale in miles
0   500   1000

Don Morris

47

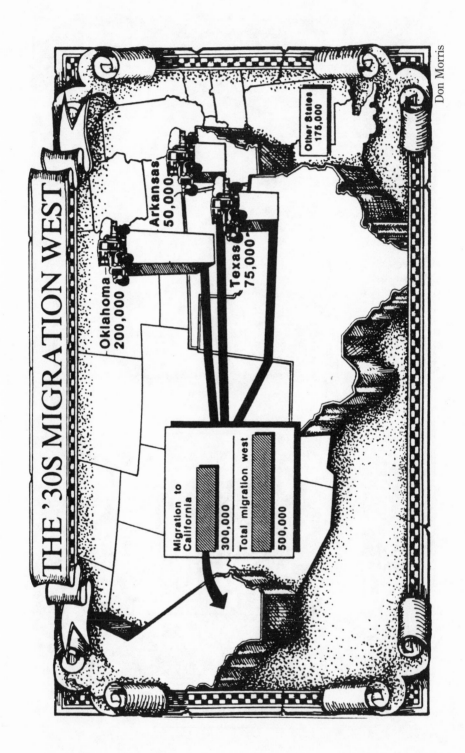

THE '30S MIGRATION WEST

Other States
175,000

Arkansas
50,000

Oklahoma
200,000

Texas
75,000

Migration to
California
300,000

Total migration west
500,000

Don Morris

48

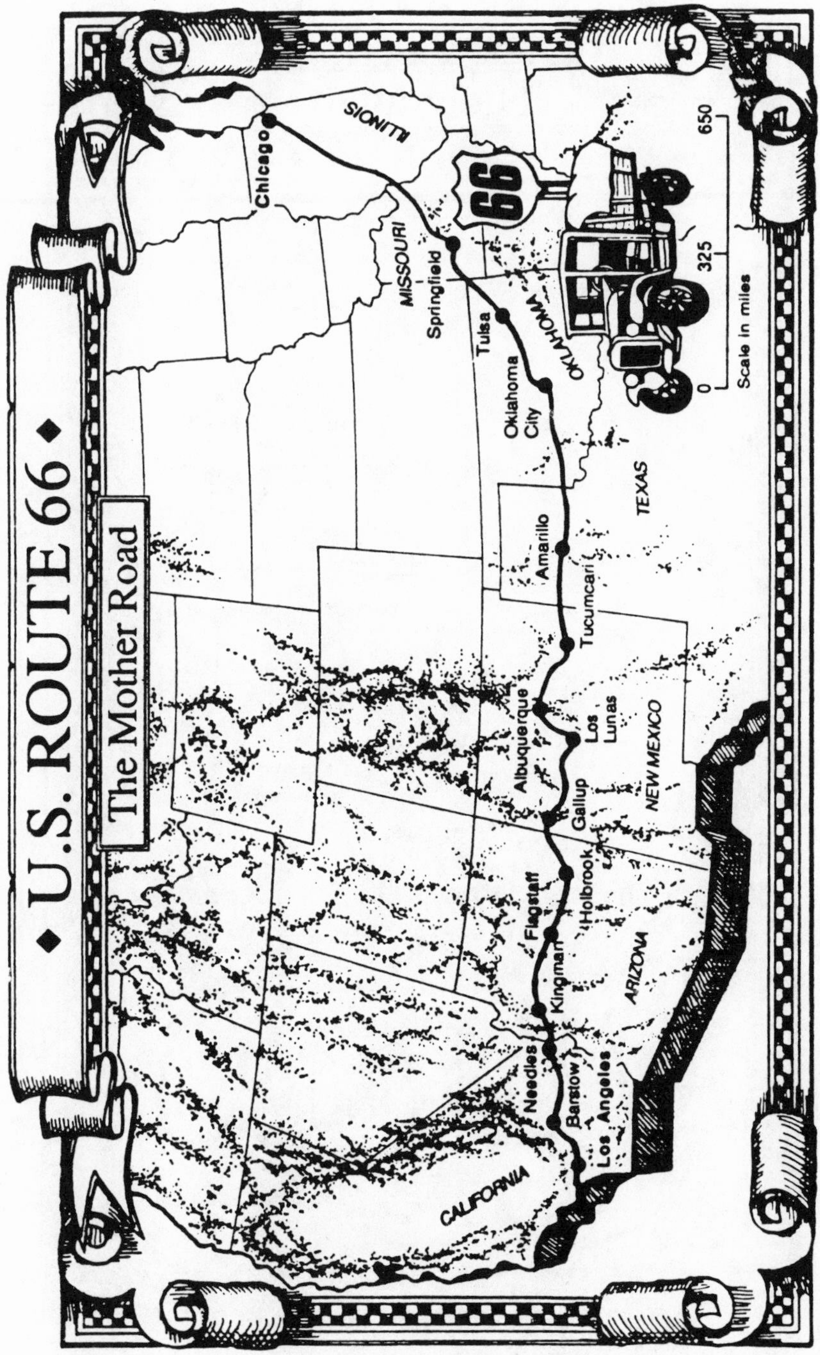

◆ U.S. ROUTE 66 ◆

The Mother Road

Don Morris

Chicago

ILLINOIS

MISSOURI

Springfield

Tulsa

OKLAHOMA

Oklahoma City

TEXAS

Amarillo

Tucumcari

Albuquerque

Los Lunas

Gallup

NEW MEXICO

Flagstaff

Holbrook

Kingman

ARIZONA

Needles

Barstow

Los Angeles

CALIFORNIA

Scale in miles

0   325   650

49

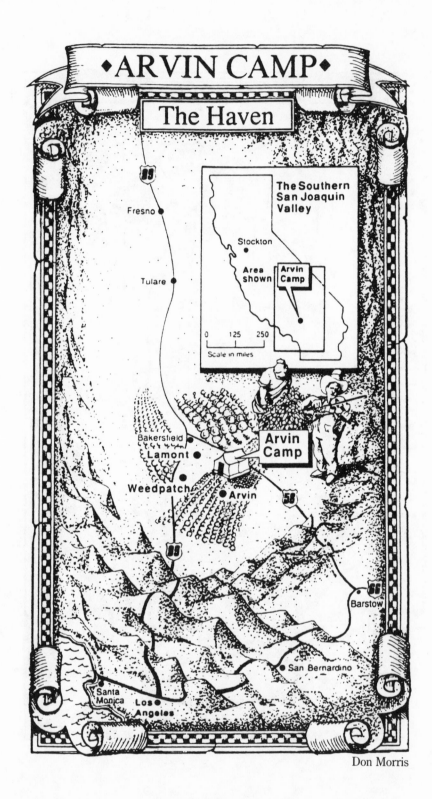

Don Morris

Articles and Essays

The Background to the Composition of *The Grapes of Wrath*

Jackson J. Benson*

Strange, but John Steinbeck wrote hardly a word about farm labor during his long apprenticeship — the one exception involved a few scenes of migrant workers, Filipinos, in a peculiar short story published in the *Stanford Spectator* called "Fingers of Cloud."[1] The omission seems odd because in retrospect the farm family, the farm worker, and the migrant seem to have been his natural subjects. These, after all, were people and settings of which he had extensive personal knowledge, growing up, as he did, partly on a ranch, knowing many farm families, and working, both as a teenager and a young man, in the fields of the Salinas Valley.

But he was ignorant of or chose to ignore the dictum that was to guide so many other American writers in our century: write what you know. Steinbeck began from another direction, perhaps guided by his love for Malory's *Morte d'Arthur*. This book, which led him, as he has stated, to becoming a writer, may also have led him to love romance, legend, fantasy, and allegory — elements that dominated his early stories and his first novels. Indeed, even the California settings that we so naturally associate with the Steinbeck name were to come into his work only gradually, coming at first by accident as he took over a manuscript from a friend, which became his second novel by composition, *To a God Unknown*.

Although his third novel by composition, *The Pastures of Heaven*, deals with farm families in a California valley, the author's attention is far more on the myth and mystery he attaches to his people than on the realistic hardships of their lives. Like his previous books, this also was a work essentially of romance and imagination. It is not until *In Dubious Battle*, his fifth novel (1936), that he takes up the subjects of farm labor and the dispossessed and takes up the method of writing from life. Here, in

*Revised from "John Steinbeck and Farm Labor Unionization: The Background of *In Dubious Battle*" (with Anne Loftis), *American Literature* 52 (May 1980): 194–223; "The Background of *The Grapes of Wrath*," *Journal of Modern Literature* 5 (April 1976): 151–232, © 1976 Temple University; and chapters 19, 20, and 21 of *The True Adventures of John Steinbeck, Writer* (New York: Viking Press, 1984).

his preparation for this earlier work, the seed for his epic, *The Grapes of Wrath*, was planted. Here our story begins.

I

Once again, as when Steinbeck's attention was turned to the use of a California setting, a major turn in his career was taken largely by accident. A writer not much concerned with social problems at that time — simply getting enough to eat and becoming the artist he wanted to become had taken nearly all of his attention — he would become the most prominent social-political novelist of the period, although he, himself, would remain largely apolitical. Above all things, he was interested in finding a good story.

Although Steinbeck was not much interested in politics, his wife, Carol, was. Contrary to the Republican views of all the rest of his own family, John had early in life developed rather generalized, liberal sympathies, but his wife had become, during the early years of the Depression, a rather vehement and outspoken political radical. It was one of her friends, Sis Reamer (who thought John to be too uninvolved and aloof from the "class struggle"), who gave him the story opportunity he was looking for.[2]

Sis, who was involved in local groups who were raising money and supplies to support the Communist efforts to organize farm labor through the Cannery and Agricultural Workers' Industrial Union, brought news to the Steinbecks, in early 1934, of two men who had worked for the union who were now in hiding. They were in the attic of a local union official who lived in Seaside, near Monterey. One of these men, Cicil McKiddy, in hiding from the retribution of California law intolerant of union activities, would provide the author with much of the material he would use for *In Dubious Battle*.

McKiddy was part of an extended family that moved, during the twenties and thirties, from Oklahoma, where some of them had homesteaded, to California. By the time McKiddy arrived, in the early thirties, conditions were very bad. Wages were at an average of fifteen cents an hour, farm labor had been denied protection under the newly enacted National Industrial Recovery Act (which had given workers in industry the right to organize), and an overabundance of farm workers was stoking the fires of intolerance toward the Dust Bowl migrants. It seems likely that through his conversations with McKiddy Steinbeck was made aware for the first time of the extent of the great Dust Bowl migration and of the depth of hostility in the reception given the Okies in the Golden State. McKiddy's family was apparently radicalized by these conditions, for both McKiddy and his uncle, Bill Hammett, went to work for the union, and McKiddy became a Party member.

While McKiddy seems to have contributed to the composite that would make up the character Tom Joad, his uncle—a sometime-preacher who was converted by the frustrations of migrant life into a worker leader—seems to have formed the basis for the character Jim Casy. Bill Hammett, who, according to Anne Loftis "had a natural authority of manner and gift for public speaking," is quoted as saying, "What do we care whether we are Reds or what we are, if we can get our wages raised?" Even more convincing evidence that McKiddy's stories were on Steinbeck's mind as he moved over a several-year period to the composition of *The Grapes of Wrath* is that one of the strikes the fugitive told him about was the Peach Strike on the Tagus Ranch in the Central Valley (where his uncle was recruited to become strike leader Pat Chambers's right-hand man). Not only did the writer use incidents from this struggle in his strike novel, *In Dubious Battle*, he would use the conflict once again as the basis for the episodes in his later novel on the peach ranch near Pixley. Anne Loftis, among others, has suggested that Hammett was probably the model for the worker-leader London in the strike novel, so that it appears that there was a good deal of crossover of both incident and character, from the same source, from one novel to the other.[3]

As a result of the publication of *In Dubious Battle*, its author— strangely enough considering the circumstances—became considered an "expert" on migrant workers and farm labor unionization. Even by the radicals, the book was acclaimed as "the best labor and strike novel to come out of our contemporary economic and social unrest."[4] But Steinbeck himself had not become radicalized. Alarmed by the essentially political reception that the novel was receiving, John wrote to friend George Albee, "I have used a small strike in an orchard valley as the symbol of man's eternal, bitter warfare with himself. I'm not interested in strike as means of raising men's wages, and I'm not interested in ranting about justice and oppression, mere outcropping which indicate the condition."[5]

He thought he had transformed the particular into the universal, creating a work of literature, but many of his readers took the novel to be a work of social reform and political propaganda. The same misreading would haunt him even more painfully in the reception that would be accorded to his great novel about the Dust Bowl migration.

II

On the basis of Steinbeck's growing reputation as a farm labor expert, George West, chief editorial writer for the *San Francisco News*, asked him to write a series of articles for the *News* about California's farm workers. West was an acquaintance who John and Carol had met at the home of Lincoln Steffens, the famous muckraker, and Ella Winter, prominent activist, in Carmel. West was sympathetic to the migrants, and he worked for the only major paper in California that had anything good to say about unions. He was particularly concerned that the novelist investigate the lot of the Dust Bowl migrants in the state — a phenomenon that had gone on for years but which only recently had begun to be perceived as a possible major social problem — and efforts by federal and state governments to ease the problem by the construction of sanitary camps.[6]

At West's suggestion, Steinbeck went to see Fred Soule, the Regional Information Advisor for the Farm Security Administration, in his office in San Francisco. Soule was able to brief him about the migrant problem and the government camp program, as well as provide him with the statistics he might need for his articles. Since there was a good deal of public opposition to the programs of the F.S.A., a New Deal agency denounced by conservative lawmakers and periodicals as "socialistic," the officials of the agency were pleased to have a writer of Steinbeck's stature and sympathies investigating the problem and their efforts to alleviate it. So important to them was John's projected series of articles that Eric H. Thomsen, Regional Director in Charge of Management, took two weeks from his regular duties to personally escort John on a tour through the Central Valley.[7]

He and Thomsen, in John's old Chevy, toured the farms and labor camps, the Hoovervilles and shanty towns, observing living conditions and interviewing laborers and their families. Near the bottom of the Valley below Bakersfield, they arrived at the Arvin Sanitary Camp, more familiarly called "Weedpatch." This was the model that Thomsen wanted John to compare to the filth and degradation they had seen in the cardboard-shack villages that had sprung up along the hookworm-invested banks of irrigation ditches.

The camp program had begun as a state program, the idea of Paul S. Taylor, an economics professor who acted as consultant to Harry E. Drobish, State Director of Rural Rehabilitation. It was Taylor who, while doing field research, first realized the dimensions of the Dust Bowl migration as a major population movement.[8] Starting in the early 1930s, over a half million fled the Okie states during the Depression, and of these, about 300,000 ended up in California. Most of these were semiliterate, unskilled workers — farmers and sharecroppers and their families who either had been dusted off primitive, subsistence farms or, outside the region of blowing dust, had been forced to leave by harsh economic conditions. When they came to California, which already had a surplus of farm labor, they found that there was no place for them to go. The land was all taken, and even when available, farm labor paid so poorly that a whole family working from sunrise to sunset earned hardly enough to eat that day.[9]

Local governments' efforts to "solve" the problem of masses of indigent people in their jurisdictions ranged from turning the migrants back from California at the state line, to evicting them from areas where their labor was no longer needed (either by force or by bribes of gifts of gasoline), to a policy of constant harassment in the hope that the migrants would somehow disappear, become someone else's problem, or go back to where they came from. Law enforcement, relief agencies, and employment bureaus all tended to take a hard line toward the Okies, cooperating with grower demands, and even in several instances cooperating with vigilante actions directed against the "Red threat" of union organizing in the fields and groves.

The camp program was one of the few bright spots in a bleak picture of prejudice, exploitation, and mass human misery. But even it, although the motives of its promoters were humane, was partially a response to health fears by the native population. The "sanitary" camp, as it was called, not only gave the migrants a temporary safe haven where they could wash, rest, and recover their dignity, it also gave the state and local jurisdictions the opportunity to bring in public health nurses to control communicable diseases. Such camps also gave growers the chance to try to control worker populations and to monitor them for signs of union activity, although the larger growers in each locality usually opposed construction of the camps in the first place.

As a matter of fact, opposition from the farm establishment — the Associated Farmers, banks and large landowners, and rural press — was so vehement in response to the initial state plan that it came close to being dropped. However, the state agency, which had been federally funded anyway, was taken from the state and made part of the federal Resettlement Administration (later the Farm Security Administration) in early May of 1935. The first camp opened in the summer of 1935 near Marysville, about fifty miles north of Sacramento, and in the fall, another, the one that was to play a part in *The Grapes of Wrath*, was built at Arvin, near the other end of the Central Valley.[10]

The state plan in 1935 had been to build a whole chain of camps up and down the state, enough to house a considerable portion of the migrants. However, unremitting hostility by Congress and by a conservative press forced the F.S.A. to scale back its program to a limited number of "demonstration" camps. Even this plan, for twenty-five camps, was eroded through lack of funds, so that by 1940, only fifteen camps had been completed or were under construction.[11]

If the idea of the demonstration camps was that the facilities would be duplicated by the growers or local governments, then the program was a failure. However, the camps did offer an opportunity for respite from unbearable poverty and filth for several thousand of the most desperate worker families, and perhaps most valuable of all, it gave some of them, through the genius and compassion of the camp managers and staff, back their sense of dignity and some hope for the future.

III

Years ago, when I first read John Steinbeck's *The Grapes of Wrath*, I noticed the second part of the novel's dedication, "To TOM who lived it," and it added a certain excitement to the novel. I thought, as perhaps most readers also thought, that the dedication referred to some real-life counterpart of the novel's central character, Tom Joad. And in thinking about the novel, I began to consider it, in part, a testimony to a friendship. Through the years I have had it in my mind's eye that Steinbeck traveled to Oklahoma and hooked up with a family, the Joads, which had been dusted off of its farm and was headed West. I saw the writer becoming a companion to the older son, while the family made its way in an old battered car made into a truck, across the desert and mountains into California. And in my imagination I saw John Steinbeck, squatting on his heels with a tin cup in his hand in front of a roadside campfire, probing the heart and mind of a Tom Joad dressed in overalls and looking a little like Henry Fonda.

But it didn't happen that way. First, contrary to the story that has become part of American folklore, John did not travel to Oklahoma and then make a trip back to California with a migrant family. He made four trips to the Central Valley, and on one occasion drove on from Bakersfield over the Tehachapi Mountains through the Mojave to the state line near Needles. When he came back, he talked about the "Okies," and his friends assumed he had gone all the way to Oklahoma. John loved being mysterious, and several years later when acquaintances would mention the "Oklahoma trip," he would only smile, without comment. Many years later he began to talk of the trip with the migrants from Oklahoma as if he had actually made it.[12]

Second, the Tom in the dedication did not refer to a real-life Tom Joad or to a migrant at all, but to Tom Collins, the manager of the Arvin Sanitary Camp. Collins was a very unusual man who would provide a great deal of background information for Steinbeck about the migrants, their customs, speech, and behavior, and at the same time, he also would make a considerable contribution to the spirit of the novel, its attitudes and values.

When John, accompanied by Eric Thomsen, arrived at Arvin on his first research trip to the Valley, it was just nightfall and raining. The wheels of his car threw up muddy water as he drove by the rows of dripping tents to the canvas shelter that was the temporary office. Inside, sitting at a littered table and surrounded by a throng of people who had come in to stand out of the rain, was Tom Collins, a small man in a damp, frayed, white suit. As John recalls the scene,

> The crowding people looked at him all the time. Just stood and looked at him. He had a small moustache, his graying, black hair stood up on his head like the quills of a frightened porcupine, and his large, dark eyes, tired beyond sleepiness, the kind of tired that won't let you sleep even if you have the time and a bed.

Thomsen introduced John to Tom, and the latter invited them to his own tent for coffee. It was made, but not drunk, for reports kept coming in from all over the muddy camp: there was an epidemic, and every kind of winter disease had developed — measles, whooping cough, mumps, pneumonia. And this one man was trying to do everything in this gathering of two thousand people because there was no one else to help. Even if the residents wanted to help, they couldn't for lack of knowledge. Back and forth he went, nursing, advising, settling arguments, and doing whatever he could to help the suffering, console the worried families, and keep the peace until morning should finally come.[13]

This was Steinbeck's introduction to the man who became the most important single source for his novel. Later, during three additional trips to various parts of California, Collins would accompany the writer. In John's words, "[we] sat in the ditches with the migrant workers, lived and ate with them. We heard a thousand miseries and a thousand jokes. We ate fried dough and sow belly, worked with the sick and the hungry, listened to complaints and little triumphs."[14]

It was not only Collins's endurance and capacity for work that attracted Steinbeck's admiration, but his love for people, no matter how poor or how ignorant, and his very large capacity for acceptance. Collins's background was that of a man who had trained for a time for the priesthood and then quit to become a teacher. After teaching for the Navy in Alaska and Guam, he started his own school for delinquent boys, and when that enterprise went bankrupt, he found a job as head of the Federal Transient Service Facility (the Depression era soup kitchens) in Los Angeles.[15] He was an idealist, a utopian reformer, a romantic, and, at his worst, something of a con artist; at the same time he was also a good administrator, a compassionate man, and experienced enough not to be too surprised at the foolish and stupid things that men do both to themselves and to each other.

After leaving the Federal Transient Service, he worked for the Resettlement Administration and Farm Security Administration from 1935 to 1941. He was very good at this work, and this period no doubt became the high-water mark of his life. Although he was not an administrator who could make decisions about the camps as a whole, he probably had more impact on the camp program than any other individual, for he was the first camp manager and designed the way the camps would actually operate. After his tenure at the Marysville camp, he had become so well regarded by his superiors that he was assigned to open most of the camps as they were built and to train new managers.[16]

Collins made the camps work by giving most of the day-to-day responsibility for running the camps to the residents themselves. He established a simple democracy, in which the camp was governed by a camp committee made up of one representative from each of the sections of the camp. Each unit elected its representatives to this town council, as well as electing representatives to various operating committees that dealt with fire, recreation, children's playground, and children's welfare, and the governing board of the Women's Club. (This club, which figures prominently in the government camp section of the novel, was later called the "Good Neighbors Society.") The camp committee at Weedpatch had the primary responsibility for setting up the rules and enforcing them, a job it took seriously.[17]

Tact is probably the key quality that made Collins so successful as a manager. He was conscious of the fact that those who came to the camp had been pushed around, insulted, and looked down upon, and he made every effort to allay their natural hostility and suspicion and restore their sense of self-worth by treating each resident with dignity. Milan Dempster, who came into the camp program as a manager in 1937, recalls that both Collins and Robert Hardie, who replaced Collins at Weedpatch, were extremely sensitive to the temper of the people in the camps, constantly cultivating a sense of their instincts and ways.[18]

Taking charge of the initial planning and organization for one camp after another as each opened, Collins would usually work with two hundred to a thousand people, many of them ignorant of basic sanitation, many of them either hostile and suspicious or worn out and desperate, to help them mold themselves into a cohesive, self-governing society. Even though this was a society of migrants, a society whose members were always changing, the residents achieved a continuity, always passing on from the old residents to the new the spirit of what Collins called "the good neighbor." It was an old-fashioned virtue that both Collins and his Okies could believe in.

Steinbeck spent several days with Collins on this first visit, carefully observing the operations of the camp, following Collins in his work, mingling with and talking to the campers—blending in with ordinary people inconspicuously and talking to them convincingly about their own interests were two of the author's major talents. He attended a camp committee meeting, watched the Good Neighbors Society welcome new arrivals, and went to one of the weekend camp dances. Since it was part of Collins's job to keep track of conditions at nearby squatters' camps, Steinbeck also accompanied him on these trips and visited nearby farms, where he not only gathered material for his News articles, but also stored away bits and pieces of material that he would later use in The Grapes of Wrath.[19]

One of the squatters' camps they visited was just north of Arvin at Lamont where they talked to the young son of the chairman of the Weedpatch Camp Committee who was a fugitive from the law, staying away from his family for fear of bringing them trouble. Dewey Russell, a manager of the camp after Collins, has said that Collins told him that the model for the Joad family was that of Sherm Eastom, the camp committee chairman at the time Steinbeck visited Weedpatch. Collins also told Russell that the model for Tom Joad was "the son [of Eastom] who was a fugitive, lived under another name, out in Lamont."[20]

IV

In the words of a friend and neighbor who saw Steinbeck on his return from his trip to the Valley, the writer came back with "a pile of material" given to him by Collins "on the Okies and the government camp he managed, with observations and dialogue."[21] This stack of material was composed of copies of Collins's camp reports, a rich vein of detailed information that John would use for his *News* articles and in *The Grapes of Wrath*. These reports, which were sent to the Farm Security Administration sometimes weekly, sometimes biweekly, were often very long, running to twelve, fourteen, even twenty pages. They included observations, statistics, and anecdotes covering almost every aspect of camp life, as well as some information about migrant life outside the camp. In the reports there are many discussions of the kinds of items one would expect — of the physical facilities and what was needed (at Weedpatch it was spraying equipment for the insects, and shade trees), of supplies (they were always running short of toilet paper), of efforts at make-do (Collins showed the baseball team how to make a baseball out of an old golf ball he had), and of social activities (the weekly dances are frequently mentioned).[22]

But there was also a great deal of material that one might not expect. Collins apparently fancied himself a social scientist, for he presents numerous surveys, lists, polls, and investigations. He seems to have counted everything countable, including the number of campers per bed each month. There are classifications of campers by occupation and state of origin, and lists of the kinds and years of cars in the camp. He kept a log of all the visitors and took surveys of work opportunities, attitudes of nearby farmers, and conditions in local squatters' camps. He counted the sick, those who had jobs, and those who caused trouble. He also investigated (by inviting himself to dinner) the diets of the campers.

In addition to the lists and statistics, which are probably more interesting to us today than they were to the officials at Farm Security Administration headquarters who had to read them, he told of his own experiences with various campers, sometimes at great length. He also included the words to some forty songs sung by the migrants, ranging from "It's the Wrong Way to Whip the Devil" to "The Lily of Hill Billy Valley" and "Why Do You Bob Your Hair, Girls?" But of all the miscellaneous matter that Collins put into his reports, the most interesting items, as well as the most useful to those such as Steinbeck who tapped the reports for material, are the narratives. These run from short anecdotes, which Collins usually included at the end of the reports under the title "Bits of Migrant Wisdom," to long stories with their own titles ("A Bird of Prey," "A Romance," "We Commit a Mortal Sin"), which might run to several pages. Collins had an ear for voice and intonation, for colorful dialogue, phonetically spelled to reproduce migrant dialects:

All wimen shuda be in bed and tucked under by 8 oclock. Aint no good womn afoot and aloose after that air hour less she be agoin to cherch.

Kaint see how cum folks kinda hate us migrants. The Good Book says as how Jesus went from place to place when he wus on erf. Aint it so Jesus wus a migrant?

Gawd is good to us farm lab'rs. When we aint got wuk and every' thing luks blue he sends us a new baby ter keep us happy.

In writing *The Grapes of Wrath* Steinbeck used Collins's reports as a kind of handbook of migrant attitudes and behavior, describing as they do ways of speaking, patterns of reaction, and conditions of life and work in various settings. In the novel there are names, characters, incidents, and pieces of dialogue that have direct ties to the reports, and bits and pieces of Collins's color are sprinkled here and there. For example, Gramma's "ancient creaking bleat" in the first part of the book, "Pu-raise Gawd fur Vittory! Pu-raise Gawd fur Vittory!" when she hears of Tom Joad's return home from prison, is taken exactly from Collins's report of the favorite expression of a woman that he employed as a part-time housekeeper. This woman, called the "Holy One" by Collins, appears to be the model for the woman in the novel who causes so much grief to others through her religious fanaticism (Collins employed her to keep her away from the camp and out of trouble).

Quite naturally, many of the anecdotes adapted from Collins's reports appear in the section of the novel (roughly a hundred pages) that is set in the government camp. And many of these relate to the sanitary facilities of the camp, which were new and strange to most of these people who, by and large, had grown up and lived all their lives on the same poor farm without flush toilets, showers, or modern laundry tubs. Less directly, almost every major scene or incident that appears in the camp section of the novel — such as the Joad arrival in camp, the camp committee meeting, and the dance — has its roots in one or more descriptions in the reports.

Beyond such connections between Collins's material and Steinbeck's novel, there were deeper influences flowing from the camp manager to the author, influences of emotion and attitude, which are difficult to measure or locate precisely. Both men had faith that our democratic institutions, through the pressure of an enlightened citizenry, could and would correct the inequities that appeared to be tearing the fabric of society apart. Although they hated the abuses of capitalism and favored labor unionizing, they really didn't see the problem in political terms. They saw it as a matter of attitude.

But most important, at least when assessed from the point of view of the novel and its qualities, both Collins and Steinbeck had an idealized view of the common man and attributed somewhat more dignity, wisdom, and courage to the migrants than they actually as a whole probably possessed — or at least more than most observers would be inclined to assign to them. While Steinbeck's idealism was usually moderated by a rather skeptical view of individual human nature, Collins sometimes lapsed into an uncritical sentimentality.

His camp reports reveal a vision of the migrants as a sort of displaced American yeomanry, blessed with old-time American virtues, but misunderstood and abused for a rural simplicity that clashed with the sophistication of their new surroundings. There was no doubt more truth in this view than in the contrary position, widely held in parts of California, that the migrants were little more than animals and need not be treated any better. Nevertheless, Collins's position in reaction to the abuse of the migrants, which he resented so deeply, was in its own way extreme: seldom do the reports ever mention migrant misbehavior that was seriously reprehensible. All migrant misbehavior seems to be of a minor nature, and always it is subject to treatment by education. By and large, the reports picture a people who are quaint: they are the salt of the earth, the charming subjects of a study in folklore. Over and over again Collins notes that once they can get themselves clean and settled, they are happy, and their happiness is stabilized and their dignity restored by participation in the representative government of the camp.

Collins had a great faith in a kind of basic Jacksonian democracy that he felt was not only the natural preference of the migrants but also the natural condition toward which all men aspired or should aspire. The problem was that society at large was in error insofar as it did not emulate the society that he had helped to create in his camps. For Collins, the camps were indeed a "demonstration." They gave flesh to the vision of man's possible social perfection, wherein all men were "good neighbors," responsive to each other's needs, and responsible citizens in a democratic society that was responsive to the general welfare.

Some of these ideas held by Collins no doubt rubbed off on Steinbeck, for good or ill, as we seem to be able to detect in the general tenor and value system of the novel. But, since Steinbeck was leaning toward, if not in fact already possessing, many of these values, there is no way to tell how much came from Collins, and there is little in Collins's vision that was original except in its application to the migrants. The utopian, visionary-Romantic was not an uncommon figure in his time — both popular and serious literature frequently featured it. What we seem to be dealing with here is not just influence, in the strictest sense, but the transmission and reinforcement of feelings and attitudes by the man who Steinbeck felt was closest to the Dust Bowl migrants. In this sense, the most important contribution by Collins to *The Grapes of Wrath* may well have been to the spirit at the heart of the novel, rather than to the details and color of its surface. It was Steinbeck's gift to make both the details on the surface and the vision beneath it both believable and moving.

V

In September of 1936, Helen Horn, an employee of the F.S.A.'s Division of Information in San Francisco, wrote to Collins, asking, "How did you like John Steinbeck and isn't it slick that the San Francisco News will let him do a series? That ought to do us a lot of good unless they start adulterating the copy which they promised they won't."[23] Steinbeck, in the meantime, was sorting out his experiences with Thomsen and Collins, organizing the background material he had gathered, and shuffling through Collins's reports for usable material. The background information that he had gathered earlier in the summer was the basis for a short summary of the migrant situation in California that appeared in the September 12th *Nation*, about a week and a half after his return from Weedpatch.[24] He wrote to Collins soon after he returned:

> I want to thank you for one of the very fine experiences of a life. But I think you know exactly how I feel about it. I hope I can be of some kind of help. On the other hand I don't want to be presumptuous. In the articles I shall be very careful to try to do some good and no harm.[25]

During the last weeks of the month, he finished his series for the *News*, called *The Harvest Gypsies*, an excellent example of what we today would call "investigative, advocacy reporting." Under the circumstances of Steinbeck's emotional commitment at the time, it was a tribute to his self-control that the articles were so calm and carefully presented. The articles, seven of them, trace the background of migrant labor in California, identify the new migrants from the Dust Bowl, describe the living conditions of the squatters' camps, discuss the large corporate farm structure of much of California's agriculture and large grower-migrant labor relations, examine the government camp program, and make recommendations for the future.[26]

At the end of September he went back to Weedpatch to talk again to Collins and observe life at the camp. A week later he wrote to his literary agents, "I just returned yesterday from the strike area of Salinas and from my migrants in Bakersfield. This thing is dangerous. Maybe it will be patched up for a while, but I look for the lid to blow off in a few weeks. Issues are very sharp here now. . . . My material drawer is chock full."[27] The Salinas lettuce strike, which he refers to here, had started about the first of September, and although Steinbeck did not profess much love for his hometown during these years, he was both hurt and angered at the outrageous vigilantism that swept through the area and within a month crushed the strike.

This strike was a major test case of its time and was much on the minds of all those concerned with farm labor, employers and employees, throughout the state. The way it was handled set a very frightening precedent. The usual fears of Red revolutionaries and economic displacement led Salinas to place its police and judicial powers, extralegally, in the hands of a retired army officer, who declared his own version of martial law and formed a local militia to resist the strike and scatter the strikers. Civil rights were voided and an internment camp set up, and neither the county nor state governments interfered to any significant extent in one of the largest vigilante actions ever to take place in California.

Steinbeck's letters suggest that he was furious, but also depressed by the easy abandonment of Constitutional principles by the average citizen in response to the fear spread by large growers motivated by greed. The parallel to Hitler's methods used in the recent past to take over Germany was a strong one, and Steinbeck was only one among many who feared that the hysteria and the bullyboy tactics inspired by the wealthy in Salinas might spread across the country.

Closer to home, however, the novelist, who had seen the hopelessness of migrant families in their makeshift camps, riddled with disease and existing often on the edge of starvation, felt that the defeat of the strikers was a defeat for all the migrants. Actually, while this was true in principle perhaps, the workers in Salinas were a slightly different group, more akin to the professional pickers he had pictured in *In Dubious Battle* than the Dust Bowl migrants near Bakersfield who were the subjects of his *San Francisco News* articles. Yet, it was the bringing together in his own mind of these two extremes, the brutality and blind selfishness of the Salinas strike with the helpless misery of the most unfortunate of the Okies, that apparently created the drama that was the main stimulus for the first version of the book that would become *The Grapes of Wrath*.

This first draft, called "L'Affaire Lettuceberg," was planned as another strike novel. It would combine the material to be drawn from Collins's accounts of the Dust Bowl migrants with the Salinas strike, focusing on the outrageous behavior of the growers and vigilantes. Carol, John's first wife, recalls it as a satire filled with caricatures of Salinas "fat cats."[28]

For a time, however, John's efforts to get his "big book," as he began calling it, under way were stalled by an anger so deep that it poisoned his thinking. Out of frustration, he wrote a satirical allegory called "The Great Pig Sticking," which, having partially relieved his feelings of outrage, he threw into the stove. By the end of the year, he was able to get a start on his novel, but in January he wrote his agent, Elizabeth Otis, "The new book has struck a bad snag. Heaven knows how long it will take to write. The subject is so huge that it scares me to death. And I'm not going to rush it. It must be worked out with great care."

But outside events now conspired to delay the writing. *Of Mice and Men* was published in February 1937 — a book about another kind of farm laborer, the bindlestiff — and its selection by the Book-of-the-Month Club and sale to Hollywood gave the Steinbecks enough money to go to Europe. On the way back, during the summer of 1937, Steinbeck stopped off at the

George Kaufman farm in Pennsylvania where he and Kaufman worked on the stage script of the short novel. John did not like New York—he felt, as he said later, that he had achieved a kind of "fifth-rate celebrity" and was suspicious that being wined and dined in the big city would somehow corrupt him. What he didn't say, and what must have been the case, was that he felt in his bones that high living at this moment was totally inappropriate to what was on his mind and the task ahead.

His book was much on his mind, and he was impatient with the playwriting. He wrote Tom Collins from New York:

> Dear Tom:
> Your letter was waiting when we got in [to New York from Europe]. Be home in about a month. Then in the house about two weeks and then I'm going to visit you for a while. Let me know where Gridley is and how to find you. I've got to get the smell of drawing rooms out of my nose. A squatter's camp is a wonderful place for that. So I'll be seeing you pretty soon and will be very glad to. . . .
>
> Sincerely,
> John S.
> (8/37)

And then later on a postcard he wrote, "In a few weeks I want to go up to your camp to see you. I'll bring blankets and stay a while if I may."

As soon as possible after the script for *Of Mice and Men* was finished, and even though Kaufman wanted him to stay to help stage the play on Broadway, John, with his wife, left on the train for Chicago. There, they bought a car and then drove back to California, following the migrants' route along through Oklahoma and then through the Central Valley. Back home, the conflict between newfound wealth and celebrity, on the one hand, and compassion for the plight of "his" migrants, on the other, once again came to the fore as he prepared to return to the field. His battered old Chevy would have been appropriate, but he could hardly mingle among the desperately poor migrants in a new car. So he bought an old bakery wagon and piled his blankets and cooking gear in the back.

Many years later, in a somewhat similar situation when he was outfitting "Rocinante" for the voyage he took with Charley to rediscover America, he compared the pickup with its camper to the pie wagon he took to the Central Valley. In both instances he wanted to get out among the people without being conspicuous. About the end of October 1937, he left his home in Los Gatos and headed east to Stockton, then north through Sacramento, Marysville, and on to the government camp at Gridley, where Tom Collins was the manager.

VI

John stayed in town for a couple of days, coming into the camp frequently to visit with Tom and talk to the campers. Then, Tom and John went out together for a few days to work in the hop fields and to stay the night on a ranch here and a squatters' camp there. During this period John wrote a card posted from the Gridley camp to Larry Powell, his first bibliographer:

> Dear Larry:
> I have to write this sitting in a ditch. Carol forwarded your letter. . . . I'll be home in two or three weeks. I'm out working—may go south to pick a little cotton. All this—needless to say is *not* for publication—migrants are going south now and I'll probably go along. I enjoy it a lot.
>
> Very flattering article—thanks.
Sincerely,
John

This was the trip that Steinbeck's Los Gatos friends thought was being made to Oklahoma. Actually, he and Tom Collins traveled in the pie wagon south, down Highway 99 to Stockton, Fresno, and Arvin, staying a few days at Collins's old camp with the idea of joining up with the migrants to pick cotton. But Steinbeck and Collins found the situation around Bakersfield chaotic and dangerous, ready to explode. Attracted by the cotton harvest, 70,000 migrants had gathered in the San Joaquin Valley during the end of the summer. There was no work, because the crop was late, and due to the vast surplus of labor, not much chance of work once the crop came in. So most of these people found themselves stuck in the Valley with no opportunity to get money and no resources with which they could either continue to live in the Valley or move elsewhere. They roamed the countryside like wild animals, trying to find some means of subsistence.

Steinbeck and Collins continued their survey of conditions by driving on to Barstow and following Highway 66 to Needles at the state line, and from there, going on to Brawley, in the Imperial Valley, by way of Blythe and El Centro. After a trip of about four weeks, Steinbeck came home from the south, stopping by to see his sister Esther in Watsonville (the pie wagon in genteel company proved embarrassing—his brother-in-law was a conservative farmer). Home in Los Gatos before Thanksgiving, he started to work again on his manuscript, writing steadily in ink in a large bookkeeping ledger and at the end of each day counting his words and entering the total in a column at the back. He was very troubled by what he had seen, and working like an accountant (his father's occupation) was part of his self-discipline.

In the meantime, the thousands of transients in the Central Valley were, in the words of Carey McWilliams, herded about like cattle and "permitted to eke out an existence in the fantastic hope that they would ultimately disperse, vanish into the sky or march over the mountains and into the sea or be swallowed up by the rich and fertile earth. But they did not move, and with the winter season came heavy rains and floods. Soon a major crisis was admitted to exist, with over 50,000 workers destitute and starving."[29] The people at various social agencies knew what was happening but were frustrated by an inability to act. After beating back the temporary challenge of union organizing in the early and middle thirties, the large growers and their corporate allies had once again assumed almost absolute power in the state's agriculture industry. By putting tremendous pressure on both the state's administration and the Congress, they were able to use their opposition to any sort of government aid for migrant workers to insure a "go slow" policy. They were afraid that help for the workers would encourage them to stay where they were not needed, and they opposed aid on the grounds that it would give the workers enough independence so that they might try once again to organize.[30]

At the height of the floods around Visalia, the Farm Security Administration was called in to provide relief, but for many, it was too little and too late. For the frustrated F.S.A. administrators, it was a heartbreaking struggle. Conditions were so bad that field-workers trying to get food to the migrants and to rescue the sick could not get the supplies in where they were needed. Powerful trucks borrowed from the National Guard, fitted with tire chains, slipped, slid into ditches, and bogged down in the mire. In the sea of mud that confronted them, rescuers could not even find the stranded and half-buried enclaves of migrants who had hidden themselves here and there across thousands of square miles of drenched farmlands to escape the wrath of local authorities. The F.S.A. realized it was not only fighting the elements in order to save lives, but it was fighting a political battle as well. To make any progress with the problem over the long haul, it would have to rally public opinion.[31]

Steinbeck had letters from Fred Soule, at F.S.A. Information, and Tom Collins describing the situation in the Valley. Soule asked him if he couldn't go down to the flood area and help by reporting what was going on. This is how John described his mission to his agent, Elizabeth Otis:

> I must go to Visalia. Four thousand families, drowned out of their tents are really starving to death. The resettlement administration of the government asked me to write some news stories. The newspapers won't touch the stuff but they will under my byline. The locals are fighting the government bringing in food and medicine. I'm going to try to break the story hard enough so that food and drugs can get moving. Shame and a hatred of publicity will do the job to the miserable local bankers. . . . Talk about Spanish children. The death of children by starvation in our valleys is simply staggering. I've got to do it. If I can sell the articles I'll use the proceeds for serum and such. Codliver oil would give the live kids a better chance.
>
> (2/14/38)

Collins had been pulled away from his camp-manager post to join other F.S.A. personnel in the stricken area who were administering relief. After receiving his letter, Steinbeck wrote back: "Will you write as soon as you get this letting me know where you can be found at various times of the day or night? And Tom — please don't tell anyone I am coming. My old feud with the ass[ociated] farmers is stirring again and I don't want my movements traced." One of the reasons it has been so difficult for scholars to discover the details concerning Steinbeck's trips among the migrants is that he worked hard at the time to conceal them. From the time that *In Dubious Battle* and "The Harvest Gypsies" were published until several years after the publication of *The Grapes of Wrath*, Steinbeck had a genuine fear of retribution by the Associated Farmers for his pro-farm labor writings. He had seen what he believed to be evidence of intimidation by violence, blackmail, and extortion on the part of the Associated Farmers and other grower organizations and believed that they were capable of anything. Indeed, he and others familiar with the union movement in California were convinced that several "unsolved" murders of union leaders had been carried out by law enforcement officers at the behest of wealthy landowners. So it is not an exaggeration to say that since he had already become a symbol of the fight to help the dispossessed, he had some justification to fear for his life and was acting with courage, both in his direct actions to aid the migrants and in his determination to write his novel.

In mid-February of 1938, Steinbeck went to Visalia and spent about ten days in the company of Collins, helping in whatever way he could. As he wrote his agents, "I've tied into the thing from the first and I must get down there and see if I can't do something to help knock these murderers on the heads" (2/38). In an unpublished autobiographical novel, Collins described some of their experiences:

> When we reached the flooded areas we found John's old pie truck useless, so we set out on foot. We walked most of the first night and we were very tired. . . . For forty-eight hours, and without food or sleep, we worked among the sick and half-starved people, dragging some from torn and ragged tents, floored with inches of water, stagnant water, to the questionable shelter of a higher piece of ground. We couldn't speak to one another because we were too tired, yet we worked together as cogs in an intricate piece of machinery. [At two o'clock in the morning they both just collapsed in the muddy fields and slept.]
>   . . . [At dawn] I found John lying on his back. He was a mass of mud and slime. His face was a mucky mask punctuated with eyes, a nose and a mouth. He was close beside me, so I knew it was John. How long we had slept in that mire we knew not. . . . [It began to rain again. Ahead of them, some yards away, they spied another tent.] We frightened the little children we found in the tent, the two little children. . . . We must have looked like men from some far-away planet to those two children, the sunken cheeks — the huge lump on the bed — they frightened John and me. Inside the tent was dry because it was on high land, but it was an island in a sea of mud and water all around it. Everything under that bit of canvas was dry — everything — the make-

shift stove was without heat; all shapes of cans were empty; pans, pots and kettles—all were dry. Everything, for there was not a morsel of food—not a crumb of bread.

"Mommy has been like that a long time. She won't get up. Mommy won't listen to us. She won't get up." Such was the greeting cried to us by the two little children.

Mommy couldn't get up. She was the lump on the old bed. Mommy was ill and she hadn't eaten for some time. She had skimped and skimped so that the children would have a bite. . . .

"How far is it to the nearest store? Is there an old car near here? Is the store East or West?" But the children only stared as John threw the questions to them. Well did he know that the big food trucks could never get off the roads and travel two miles or more over the muddy, drowned fields to that tent! So John faded into the early morning. . . .

[Sometime later John returned.] John and I sat on the dirt floor. We sat there and the five of us ate the food which John had obtained from the little store some muddy distance away. We sat there and ate a bite—a bite that was a banquet. . . .

Then names and ages of our new-found friends for delivery to the government agency which would succor the isolated family, and we were off again to find other mothers and children out there in that vast wilderness of mud and deep water.[32]

After more than a week, John went into town to clean up and rest. With Collins and several other relief workers, he went to a restaurant to get his first solid, cooked meal in many days. He had two breakfasts of steak and eggs, much to the dismay of one of the workers, Sis Reamer (the very same woman who took John years earlier to meet Cicil McKiddy), who was very angry that he could bear to eat so well, considering that they were surrounded by people who were starving. This reaction would seem to foreshadow a conflict that would envelope John for the rest of his life: while conservatives like the Associated Farmers would continue to denounce him as a Communist, liberals would attack him for his lack of total commitment to the welfare of the poor. He cared deeply about the poor, but his commitment was to writing, not to political solutions.[33]

VII

John went home for only two days and was back again in the flood area. Returning from this second trip, he wrote to Elizabeth:

Just got back from another week in the field. The floods have aggravated the starvation and sickness. I went down for Life this time. Fortune wanted me to do an article for them but I don't. I don't like the audience. The Life sent me down with a photographer from its staff and we took a lot of pictures of the people. They guarantee not to use it if they change it and will send me the proofs. They paid my expenses and will put up money for the help of some of these people. . . .

It is the most heartbreaking thing in the world. If Life does use the stuff there will be lots of pictures and swell ones. It will give you an idea of the kind of people they are and the kind of faces. I break myself every time I go out because the argument that one person's effort can't really do anything doesn't seem to apply when you come on a bunch of starving children and you have a little money. I can't rationalize it for myself anyway. So don't get me a job for a slick [magazine]. I want to put a tag of shame on the greedy bastards who are responsible for this but I can best do it through newspapers.

(2/38)

But *Life* did not print the article, apparently because he would not let them edit it and some of the language was too liberal for the editors to swallow. The irony was that the big money magazine, *Fortune*, got someone else to do an article which, even though it was sympathetic to the migrants, *was* published.[34]

John's experiences in the flood had a profound effect on him. They would eventually lead to the dramatic final scenes of his finished novel, but in the meantime they sat in the back of his mind, like a conscience prodding him toward a deeper, more significant creation than the one he was presently working on. He was not satisfied with the tenor and direction of "L'Affaire Lettuceberg," and when he was nearly finished with the draft in early May of 1938, he revealed his doubts to his agent, telling her that if she thought it was no good, then he would "burn it up and forget it."

When he began the project, almost two years earlier, he had the idea that he had gained enough monetary security so that he could take several years to write a long, complex novel which he would attempt to make an important work of art. Soon afterward, however, he was pulled by his sympathies toward launching a satirical attack on those responsible for the horrors of migrant life and the terrors of vigilante violence. For these many months he had been drawn by his emotions in one direction, and by his artistic aspirations in another, yet he was unwilling to recognize that he could fulfill one goal or the other but probably not both. Now that the draft was nearly completed, he claimed, in a letter to his agent, that "I don't care about its literary excellence . . . only whether it does the job I want it to do. . . . It is a mean, nasty book and if I could make it nastier I would" (5/2/38).

But in the end, the artist won out over the propagandist. Carol, as committed as she was to the cause of the underdog, hated the draft and argued against it. John himself found that he could not stomach it, and writing once again to his agent, Elizabeth Otis, explained why he had decided to burn it, after all: "Not once in the writing of it have I felt the curious warm pleasure that comes when work is going well. My whole work drive has been aimed at making people understand each other and then I deliberately write this book, the aim of which is to cause hatred through partial understanding" (5/38). The most persuasive argument against "L'Affaire Lettuceberg" would not have been possible damage to his reputation, which he cared little about, but, following his traumatic struggle to save lives in the mud of the San Joaquin Valley, that a cheap treatment would not do justice to the dignity of his subject.

So he started all over. This time the book would focus on the migrants themselves, rather than on his hatred of those who had persecuted them. By the first of June he was well on his way and pleased with his progress, writing to Elizabeth Otis that "it is a nice thing to be working and believing in my work again" and "I don't yet understand what happened or why the bad book should have cleared the air so completely for this one. I am simply glad that it is so" (6/1/38).

There was something in John's makeup that seemed to make it impossible for him to slowly plan, develop, and then deliberately write a long work of fiction. The excitement of the material and emotion would cook in his mind, so that the pressure built to a point that slow, careful composition became impossible. When at last he found his true direction and began writing the final draft of *The Grapes of Wrath*, he made it a long sprint, rather than a marathon run, and the strain very nearly destroyed him. From the beginning of June to the end of October, he wrote the manuscript, and then during November and early December, he revised and made corrections. Although he repeatedly told himself to slow down, the pace gradually quickened until, during the last weeks, he was working day and night. It was a remarkable period of work: in six months he wrote a 200,000-word novel that was highly complex in structure, detailed in fabric, and quite varied in tone and style.

In early September he reported to Elizabeth Otis that

> Carol is typing ms (2nd draft) and I'm working on first. I can't tell when I will be done but Carol will have second done almost at the same time I have first. And—this is a secret—the 2nd draft is so clear and good that it, carefully and clearly corrected, will be what I submit. Carol's time is too valuable to do purely stenographic work.
>
> (9/10/38)

Carol was in fact writing the revision, that is, correcting errors and editing for contradictions and awkwardness, while John was doing the initial draft. In the same letter he reported that his wife had come up with a brilliant idea for the title of the new book. "The grapes of wrath" from "The Battle Hymn of the Republic" gave the book a dynamic focus, and the words of the hymn could be applied in numerous ways to the novel's contents:

> I . . . like it better all the time. I think it is Carol's best title so far. I like it because it is a march and this book is a kind of march—because it is in our own revolutionary tradition and because in reference to this book it has a large meaning. And I like it because people know the Battle Hymn who don't know the Star Spangled Banner.

He particularly liked the title because it gave an American stamp to his material. From previous experience he knew that there would be those who would try to smear the book as foreign-spirited, and he wanted to blunt such an attack from the outset because he felt very strongly that what he was describing was an American phenomenon.

VIII

The Grapes of Wrath, when it was published in April 1939, was an enormous popular and critical success. It was on the best-seller lists throughout the rest of that year and much of the following one, and brought the author the Pulitzer Prize for fiction. John Steinbeck became one of the two or three best known American writers, and the novel, repeatedly reprinted (some two-dozen times in the U.S. to the present) and published in countries around the world, became the centerpiece for the career that was honored in 1962 with the Nobel Prize.

At the same time, Steinbeck's achievement exacted a heavy price. A shy and modest man, the author found his anonymity and ability to blend in with the common man, on which he had depended so much, taken from him by the notoriety generated by the book. Both he and his wife finished the book physically exhausted and emotionally drained. John had developed an infection that spread throughout his body and made it painful for him to sit or walk. The friction that developed between him and his wife during the strained period of composition, as well as the emotional pressures of the controversy that followed the novel's composition, were major factors in the break-up of their marriage. And the antagonism expressed toward him by his neighbors following the publication of the book, as well as the jealousy of his success expressed by some of his friends, made it impossible for him to continue to live and work in California. He had gained everlasting fame, but had lost the wellspring of his inspiration, his deep connection to the land and his own people.

As for Tom Collins, he was given the job of technical advisor to the filming of the novel, on Steinbeck's recommendation. The status this gave him, plus the $15,000 fee he earned, aroused jealousy among his colleagues, and he was the subject of some controversy until he left the Farm Security Administration in 1941. There were complaints from his superiors that he had become difficult and contentious and that he tended to go over the heads of his superiors rather than through official channels.

In addition to problems with his colleagues and superiors, there had been a subtle shift in the atmosphere of the camps over the years from their inception. Instead of hiring in managers who like Collins were older and had knocked around a bit, the tendency was to hire young graduate students out of the University of California at Berkeley. Managers of this sort had great difficulty, apparently, putting Collins's ideas into practice. They thought his ideas "corny" and his structure of relationships and attitudes old-fashioned.

There was resentment and strife in many of the camps. But some of the strife was not due to manager ineptitude so much as it was due to changes in the attitudes of the migrants themselves. By 1939 and 1940, the migrants were less dependent on the camps for refuge from destitution or persecution. The job and wage picture had brightened a bit. In short — and this is a harsh judgment to make — the success of Collins's policies was due not only in great measure to the rather unique talents of Collins himself, but to some extent also to the extreme desperation of the migrants during the early years of the program. Once they were not quite so desperate, the spirit of community cooperation and democracy in the camps so nourished by the vision of Collins seemed to collapse.

At Thornton in 1940, two things happened that very much upset the F.S.A. hierarchy and which reflected on Collins, even though his responsibility for these things may have been slight — one was a knifing incident between two migrant workers, and the other was an outbreak of infectious diphtheria. Both resulted in adverse publicity at a time when the F.S.A. was coming once again under severe and hostile Congressional pressure and the Associated Farmers had, in the words of the district administrator, been "making life pretty miserable for all of us."[35]

Collins resigned, somewhat disgruntled and unhappy, on 30 April 1941. He married a public health nurse who had also served in the camps, and the two of them moved to a fifteen-acre apricot ranch owned by his wife near San Juan Bautista, California. There, Collins worked on the ranch and attempted to emulate the success of his author friend by himself becoming a writer. He had had some encouragement along these lines earlier from Steinbeck who, so impressed by the material of the camp reports, had tried to get them published. Collins attempted to write his memoirs, with emphasis on his camp experience, and get them published as a novel. He wrote several drafts, one of which, called "They Die to Live," was accepted for publication by a West Coast publisher, Lymanhouse. Notices of publication appeared in several newspaper columns, and Collins proudly informed his friends and former co-workers of the impending publication scheduled for the fall of 1941. However, the publisher, Edward Lyman, came to feel that the market for such a book had really already been met by *The Grapes of Wrath*, and using the excuse of the wartime shortage of paper, backed out of the contract.[36]

Failing as both a writer and a farmer, Collins in 1943 moved his family to the area near Fresno. Here he was employed first as a consultant to California Cotton and then to the California Wine Institute. In July 1946 he was divorced from his wife, and by this time, had given up trying to get his novel published. For the next ten years, he became a migrant himself, managing or acting as desk clerk for a series of hotels for transients in Salinas, Marysville, Willows, and Sacramento. A reporter for the *Sacramento Bee*, working on a story about farm labor, ran into a wiry, grizzled old-timer in an area of the city where derelicts are often hired by labor contractors to work in the fields. The old-timer claimed to have been the Tom that Steinbeck wrote about. Perhaps the reporter was thinking of Tom Joad, rather than the Tom in the dedication "To TOM who lived it." At any rate, he did not believe him.[37]

Notes

1. "Fingers of Cloud: A Satire on College Protervity," *Stanford Spectator* (February 1924), 149, 161–64.

2. Interview, Mrs. Carol (Steinbeck) Brown, 31 May 1974.

3. Material concerning McKiddy's conversations with Steinbeck based on interviews with Mrs. Carol Brown and with Francis Whitaker, 18 October 1976. Material concerning Bill Hemmett from Anne Loftis, "The Man Who Preached Strike," *Pacific Historian* 30 (1986): 63–75. For Hammett as a model for London, see Cletus E. Daniel, *Bitter Harvest: A History of California Farmworkers, 1870–1941* (Ithaca: Cornell University Press, 1981), 321, n. 45.

4. Fred T. Marsh, review of *In Dubious Battle, New York Times Book Review*, 2 February 1936, 7.

5. *Steinbeck: A Life in Letters*, ed. Elaine Steinbeck and Robert Wallsten (New York: Viking Press, 1975), 98.

6. Interview, Mrs. Carol (Steinbeck) Brown, 31 May 1974.

7. Letter, Robert Hardie, 30 April 1971; papers in the Farm Security Administration collection at the Federal Records Center, San Bruno (hereafter abbreviated as "F.S.A./San Bruno" and the F.S.A. papers collected at the National Archives in Washington, D.C. (hereafter abbreviated as "F.S.A./Wash.").

8. Letters, Laurence I. Hewes, Jr., 17 July 1973, 24 August 1973, and 22 September 1973.

9. Walter J. Stein, *California and the Dust Bowl Migration* (Westport, Conn.: Greenwood Press, 1973), 16. Carey McWilliams, *Factories in the Field* (Boston: Little, Brown, 1939), 163–64.

10. Hewes; F.S.A./Wash.

11. F.S.A./San Bruno; F.S.A./Wash.

12. Interview, Mrs. Carol (Steinbeck) Brown, 20 July 1970; interview, Mrs. Gwyndolyn Steinbeck, 6 March 1971.

13. John Steinbeck, "Foreword" to Windsor Drake (Tom Collins), "Bringing in the Sheaves," *Journal of Modern Literature* 5 (April 1976): 211–13.

14. Ibid.

15. Interview, Patricia Collins Olson, 14 April 1974.

16. F.S.A./Wash.

17. Arvin Migratory Labor Camp Reports, F.S.A./San Bruno.

18. Interview, Milan Dempster, 16 June 1971.

19. Arvin Migratory Labor Camp Reports, F.S.A./San Bruno; interview, Reginald Loftus, 23 June 1971; interview, Helen Hosmer, 25 June 1971.

20. Interview (by John Berthelsen), Dewey Russell.

21. Interview, Reginald Loftus, 23 June 1971.

22. The material in this and the following paragraphs has been taken from the Arvin Migratory Labor Camp Reports, Lubin Collection, Bancroft Library, University of California, Berkeley.

23. F.S.A./Wash.

24. "Dubious Battle in California," 302–04.

25. August 1936. Letters from John Steinbeck to Tom Collins are reproduced here by permission of Mary Alice Johns and by McIntosh and Otis, Inc., acting in behalf of the John Steinbeck estate.

26. *San Francisco News*, 5–12 October 1936.

27. October 1936. Letters from John Steinbeck to his agents are reproduced by permission of Elizabeth Otis and McIntosh and Otis, Inc., agents for the John Steinbeck estate. These letters are now in Special Collections, Stanford University Libraries.

28. Interview, Mrs. Carol (Steinbeck) Brown, 31 May 1974.

29. McWilliams, *Factories in the Field*, 315.

30. Hewes.

31. F.S.A./Wash.; F.S.A./San Bruno.

32. Windsor Drake (Tom Collins), "From *Bringing in the Sheaves*," *Journal of Modern Literature* 5 (April 1976): 221–24.

33. Ibid.; interview, Francis Whitaker, 18 October 1976.

34. Published "by the editors," "I Wonder Where We Can Go Now," and "Along the Road," *Fortune* 29 (April 1939): 90–94, 96–100, 112–20.

35. Interview, Helen Hosmer, 25 June 1971; F.S.A./Wash.

36. Correspondence between Edward D. Lyman and Tom Collins in the Tom Collins papers, provided by his daughter, Mary Alice Johns.

37. Interview, Mary Alice Johns, 2 October 1974; interview and letter, John Berthelsen.

The Reception of *The Grapes of Wrath* in Britain: A Chronological Survey of Contemporary Reviews

Roy Simmonds*

On the Sunday evening of 9 July 1939 an American commentator, speaking on the BBC National radio program, devoted almost the whole of his quarter-hour talk to eulogizing a novel that had been published that April in New York and that was currently topping the best-seller lists in the United States. Indeed, he implied that no one on his side of the Atlantic seemed to be reading anything else. The commentator was Alexander Woollcott, and the novel was John Steinbeck's *The Grapes of Wrath*. Woollcott, delivering his weekly "Letter from America," spared his British listeners no superlatives. "I am not," he declared, "forgetting such books as *Moby-Dick* and *Leaves of Grass* and *Life on the Mississippi* and *Death Comes for the Archbishop* when I say *The Grapes of Wrath* seems to me as

*This essay was written specifically for this volume and is published here for the first time by permission of the author.

great a book as has yet come out of America." Elsewhere during his talk, he described the book as "an American *Les Misérables*," and linked Steinbeck's name with that of the incumbent president, Franklin D. Roosevelt, as the two men whose voices were *the* representative ones through which America should be heard and judged at that moment in history.[1] Less than a month later, on 3 August, H. G. Wells's new book, *The Fate of Homo Sapiens*, was published in London. Wells added his voice to what was rapidly to become a virtual chorus of prepublication praise for Steinbeck's book:

> Sometimes [Wells wrote] a work of art can do more to present reality than a whole library of reports and statistics, and that tremendous genius, John Steinbeck, in his *The Grapes of Wrath* (1939), has given an unforgettable picture of the last stage of that process of material and moral destruction and disillusionment with which the story of sturdy individualism in America concludes. He gives it all, from the exhausted soil dribbling down to dust, to the broken pride, the hopeless revolt and the black despair of the human victims, without rhetoric, without argument, but with an irresistible effect of fundamental truth.[2]

The novelist, short-story writer, and biographer Arthur Calder-Marshall had also read *The Grapes of Wrath* in its U.S. edition, and in the September issue of the *Fortnightly Review* stated that, apart from the ending of the book, which he found to be "artificial and symbolical," he had "no hesitation in saying that [the book] is the most important novel to come out of America for twenty years." He concluded: "[The book] has already been heralded by discerning English critics, and when it is published by Messrs. Heinemann on September 7, I am prepared to prophesy that its success in this country will be as immediate and as widespread as it was in America."[3]

It could be said that, in many respects, it was probably not the most propitious of times for the launching in England of one of the key novels of twentieth-century American literature. The threat of European conflict, seemingly now inevitable, had hung over the country during the whole of that summer. On Sunday morning, 3 September, just after eleven o'clock, the British prime minister, Neville Chamberlain, announced over the radio to the British people that, after nearly twenty-one years of uneasy peace, their country was again at war with Germany. When, a mere four days later, *The Grapes of Wrath* appeared in the bookshops, people were still coping in their own individual ways with the reality that war, and the very potent danger of immediate air raids, was upon them and that within a few days or weeks they might be maimed or killed. Indeed, the following day, 8 September, the *Manchester Guardian's* book reviewer, Wilfrid Gibson, confessed that "when the world is actually crashing into war it is difficult even for the most conscientious reviewer to give to the consideration of works of fiction the undistracted concentration that is essential to a just assessment of their values." For all that, he did not hesitate to maintain that *The Grapes of Wrath* was one of the most vital stories he had read "for some time," and that under different circumstances it would have been a story that would have held him completely absorbed. "This is a terrible and indignant book," Gibson went on, "yet it is not without passages of lyrical beauty, and the ultimate impression conveyed is that of the dignity of the human spirit under the stress of the most desperate conditions."[4]

Philip Jordan, writing that same day in the London *News Chronicle*, had, however, an overall more positive attitude. The heading to his review exhorted his readers: "War Or No War: Read This Book." Observing that the arts are the first victims of war, he warned that it was essential to remember "that great literature must not be totally obscured from the public mind." He continued: "Fortunately we have in Steinbeck's contribution to human understanding a work that no amount of human misery can stifle; for he has written one of the major stories of our age, and has written it with an effortless power more considerable, more important than all the warring follies of rival imperialist dreamers." Noting that he had never before used the word "genius" to describe any of his contemporaries, he wrote that he was now obliged to endorse H. G. Wells's judgment. "For months, for years perhaps, the creative spirit of civilized men will be in chains; and it is our good fortune that this prophet of the dispossessed has chosen this time to speak, and to remind us that the creative spirit cannot die." Somewhat obviously, given the circumstances, he compared the migration of the Oklahoma farmers with the flight of the European refugees. Although he looked upon Alexander Woollcott as "a whimsical old puss," Jordan admitted that he had to agree with Woollcott that Steinbeck's novel "stands beside the contributions which America has made to the literature of the world." *The Grapes of Wrath*, in his view, did belong with *Moby-Dick* and *Leaves of Grass*. "And you cannot put anything much higher than that."[5]

The London *Times* review, also printed on 8 September, was a somewhat more sober and balanced piece, seeing Steinbeck's theme as being based on the premise that money, once a convenience, has become an incubus, but observing that although the author had been absorbed in presenting his sociological and political theme he had successfully avoided the trap of reducing the book to mere propaganda or polemics. His characters lived and held an interest for the reader "at least commensurate with that of the general theme."[6]

The following day, the reviewer in the *Times Literary Supplement* expressed a similar opinion. While he saw *The Grapes of Wrath* as "a campaign," with Mammon as the enemy, he was careful to stress that the book was not simply a tract:

> Mr. Steinbeck looks beyond his people and he sees the universal reverence for profits, but he sees his people first. If he despises and derides Mammon, he does so not because he dislikes a theory, but

because he sees the practical effect in human misery. Are not his Joads the victims of a system for which no man will take the responsibility? The Joads are certainly not the puppets of a theory. Their essential decency and good citizenship are evident beneath their various raffish surfaces, but they are not mere personifications of these qualities. . . . [T]hese are individual men and women.[7]

The reviews in the two London quality Sunday papers, the *Observer* and the *Sunday Times*, were almost uniformly favorable, both critics having certain well-defined reservations. In the *Observer*, the novelist Frank Swinnerton regretted the fact that the book had appeared at this particular time, for he feared that the outbreak of war would prevent it from sweeping England as it had already swept America. But, putting aside his misgivings, he nevertheless anticipated the possibility that the book would succeed:

[Steinbeck] has great power, intense feeling, and a strong sense of the evil of a system which allows prosperity to a few and nothing but eventual serfdom to the many. He has extraordinary mimetic skill, by means of which he creates unforgettable impressions of the American highway and American types. He makes his travelling family always real and sometimes poignantly pathetic. If he is sometimes conventionally dithyrambic, and his collapsing house is a flick picture, these are specks in a fine, graphic panorama, the argument of which seems to me irresistible. In normal times *The Grapes of Wrath*, despite its American scene, would have come home to Englishmen as powerfully as *The Jungle* did in its day. It may still do so; for though it is local and topical it never loses sight of essential human values.[8]

If Swinnerton tentatively thought that *The Grapes of Wrath* stood a good chance of surviving, his counterpart, Ralph Straus, in the *Sunday Times* expressed his doubts, ending his review with the observation: "*The Grapes of Wrath* may not belong to the ages, but it has depth and is finely human: the work of a novelist who is also a true poet." Earlier in the piece, Straus agreed that the book did possess "many of the qualities which go to the making of a real work of art," and that it was written "not only with the absolute sincerity that you expect, but also with the kind of white-hot enthusiasm which can act on the reader like a magnet." On the debit side, however, he observed:

[I]t may be that in this country there will be readers who wish that much that is described in almost Zolaesque detail could have been merely suggested; readers, too, who may find a touch of monotony in the chatter of humble folk forced to live in conditions which, even with Mr. Steinbeck playing guide, must seem on this side of the Atlantic so strange and aloof. There is, perhaps, just a little too much detail, though I can well understand the author's desire to include it all. . . . As a result, the book, though always vivid and always dynamic, is, to my mind, on the long side.[9]

Another novelist, Phyllis Bentley, writing three days later in the *Yorkshire Post*, began her review by stating the proposition that in order to earn the accolade "great" a work of literature had, among other considerations, to possess the complementary characteristics of being both thoroughly local and thoroughly universal. "For a work that is not local," she wrote, "not deeply rooted in some particular spot of earth, is apt to be like all rootless things, sapless and shrivelled; yet a universal significance, a symbolic relation to the common human lot, is necessary if the work is to have real and permanent validity." She felt that Steinbeck's fiction prior to *The Grapes of Wrath*, while possessing a strong local quality, did not quite attain the universal, because she had "not been quite able to accept as universally valid the values on which his conflicts depend." While *The Grapes of Wrath* still contained passages that lacked this universality, she nevertheless considered that the book as a whole had the two essential local and universal qualities: "it is both an epic of America and an epic of all the injured and oppressed." In the long run, however, her conclusion was that the book had not attained unqualified greatness: "It is, to speak soberly, a very fine novel, indeed: not to be compared with Hugo, Zola and Dostoievsky, as some have compared it, only because it excites anger and pity for the Joads' collective material situation, rather than grief for their individual spiritual tragedies."[10]

Three of the least favorable and, in some respects, most openly critical of all the reviews appeared later that week in the national weeklies the *Listener*, the *Spectator*, and the *New Statesman & Nation*. In the first of these, Edwin Muir, the poet and (with his wife) the translator of Kafka, seemed to be damning the book with faint praise. Certainly, his reaction was markedly lukewarm. He disagreed on one specific point with both the *Times* and the *Times Literary Supplement* reviewers. "The weakness of the book," he wrote, "is a weakness of imagination. Mr. Steinbeck can describe physical hardships vividly, and the story is mainly an account of physical hardships. But he does not seem to have any grasp of character. When these tough Oklahoma farmers and their families cease enduring and begin to feel, all that comes out of them is a stream of sentimental generalities."[11]

In the *Spectator*, Kate O'Brien, while conceding that the theme of the novel was "quite magnificent" and that it was "a vivid, generous sermon on modern misery, on the crassness and savagery of some who create it, and the nobility of its victims," considered that in the ultimate analysis, because of a failure of language, Steinbeck had not succeeded in what he had patently set out to do:

> Mr. Steinbeck gives us an enormous, vivid setting; he fills it with odd and lively characters; he uses an attractive Western States patois, and he tells a terrible, moving story of universal and immediate significance. Why, then, am I not enthralled by his book? Simply because, right or wrong, I dislike the manner of his writing, which I think epitomises the

intolerable sentimentality of American "realism." I think that he wrecks a beautiful dialect with false cadences; I think he is frequently uncertain about where to end a sentence; I think his repetitiveness is not justified by emotional result; and whereas the funny, niggling coarseness which he jovially imposes on his pathetic migrants may be true to type, it seemed to me out of tone, and to offend against the general conception.

For all that, she pronounced that "the book is good, interesting and generous, and its wide popularity would be a beneficial thing."[12]

Anthony West, in his *New Statesman* review, was, on the other hand, uncompromisingly hostile in his rejection of the book. It was, he wrote, "a horrible story," and it had "great defects as a novel," its form (the parallel accounts of the Joads' experiences and the generalized accounts in the interchapters of the migration of the dispossessed farmers) being, in his opinion, "astonishingly awkward." West concluded his review with a final dismissal of the whole work:

Mr. Steinbeck makes his points with the delicacy of a trip hammer, the book lacks form and ends simply because the characters have reached the ultimate believable degradation and the length has reached the limit which publishers and public can stand. Pity and sympathy cannot tempt one to suspend purely artistic standards, but this cannot be called a good novel. Its virtue lies in the burning sincerity which has captured the imagination of the American public and awakened them to the human aspect of the dust-bowl disaster. *The Jungle* is dead mutton as literature but it is alive in the American legislation which has amplified the Meat Inspection Bill and the Pure Food Bill of 1906, which the novel called into being within a few months of publication. *The Grapes of Wrath* will take a place beside it in the social history of the United States, but it is its literary fate to lie in that honourable vault which houses the books that have died when their purpose as propaganda has been served.[13]

By now, Britain was in the third week of war, and Helen Cockburn in the *Burton Observer* also bemoaned the fact that it was unfortunate that *The Grapes of Wrath* "should come out at a time like this, when most of us are more anxious for war news than for new novels." Echoing Philip Jordan, she urged her readers: "War or no war, it must be read." She declared it to be "a masterpiece."[14] In the *Daily Telegraph*, John Brophy also touched on the effect of war on the book trade and suggested that in setting down to a strange new routine of life people should not forget that "at the nearest bookshop or library they will find an attractive choice of novels both new and good." First place, he maintained, belonged without doubt to *The Grapes of Wrath*.[15] The anonymous reviewer in the *Inverness Courier* referred to the novel as "powerful" and as "a book to read," but, like Kate O'Brien, found Steinbeck's style "curious and in some ways difficult to read," and, like Ralph Straus, criticized the author for being "so intent on leaving no detail to the imagination that his book is overburdened with matter that might well be omitted."[16]

This last was a fault that another novelist, Lettice Cooper, writing in another of the country's national weeklies, *Time and Tide*, also picked upon. The book, she complained, "is told with too much detail — when will American novelists learn that it is not necessary to give the menu for every meal?" Although she found occasional lapses into sentimentality, her final assessment of the book was that it was as a whole "absorbing, deeply moving, on a grand scale, and informed with humanity and tenderness." She did not agree with those other reviewers who had felt dismay that the book should appear when it did. She argued:

> It is a great mistake to assume that because war has broken out people will want to relax their minds by reading only trivial novels and hearing only light facile music. Undoubtedly these should be there and will be there for those who have always wanted them and will continue to want them. Those who have acquired in their reading quality, something for the mind to bite on, and something to liberate the imagination will want it more than ever, and for such as these *The Grapes of Wrath* is better reading for war time or any other time than a dozen lesser novels. It is, I think, a particularly good book to read this week, for it reminds us, although indirectly, that the betrayal of socialism by a great nation is only the failure of that nation and not an answer to the fundamental problem, "How can the poor, the simple, and the weak be protected from exploitation by the greedy and the powerful? How can the greedy and the powerful be saved from destroying their own humanity by exploitation of the weak and the poor?"[17]

Lettice Cooper's sentiments were near to the heart of those of yet another of England's popular novelists of those days, Sir Hugh Walpole. In an article in the *Daily Sketch* on the same day that Lettice Cooper's review appeared, Sir Hugh wrote:

> I have been conscious this week of another thing for which England and France are fighting, and that is culture. Culture is a horrible word, but I mean the books and the painting and the music that are the lasting food and enrichment of mankind. . . .
> I think it is the duty of all of us to read fine things and talk of them. . . . Therefore, so long as I am free to do so, I shall, week by week, name new books that are worth the reading whatever the war news is. . . .
> There is Steinbeck's fine *The Grapes of Wrath*. He wrote *Of Mice and Men*, and this is a novel about Americans who travel to California in search of homes and are bitterly disappointed with what they find there.[18]

Certainly, as a review of the book, Walpole's piece left a great deal to be desired, but his name was much respected in the literary establishment of the day and his endorsement was not to be decried.

Two further reviews by influential literary figures appeared before the end of the first month of the war. These were V. S. Pritchett, the present doyen of the British short story, and the Communist poet Randall Swingler, who was for a time the editor of the radical magazine *Left Review*. V. S. Pritchett's review appeared on the 27th of the month in the coffee-table glossy the *Bystander*. Pritchett pronounced *The Grapes of Wrath* "an impressive American tract," but he was irritated by the "March of Time prose which cuts up so easily into verse," and while he thought the book magnificent in some of its aspects he criticized it for lacking "the variety of the great novels of indignation." He was particularly vexed, it would seem, by the interchapters. "I think," he wrote, "the generalised incantations about all the other families on this defrauded trek, and the undertone of uplift, are mistakes. Among other things, they make the book monotonous." But, for all its faults, he regarded *The Grapes of Wrath* as an "epic Exodus with the splutter of an old engine and the cackling talk of the cotton field replacing the poetic wailing of the Jews," and he admitted that there was "certainly no English novelist who could begin to grasp a theme like this, tract or no tract."[19]

As was to be expected, Randall Swingler in his review in the *Daily Worker* that same day referred back to Steinbeck's previous sociopolitical novel:

> Ever since I first read *In Dubious Battle*, I knew John Steinbeck was a writer who would eventually write a big book. He has worked and struggled with the people about whom and for whom he writes. He writes in their language, he thinks in terms of their experience.
>
> Since *In Dubious Battle*, he has very wisely and patiently been perfecting his powers in one or two experimental works. Now he has launched his first really big and important novel, *The Grapes of Wrath*. . . . Steinbeck's novel can . . . justly be called an epic. Read this before any other novel you have in mind.[20]

On the last day of the month, Vernon Fane in the *Sphere* referred to *The Grapes of Wrath* as "a Titan in contemporary literature," and rated it "beyond any doubt the book of the year—perhaps even of our time."[21]

The fears voiced by the faint-hearted among those in the book trade that one of the immediate effects of the war would be that people would stop buying books, was proved to have been based on a false premise. People, in fact, carried on with their lives pretty much as before. Heinemann's prepublication publicity campaign and the almost unanimous support of the reviewers in the London national papers and magazines had ensured that the reading public, war or no war, even with the continuing threat of catastrophic bombing raids, was eager to purchase and read *The Grapes of Wrath*, together with all other new novels of worth that the publishers were still bringing out. The *Observer* of 24 September, after consulting four of the leading London bookshops, produced a list of the recently published books that were proving to be best-sellers in the capital. *The Grapes of Wrath* was included as one of "four good books doing splendidly." The other three were Hugh Walpole's *The Sea Tower*, Frank Swinnerton's *The Two Wives*, and Noel Coward's *To Step Aside*. Other best-sellers mentioned were P. G. Wodehouse's *Uncle Fred in Springtime* and Francis Brett Young's *The City of Gold*. It is perhaps worthwhile to note that in this time of understandably increased patriotic fervor only one American book was included in this list of six.[22] In the "Books and Writers" column of the *Yorkshire Post* of 1 November, a further survey of forty-three bookshops throughout the country revealed that during the first month of the war the four leading best-sellers were all works of fiction and were, in order of popularity: *The City of Gold*, *The Sea Tower*, *The Grapes of Wrath*, and Richard Llewellyn's *How Green Was My Valley*.[23] The literary correspondent of the *Inverness Courier* reported on 13 October that *The Grapes of Wrath* was already in its fourth printing and that when he had asked a local bookseller the previous week what books were selling he was told that the two top sellers were James Bridie's autobiography and *The Grapes of Wrath*.[24]

Laudatory reviews continued to be published. The unnamed reviewer in the *Southport Guardian* considered that with *The Grapes of Wrath* Steinbeck had placed himself "in the foremost rank of contemporary American writers," and again evoked a passing comparison of the book with *The Jungle*. Setting *The Grapes of Wrath* firmly in the agrarian tradition of American literature, the reviewer continued:

> In America the novel has a double appeal; it is a social indictment, a novel with a propagandist purpose, and as in general with stories of this genre, may deliberately heighten its dramatic appeal to enforce its message; it not only deals with economics of agriculture, but also indicts the narrow concept of American civilization, material and mechanical, and argues that besides dollars, the hunger and feel for the land is inherent in the real American character, that the best citizens spring from the land, that a rural life and economy are necessary for a happy, prosperous American civilization. This philosophy runs through Steinbeck's former books, but never with such powerful purpose as here.

The reviewer's one adverse criticism of the book was a familiar one. While accepting that for the English reader the book's principal attraction was its literary quality and its Zolaesque realism, rather than its sociological and propagandist message, that very realism was "at times almost frankly lurid . . . and the exercise of more selection and toning down of some of the scenes would have sharpened the book and given it more artistic unity." With that one reservation, the reviewer rated *The Grapes of Wrath* "a creative work of art, vital, vivid, full of character and living in its characters."[25]

Richard King, in another of the coffee-table glossies, the *Tatler*, considered the book to be "the most outstanding novel" he had read "for a long, long, time,"[26] while W. E. Cockburn in the *Liverpool Echo* regarded it as being "as good as anything America has sent us since *Gone With the Wind*" and was inclined to the view that it was "not merely a major work, but a masterpiece."[27] Under the subheading "Novel of a Century" in the *Perthshire Constitutional*, J. H. C. Laker declared that Steinbeck had shown himself to be "the greatest prose writer of the age."[28] By then the book was in its sixth printing.

The *Grapes of Wrath* figured prominently in the end-of-year surveys of the 1939 publishing scene. Wilfrid Gibson, in the *Manchester Guardian*, reaffirmed his earlier assessment of the book by calling it "the most compellingly dynamic of all the novels that have come my way this year," and suggested that although it dealt with urgent contemporary issues in the United States it would "survive when the immediate issues with which it deals have become half-forgotten history."[29] The *Observer* drew up a list — with which, it was stressed, all the bookshops and libraries agreed — of "the outstanding favourites" since the outbreak of war, and recorded among the "really big successes" in the fictional field Noel Coward's *To Step Aside*, Hugh Walpole's *The Sea Tower*, John Steinbeck's *The Grapes of Wrath*, Richard Llewellyn's *How Green Was My Valley*, Aldous Huxley's *After Many a Summer*, Ann Bridge's *Four-Part Setting*, and J. B. Priestley's *Let the People Sing*.[30] The *Daily Worker*, predictably, selected *The Grapes of Wrath*, "that great epical novel from America," as its "obviously outstanding choice."[31] *The Grapes of Wrath* headed the list in the London *Evening Standard*, followed by Rachel Field's *All This and Heaven, Too*, Pearl Buck's *The Patriot*, and Richard Llewellyn's *How Green Was My Valley*.[32] The *New English Weekly*, while opining that the "most important single event in fiction during the year was the publication of *Finnegans Wake* by James Joyce," noted that American writers had led the field in more orthodox fiction. New works by Faulkner (*The Wild Palms*), Dos Passos, (*The Adventures of a Young Man*), Allen Tate (*The Fathers*), Hemingway (*The Fifth Column and the First Forty-Nine Short Stories*) and Katherine Anne Porter (*Pale Horse, Pale Rider*) had been published during the year, but Steinbeck's *The Long Valley* and "his widely successful *The Grapes of Wrath*" were picked out for special mention.[33] In the *Yorkshire Post*, under the heading "News and Views: Pleasing Events of 1939," the reviewer, admitting that he had read the book "at irregular intervals amid many grave preoccupations," said that he could "hardly sum it up in a trim paragraph," and "must read it again under more tranquil conditions." He averred, however, that, after he had read a few chapters, *The Grapes of Wrath* had impressed him principally "as a powerful presentment of the sombre side of American life, just as Theodore Dreiser's *American Tragedy* did."[34] The *Sunday Times* noted that there had been "some admirable novels from America" and that *The Grapes of Wrath* had been "one of the season's biggest successes."[35]

As is evident, despite the momentous events of the autumn and winter of 1939, *The Grapes of Wrath* enjoyed a very substantial and steady sale in

Britain. The reasons for this were manifold. From the very beginning, even though its publication coincided with the initial trauma of the outbreak of war, the book seems to have caught the imagination of the reading public as no other American novel since *Gone With the Wind*. Virtually all the reviewers remarked on the fact that, although the novel was propagandist in content, fiercely indignant in tone, and somber, even depressing, in its theme, it nevertheless told an engrossing story in, for the most part, a beautiful quasi-biblical prose shot through with moments of high emotion and human courage in the face of adversity. All in all, the book obviously had something pertinent to say to the people of wartime Britain. Moreover, and no less importantly, now that the normal patterns of life had been disrupted and had to be adjusted to new and unfamiliar routines and rhythms, reading had become a staple diet, a means of escape from hours of enforced boredom and the darkened world of the blackout.

The war had another, and perhaps curiously unappreciated, influence on the reception given to Steinbeck's book in Britain. In America, *The Grapes of Wrath* had been greeted in some quarters with howls of fury, not only because of its propagandist message, but also on the grounds of obscenity.[36] In England the propaganda had no relevance to the current national scene, but there is little doubt that in normal times Mrs. Grundy and her fervent associates would have risen en masse to condemn some of the language and some of the incidents reported by Steinbeck in the book. One has only to recall the reception given in Britain to Norman Mailer's *The Naked and the Dead* in 1948, when the book was hysterically denounced in the House of Commons, no less. As it was, although several reviewers had noted the occasional coarseness displayed in *The Grapes of Wrath*, they tempered their criticism with the observation that this was really all of a piece with the story Steinbeck had to tell, was thus not entirely gratuitous, and was perfectly, if regrettably, life being what it was, acceptable in its context. As far as the Mrs. Grundys and their ilk were concerned, they clearly found more pressing matters to occupy their minds, and accordingly no public outcry was ever directed against the book in Britain.[37]

By late July 1940, when John Ford's film of the book had finished its first week run at London's Odeon, the so-called phoney war was over. Norway, Denmark, Holland, Belgium, and France had been overrun and the invasion of Britain was expected any day. Although the times were fraught with deep apprehension, Ford's film had done record-breaking business during that first week, with long lines for each performance and many requests for reserved seats. The film had the effect of stimulating renewed interest in the book itself, and Heinemann reported "a sharp increase" in sales following the screening of the film. Three bookshops in Charing Cross Road — Foyle's, Collett's and Better Books — as well as Truslove & Hanson's on Oxford Street set up large window displays of the book, complemented with stills from the film. By mid-August, Heinemann was able to report that sales of the book had "increased beyond the most sanguine expectations."[38]

It is doubtful if, since the date of its original publication on 7 September 1939, *The Grapes of Wrath* has ever been out of print in Britain. Heinemann has issued many hardcover editions over the years. In 1940 editions of the book were issued by the country's two leading book clubs, The Reprint Society (World Books) and the Reader's Union. The first paperback edition was published by Penguin Books in 1951 and subsequently reprinted by them almost every year until 1975, when the British paperback rights were acquired by Pan Books.

To this day *The Grapes of Wrath* continues in Britain to be one of the most enduring of twentieth-century American novels. Certainly, it is the most enduring of the novels of the depression era. Just as it had something to say to the people of wartime Britain all those many years ago, so succeeding generations discovered that it still retained for them the powerful impact it initially had in 1939. Indeed, it still has something undeniably pertinent to say to us today as we survey the contemporary international scene. In many respects, little has changed.

Grateful acknowledgement is made to W. Roger Smith of William Heinemann Ltd. (Steinbeck's British publishers) for his invaluable assistance in the preparation of this essay.

Notes

1. Information concerning and quotations from Alexander Woollcott's talk have been culled from reviews in the *Yorkshire Post* of 6 September 1939, the *Spectator* of 15 September 1939, the *South Wales Evening Post* of 20 September 1939, the Johannesburg [South Africa] *Star* of 12 October 1939, and the *Southport Guardian* of 14 October 1939.

2. H. G. Wells, *The Fate of Homo Sapiens* (London: Secker & Warburg, 1939), 272–73.

3. Arthur Calder-Marshall, "The Novels of John Steinbeck," *Fortnightly Review* (September 1939), 295–304.

4. Wilfrid Gibson, "Three New Novels," *Manchester Guardian*, 8 September 1939, 3.

5. Philip Jordan, "War Or No War: Read This Book," *News Chronicle*, 8 September 1939, 4.

6. "Another American Tragedy," *Times*, 8 September 1939, 6.

7. "Victims of Mammon," *Times Literary Supplement*, 9 September 1939, 525.

8. Frank Swinnerton, "Topical and Timeless," *Observer*, 10 September 1939, 5.

9. Ralph Straus, "Mr. Steinbeck's Success," *Sunday Times*, 10 September 1939, 5.

10. Phyllis Bentley, "An American Voice: We Are The People—We Go On," *Yorkshire Post*, 13 September 1939, 2.

11. Edwin Muir, "New Novels," *Listener*, 22 (14 September 1939): 543.

12. Kate O'Brien, "Fiction," *Spectator*, 163 (15 September 1939): 386.

13. Anthony West, "New Novels," *New Statesman & Nation*, 18 (16 September 1939): 404–5.

14. Helen Cockburn, "Californian Mirage: An American Masterpiece," *Burton Observer*, 21 September 1939, 9.

15. John Brophy, "Mr. Steinbeck's Epic Story," *Daily Telegraph*, 22 September 1939, 4.

16. "A Powerful American Story," *Inverness Courier*, 22 September 1939, 3.

17. Lettice Cooper, "New Novels," *Time & Tide*, 20 (23 September 1939): 1256–57.

18. Sir Hugh Walpole, "These Things Will Live," *Daily Sketch*, 23 September 1939, 7.

19. V. S. Pritchett, *Bystander*, 143 (27 September 1939): 472.

20. Randall Swingler, "Novels That Are Not 'Escapist,' " *Daily Worker*, 27 September 1939, 3.

21. Vernon Fane, "An Oklahoma Farmer's Fight with Fate," *Sphere*, 158 (30 September 1939): 500.

22. *Observer*, 24 September 1939, 3.

23. "Books and Writers," *Yorkshire Post*, 1 November 1939, 4.

24. "Literary Notes: Chats About Books and Bookmen," *Inverness Courier*, 13 October 1939, 3.

25. "Books of the Day: The Big Six and an American," *Southport Guardian*, 14 October 1939, 7.

26. Richard King, "With Silent Friends," *Tatler*, 154 (18 October 1939): 74.

27. W. E. Cockburn, "Defeating Depression: Books for All Fronts: Two Brilliant Novels: An American Masterpiece," *Liverpool Echo*, 28 October 1939, 3.

28. J. H. C. Laker, "Books for Perthshire Readers," *Perthshire Constitutional*, 11.

29. Wilfrid Gibson, "Reviewers' Choice," Supplement to the *Manchester Guardian*, 1 December 1939, 4.

30. *Observer*, 3 December 1939, 3.

31. Randall Swingler, "Books to Remember at Xmas," *Daily Worker*, 6 December 1939, 3.

32. "Books for Christmas," *Evening Standard*, 14 December 1939, 4.

33. Damon, "Readers Christmas Signpost," *New English Weekly*, 16 (14 December 1939): 138.

34. W. L. A., "News and Views: Pleasing Events of 1939," *Yorkshire Post*, 29 December 1939, 4.

35. Ralph Straus, "The Year's Fiction: A Personal Choice," *Sunday Times*, 31 December 1939, 5.

36. The furor that the book had caused in some quarters of the United States was fully reported in the British press. See, for example, "Wrath and the Grapes," *Cavalcade*, 2 (New Series) (30 September 1939): 14.

37. In this respect, it is perhaps worthy of note, if only in passing, that the *Macclesfield Times* of 24 October 1940, reported that a certain Reverend H. Lismer Short had used Steinbeck's novel as the subject of his sermon the previous Sunday morning. The report does not state whether the Reverend Short praised or condemned Steinbeck's novel, but the implication is that he used the book as an example of the evil done unto man by his fellowmen, and of the resilience of the human spirit.

38. Based on information culled from reports in *To-Day's Cinema* of 30 July 1940, and *Kinematograph Weekly* of 15 August 1940.

The Dynamics of Community in
The Grapes of Wrath   Peter Lisca*

The Grapes of Wrath, more than Steinbeck's other novels, remains viable not just in drugstore racks of Bantam paperbacks or in college survey courses but in the world of great literature, because in that novel he created a community whose experience, although rooted firmly in the particulars of the American Depression, continues to have relevance. Certainly one aspect of that community experience which contributes to its viability is its dimension of social change. It is not coincidence that in the last decade, full of violent social action in so many aspects of American life, we have found ourselves turning with new interest toward the 1930s, recognizing there an immediate political and emotional relevance. *The Grapes of Wrath* moves not only along Route 66, east to west, like some delayed Wagon Wheels adventure, but along the unmapped roads of social change, from an old concept of community based on sociological conditions breaking up under an economic upheaval, to a new and very different sense of community formulating itself gradually on the new social realities.

Various facets of the old community concept are solidly developed in the first quarter of the book. The novel opens with a panoramic description of the land itself, impoverished, turning to dust and quite literally blowing away. It can no longer sustain its people in the old way, one small plot for each family, and it is lost to the banks and holding companies — impersonal, absentee landlords — which can utilize the land with a margin of profit by the ruthless mechanical exploitation of large tracts. But for the old community the land was something more than a quick-money crop or columns of profit and loss in a financial ledger, more even than the actual physical sustenance of potatoes, carrots, melons, pigs and chickens. Nor is it fear of the unknown that keeps the community attached to the now useless land. For these are a people with pioneer blood in their veins. The old community is further tied to the land by memories of family history. It is Muley who speaks this most convincingly:

> I'm just wanderin' aroun' like a damn ol' graveyard ghos'. . . . I been goin' aroun' the places where stuff happened. Like there's a place over by our forty; in a gulley there's a bush. Fust time I ever laid with a girl was there. Me fourteen an' stampin' an' snortin' like a buck deer, randy as a billygoat. So I went there an' I laid down on the groun', an' I seen it all happen again. An' there's the place down by the barn where Pa got gored to death by a bull. An' his blood is right in that groun', right now. . . . An' I put my han' on that groun' where my own Pa's

*Reprinted with permission from *From Irving to Steinbeck: Studies in American Literature in Honor of Harry R. Warfel,* ed. Motley Deakin and Peter Lisca (Gainesville: University of Florida Press, 1972), 127–40. © 1972 University Presses of Florida.

blood is part of it. . . . An' I seen my Pa with a hole through his ches',
an' I felt him shiver up against me like he done. . . . An' me a little kid
settin' there. . . . An' I went into the room where Joe was born. Bed
wasn't there, but it was the room. An' all them things is true, an' they're
right in the place they happened. Joe came to life right there.

Muley rambles, but his selection is not arbitrary — copulation, birth,
death. And these are not just vague memories or abstractions. In the
presence of the actual bush, the actual barnyard, the same room, this
essential past is relived in the present. Muley asks, "What'd they take when
they tractored the folks off the lan'? What'd they get so their 'margin a
profit' was safe? They got Pa dyin' on the groun', an' Joe yellin' his first
breath, an' me jerkin' like a billygoat under a bush in the night. What'd
they get? God knows the lan' ain't no good. . . . They jus' chopped folks in
two. Place where folks live is them folks."

Here Muley speaks not only for himself, but for an entire community,
the people in whose deserted houses at night he can still sense the "parties
an' dancin'," the "meetin's an' shoutin' glory. They was weddin's, all in
them houses." So strong is his attachment that he chooses to stay with the
land and its empty houses rather than move away with the rest of his
family. Grandpa Joad, too, despite his eagerness at the beginning, was not
able to leave the land and had to be given an overdose of pain-killer and
carried off. When he dies, just before crossing the Oklahoma border, Casy
assures the folks that "Grampa didn't die tonight. He died the minute you
took 'im off the place. . . . Oh, he was breathin', but he was dead. He was
that place, an' he knowed it. . . . He's jus' stayin' with the lan'. He
couldn't leave it." This is amplified to the level of community experience in
one of the interchapters, when the choric voices intone: "This land, this
red land is us; and the flood years and the dust years and the drought years
are us."

As the land itself and its houses are imbued with a traditional
experience, so are the farm tools, horses, wagons, the household goods
whose value cannot be measured in money: the beaded headband for the
bay gelding, " 'Member how he lifted his feet when he trotted?" And the
little girl who liked to plait red ribbons in this mane. "This book. My
father had it. . . . Pilgrim's Progress. Used to read it. . . . This china dog
. . . Aunt Sadie brought it from the Saint Louis fair. See? Wrote right on
it." It is a community experience which is imaginatively voiced to the
buyers of these goods: "You are not buying only junk, you're buying
junked lives. . . . How can we live without our lives? How will we know
it's us without our past?"

In addition to the identity invested in the land, the houses and
personal possessions, all of which must be left behind, the community is
also defined in terms of social customs and mores. That it is patriarchal,
for example, is clear from the deference of the women to male decision
and authority. When the decision is made to include Casy in the group,

Ma Joad is consulted about whether there would be food enough and space, but once that decision is made, Casy, who "knew the government of families," takes his place among the planning men. "Indeed, his position was eminent, for Uncle John moved sideways, leaving space between Pa and himself for the preacher. Casy squatted down like the others, facing Grampa enthroned on the running board. Ma went to the house again." It does not matter that Grampa is senile and utterly useless. Formally, his titular headship must be acknowledged, and, at this point in the novel, Ma must leave men to men's business. Again, when the family is seating itself in their truck, ready to leave, Uncle John would have liked his pregnant niece, Rosasharn, instead of himself, to sit up front in the comfortable seat next to the driver. But he knows "this was impossible, because she was young and a woman." The traditional distinction in social role is also evident in Ma's embarrassment at Casy's offer to salt down the pork. "I can do it," he says; "there's other stuff for you to do." Ma "stopped her work then and inspected him oddly, as though he suggested a curious thing. . . . 'It's women's work,' she said finally." The preacher's reply is significant of many changes to come in the community's sense of identity and the individual's sense of his total role: "It's all work," he replies. "They's too much of it to split it up to men's or women's work."

It is fitting that this break from domestic traditions should be announced by Casy, who is the first person from his community whom Tom meets on the way home from prison, and who announces at that meeting that he, the preacher, the spiritual source and authority of that community, has already abandoned the old dispensation and is seeking a new and better one. And after hearing his short, two-sentence, unortho- dox testament of belief in an oversoul, a human spirit "ever'body's a part of," Tom says, "You can't hold no church with idears like that. People would drive you out of the country with idears like that. Jumpin' an' yellin'. That's what folks like. Makes you feel swell. When Granma got to talkin' in tongues, you couldn't tie her down. She could knock over a full- growed deacon with her fist." Later in the novel other details of this old- time religion are given, such as the mass total immersions; Pa, full of the spirit, jumping over a high bush and breaking his leg; and Casy going to lie in the grass with young girls of his congregation whose religious fervor he had excited. But Casy is through with all that now, and these particular aspects of community, like those inherent in the land, the houses and personal goods, the domestic codes — all must be left behind.

This is not to say, however, that the sense and need of community is lost or has been destroyed. Steinbeck presents this sense and need on several levels from the biological to the mythical and religious. The novel's first interchapter is that masterful description of the turtle crossing the road, surviving both natural hazards and the attempts of man to frustrate its efforts. The turtle is clearly a symbol of the unthinking yet persistent life force. "Nobody can't keep a turtle though," says Casy. "They work at it and work at it, and at last one day they get out and away they go. . . ." The fact that this turtle has been going southwest, that Tom picks it up as a present to the family, and that it continues southwest when released, clearly identifies this turtle and its symbolic attributes with the Joads and the migrants. In them, too, there exists the instinct for survival and the necessity for movement which form, on the most elemental level, the basis of community.

The last interchapter of the novel's first part (before the Joads actually start their trip) also presents a biological argument. The abandoned houses are only temporarily without life. Soon they are part of a whole new ecology:

> When the folks first left, and the evening of the first day came, the hunting cats slouched in from the fields and mewed on the porch. And when no one came out, the cats crept through the open doors and walked mewing through the empty rooms. And then they went back to the fields and were wild cats from then on, hunting gophers and field mice, and sleeping in ditches in the daytime. When the night came, the bats, which had stopped at the doors for fear of light, swooped into the houses and sailed about through the empty rooms, and in a little while they stayed in dark room corners during the day, folded their wings high, and hung headdown among the rafters, and the smell of their droppings was in the empty houses.
>
> And the mice moved in and stored weed seeds in corners, in boxes, in the backs of drawers in the kitchens. And weasels came in to hunt the mice, and the brown owls flew shrieking in and out again.
>
> Now there came a little shower. The weeds sprang up in front of the doorstep, where they had not been allowed, and grass grew up through the porch boards. . . . The wild cats crept in from the fields at night, but did not mew at the doorstep any more. They moved like shadows of a cloud across the moon, into the rooms to hunt the mice.

This life force, which manifests itself in getting the turtle across the road and in creating a new biological community around the abandoned houses, lies also in the nature of man. And because man can abstract and conceptualize, that force is present in him not only in his instinct for physical survival, but also as projected in his gregariousness and social constructs. Thus, despite the fact that the anonymous truck driver in chapter two, a not particularly likable person, is forbidden to carry riders, and may lose his very valuable job for doing so, it is his need for human contact as well as his need of being a "good guy" that prompts him to give Tom Joad a ride: "Fella says once that truck skinners eats all the time. . . . Sure they stop, but it ain't to eat. They ain't hardly every hungry. They're just goddamn sick of goin'—get sick of it. Joints is the only place you can pull up, an' when you stop you got to buy somepin' so you can sling the bull with the broad behind the counter."

Even Tom Joad, who comes into the novel aggressively independent, not only recollects how a fellow inmate at prison who had been paroled came back to prison because it made him feel "lonesome out there," but admits to the same desire for human community in himself. " 'The guy's right too,' he said. 'Las' night, thinkin' where I'm gonna sleep, I got scared. An' I got thinkin' about my bunk, an' I wonder what the stir-bug I got for a cell mate is doin'. Me an' some guys had a strang band goin'. Good one. Guy said we ought to go on the radio. An' this mornin' I didn' know what time to get up. Jus' laid there waitin' for the bell to go off.' " Casy understands this need of man for community. When he tells Tom "They's an army of us without no harness. . . . All along I seen it. . . . Everplace we stopped I seen it. Folks hungry for sidemeat, an' when they get it they ain't fed," he is saying in his own words that man cannot live by bread alone, that it takes more than a full stomach to make man happy. In one of the interchapters the choric voice defines in communal terms this "harness" which man needs:

> The last clear definite function of man — muscles aching to work, minds aching to create beyond the single need — this is man. To build a wall, to build a house, a dam, and in the wall and house and dam to put something of Manself [note he does not say *him*self], and to Manself take back something of the wall, the house, the dam. . . . For man, unlike any other thing organic or inorganic in the universe, grows beyond his work, walks up the stairs of his accomplishments. . . . Fear the time when Manself will not suffer and die for a concept, for this one quality is the foundation of Manself, and this one quality is man, distinctive in the universe.

It is this inherent feeling of "Manself," to use Steinbeck's term, which forges the link of community, making out of all the scattered, lonely individuals a huge and irresistible "WE."

Further, in *The Grapes of Wrath* these seemingly inherent biological drives toward community are supported and given authority through a continuum of historical and religious reference. The Joads trace their ancestry back to the colonization of the new world: "We're Joads," says Ma. "We don't look up to nobody. Grampa's grampa, he fit in the Revolution." Looking into the terrible desert which they are about to cross, Al exclaims, "Jesus, what a place. How'd you like to walk across her?" "People done it," says Tom. "Lots a people done it; an' if they could, we could." "Lots must a died," says Al. "Well," replies Tom, "we ain't come out exactly clean." As she consoles Tom for the necessity of suffering insults meekly (when they are stopped by vigilantes at the roadblock), Ma Joad repeats again this sense of being supported by participation in a historical community: "You got to have patience. Why, Tom — us people will go on living when all them people is gone. Why, we're the people — we go on." And one of these phrases, "We're the people," strikes echoes answered in Psalm 95: "For He is our God; and we are the people of his pasture, and the sheep of his hand," thus giving the Joads community with the "chosen people."

The details which further this association are so numerous and have been pointed out by scholars so frequently as to need little discussion here. Briefly, the twelve Joads are the twelve tribes of Judea; they suffer oppression in Oklahoma (Egypt) under the banks (Pharaohs); undertake an exodus; and arrive in California (Canaan, the land of milk and honey) to be received with hostility by the native peoples. The novel's title, through "The Battle Hymn of the Republic," alludes to Deuteronomy, Jeremiah, and Revelation, as for example "And the angel thrust in his sickle into the earth, and gathered the vine of the earth, and cast it into the great winepress of the wrath of God." In some of the interchapters the strong echoes of the King James Old Testament poetically identify the evils of the present with those decried and lamented by the Prophets:

> Burn coffee for fuel in the ships. Burn corn to keep warm, it makes a hot fire. Dump potatoes in the river and place guards along the banks to keep the hungry people from fishing them out. Slaughter the pigs and bury them, and let the putrescence drip down into the earth.
>
> There is a crime here that goes beyond denunciation. There is a sorrow here that weeping cannot symbolize. There is a failure here that topples all our success. The fertile earth, the straight tree rows, the sturdy trunks, and the ripe fruit. And children dying of pellagra must die because a profit cannot be taken from an orange.

As the numerous allusions and parallels to the Old Testament establish a historical community between the oppressed migrants and the Israelites, the even more numerous allusions and parallels to the New Testament establish a religious community in Christianity. Again, the evidence is so extensive and has been so thoroughly analyzed elsewhere that little discussion is needed here. The most important of these elements is the itinerant preacher, who has lately left off preaching. Beginning with his initials, J. C.; his rebellion against the old religion; his time of meditation in the wilderness; his announcement of the new religion; his taking on his head the sins of others; to his persecution and death crying out, "You don' know what you're doin' "; Jim Casy is clearly a modern Christ figure. The new messiah arrives in a rich context of traditional Christian symbology, and his message, like that of Christ, is one that considerably broadens man's sense of spiritual community.

It rejects theological notions of sin ("There ain't no sin and there ain't no virtue. There's just stuff people do."); it defines the religious impulse as human love ("What's this call, this sperit? . . . It's love."); and it identifies the Holy Spirit as all men, the human spirit ("Maybe all men got one big soul ever'body's a part of."). Later in the novel, Casy becomes bolder and extends this community beyond man — "All that lives is holy" — and finally embraces even the inorganic world — "There was the hills, an' there was men, an' we wasn't separate no more. We was one thing. An' that one thing was holy." His disciple, Tom Joad, repeats Casy's notion of an Oversoul, and immediately quotes from Ecclesiastes to further support the notion of community: "Two are better than one, because they have a good reward for their labor. For if they fall the one will lif' up his fellow, but woe to him that is alone when he falleth, for he hath not another to help him up." When his mother expresses fear that they may kill him, he replies, "Then it don' matter. Then I'll be ever'where—wherever you look. Wherever there's a fight so hungry people can eat, I'll be there. . . . I'll be in the way kids laugh when they're hungry an' they know supper's ready." As another said before him, "Behold, I am always with you."

These forces for community which Steinbeck presents in the novel— biological, social, historical, religious—are impressive for their strength and variety, manifesting themselves in a range from the physical functions of unthinking organisms to the efflux of divine spirit. But in *The Grapes of Wrath* we do not see the realization of utopian community, for there are anticommunity forces as well; and these, too, are strong and manifest themselves in a wide range. Even the religious impulse, which in Casy and Tom is a positive force, can be a negative one, a perversion of its real purpose. Thus Uncle John's sense of personal sin isolates him from his fellowman and drives him to debauchery and a further sense of sin and isolation. Religion is seen as an isolating force also in the fanatic Mrs. Sandry, who frightens Rosasharn with her description of the horrible penalties God visits on pregnant women who see plays, or does "clutch-an'-hug dancin'," seeing these as the causes of miscarriage and malforma-tion, rather than disease and malnutrition, as Satan, in the guise of the camp manager, claims. The greatest practical realization of community in the novel is the government camp at Weedpatch, especially the dance. Despite the strong forces against them the people foil attempts to instigate a fight which will give the corrupt police the power to break up the camp. It is important, therefore, that during the dance the religious fanatics are seen as separate: "In front of their tents the Jesus-lovers sat and watched, their faces hard and contemptuous. They did not speak to one another, they watched for sin, and their faces condemned the whole proceeding."

Back at the other end of the scale, we see anticommunity forces at work also on the biological level of sheer survival. It is not greed or hatred or even ignorance that makes Willy drive one of the destroying tractors: "I got two little kids," he says. "I got a wife an' my wife's mother. Them people got to eat. Fust an' on'y thing I got to think about is my own folks." But Muley notes what is behind the bluster: "Seems like he's shamed, so he gets mad." Mr. Thomas, the owner of a small orchard who is pressured by the Farmers Association to lower his wages, is also doing what he is ashamed of in order to survive, and he too speaks "irritably" and becomes gruff. Near the end of the novel, Ma Joad sees through the glib gibes of the pathetic little clerk in the expensive company store: "Doin' a dirty thing like this. Shames ya, don't it? Got to act flip, hugh?" Whether or not the used-car salesmen overcharging for their jalopies also feel shame we do not learn. But clearly these people, as well as many others in the novel, are working against community because of the need for individual survival. Perhaps that is one of the significances of those calm little descriptions of predatory activity in nature which are found throughout the novel. Immediately preceding the car salesmen, for example, we have this: "gradually the skittering life of the ground, of holes and burrows, of the brush, began again; the gophers moved, and the rabbits crept to green things, the mice scampered over clods, and the winged hunters moved soundlessly overhead."

Sometimes the instinct of mere survival shades into selfishness and greed, as when the large owners squeeze out the little people and pay far lower wages than they can afford. It is interesting of Steinbeck's method that selfishness as an anticommunity drive, absolutely apart from any necessity for survival, receives its barest treatment in an episode involving the Joads themselves, the children. At the government camp, Ruthie breaks into a peaceful, established croquet game, unwilling to wait her turn. Insisting, "I wanta play now," she wrestles a mallet from a player. The actions of the other children are interesting. Under the guidance of the supervisor, they simply abandon the game to her, refusing community so to speak, leaving her alone and ridiculous on the court until she runs away in tears.

A third anticommunity force is the result of still another step beyond mere survival — the creation of a system, a machine, a monster, which seems to have a life of its own. Steinbeck presents it in a hypothetical choric dialogue:

> We're sorry. It's not us. It's the monster. The bank isn't like a man.
> Yes, but the bank is only made of men.
> No, you're wrong there — quite wrong there. The bank is some-thing else than men. It happens that every man in the bank hates what the bank does, and yet the bank does it. The bank is something more than men, I tell you. It's the monster. Men made it, but they can't control it.

But a monster need not be a bank. It may be "an owner with fifty-thousand acres," or it may be the entire economic structure itself which works against community: "Men who can graft the trees and make the seed fertile and big can find no way to let the hungry people eat their produce. Men who have created new fruits in the world cannot create a system whereby their fruits may be eaten . . . the works of the roots of the vines, of the trees must be destroyed to keep up the price. . . . And coroners must fill in the certificates — died of malnutrition — because the food must rot, must be forced to rot."

In the light of certain cliches about the social message in Steinbeck's supposedly "revolutionary" novel, it is interesting that these concepts of the "monster" and of a backward religion are only two of several anticommunity forces, and that the rest lie not in social structures but in man's own nature or individuality, as with the forces toward survival and selfishness discussed above and the forces of suspicion and ignorance. It is distrust that makes the transport company place a "No Riders" sign on the windshield of its trucks. It is a suspiciousness learned in jail that makes Tom, before his conversion, say for the second time, "I'm just puttin' one foot in front a the other," and again in a few pages, "I ruther jus' lay one foot down in front a the other." He doesn't trust people enough to extend himself. So deeply engrained is this suspicion that even at the government camp he is immediately suspicious of the "committee" which he is told will visit them tomorrow, and Pa Joad is openly hostile toward the camp manager's visit, although both occasions are friendly and helpful. Casy tells the story of the organizer who got a union started to help the workers: "An' know what? Them very folks he been tryin' to help tossed him out. Wouldn' have nothin' to do with 'im. Scared they'd get say in his company. Says, 'Git out. You're a danger on us.' "

Along with suspicion and distrust is ignorance. There is the simple ignorance of the hired tractor driver who perhaps lives twenty miles away in town and needs not come back to his tractor for weeks or months:

> And this is easy and efficient. So easy that the wonder goes out of work, so efficient that the wonder goes out of land and the working of it, and with the wonder the deep understanding and the relation. And in the tractor man there grows the contempt that comes only to a stranger who has little understanding and no relation. For nitrates are not the land, nor phosphates; and the length of fiber in the cotton is not the land. Carbon is not a man, nor salt nor water nor calcium. He is all of these, but he is much more, much more; and the land is so much more than its analysis. The man who is more than his chemistry, walking on the earth, turning his plow point for a stone, dropping his handles to slide over an outcropping, kneeling in the earth to eat his lunch; that man who is more than his elements knows the land that is more than its analysis. But the machine man driving a dead tractor on land that he does not know and love, understands only chemistry; and he is contemptuous of the land and of himself. When the corrugated iron doors are shut, he goes home, and his home is not the land.

A more complex aspect of ignorance as a force against community appears in the interchapters, most clearly in that chapter wherein migrants are forced to sell their household goods to profiteers who take advantage of their need in order to pay very little for honest goods, and who are addressed by the choric voice: "you're buying bitterness. Buying a plow to plow your own children under, buying the arms and spirits that might have saved you. Five dollars, not four. I can't haul them back— well, take 'em for four. But I warn you, you're buying what will plow your own children under. And you won't see. You can't see . . . But watch it, mister. There's a premium goes with this pile of junk and the bay horses—

so beautiful — a packet of bitterness to grow in your house and to flower some day. We could have saved you, but you cut us down, and soon you will be cut down and there'll be none of us to save you." Perhaps no other passage in the novel carries so convincingly this great truth of human community, that no man is an island, that what you do unto the least of these you do unto me. The tenor of all these forces of ignorance against community is, of course, in Casy's dying words, an echo of Christ's own words — "You don't know what you're doin'."

Because it is not theological or sociological determinism, but ignorance breeding selfishness and distrust, that is so largely responsible for the forces against community, it follows that the establishment of the new community will come out of true knowledge, out of which in turn will come love and sharing. It is Casy, the spiritual leader, who first abandons the old ways and becomes a seeker for new truth. When he first appears he has already abandoned his conventional notions of sin, hellfire, and the salvation of individual souls for the doctrine of universal love and the transcendental Oversoul. He asks to go along with the Joads because he wants to learn more: "I'm gonna work in the fiel's, in the green fiel's, an' I'm gonna try to learn. Gonna learn why the folks walks in the grass, gonna hear 'em talk, gonna hear 'em sing. Gonna listen to kids eatin' mush. Gonna hear husban' an' wife poundin' the mattress in the night. Gonna eat with 'em an' learn." What he finally learns, in jail after giving himself up to save Tom and Floyd, is that man's spiritual unit must express itself in a social unity, which is why he becomes an organizer. The grace which he reluctantly gives over his first breakfast with the Joads is already groping in this direction: "I got to thinkin' how we was holy when we was one thing, an' makin' was holy when it was one thing. An' it on'y got unholy when one mis'able little fella got the bit in his teeth an' run off his own way, kickin' an' draggin' an' fightin'. Fella like that bust the holiness. But when they're all workin' together, not one fella for another fella, but one fella kind of harnessed to the whole shebang — that's right, that's holy."

It is this growing knowledge of the necessity of sharing with strangers far beyond the usual circle of family and friends that becomes the most powerful force for establishing the new community. The novel's action opens with a series of acts of sharing. The truck driver shares a ride, Tom offers to share his whiskey with him and does share it with Casy. Muley not only shares his rabbits, but makes the first statement of this new principle: " 'I ain't got no choice in the matter.' He stopped on the ungracious sound of his words. 'That ain't like I mean it. That ain't. I mean' — he stumbled — 'what I mean, if a fella's got somepin' to eat an' another fella's hungry — why, the first fella ain't got no choice. I mean, s'pose I pick up my rabbits an' go off somewhere's an' eat 'em. See?' " To this is added Mrs. Wilson's answer to Ma Joad's thanks for help: "People needs — to help." Just a few pages later Ma Joad in replying to Mrs. Wilson's thanks for help, gives the concept a further turn: "you can't let help go unwanted." It is significant that the first example of spontaneous sharing with strangers on the journey is a symbolic merging of two families: Grampa's death in the Wilson's tent, his burial in one of the Wilson's blankets with a page torn from the Wilson's Bible, and Ma Joad's promise to care for Mrs. Wilson. As Pa Joad expresses it later, "We almost got a kin bond." And Ma Joad, who starts off with a ferocious defense of her family against all comers — "All we got is the fambly" — four hundred pages later says, "Use' ta be the fambly was fust. It ain't so now. It's anybody. Worse off we get, the more we got to do." Her progress is charted by the numerous occasions for sharing which are described in the novel — their past, their knowledge, their food and hunger, gasoline, transportation, shelter, work, talent, joy and sorrow.

The narrative is saturated with the particulars of this sharing, and it is in the choric voice of the interchapters: "And because they were lonely and perplexed . . . they huddled together; they talked together; they shared their lives, their food, and the things they hoped for in the new country. . . . In the evening twenty families became one family, the children were the children of all. The loss of home became one loss, and the golden time in the west was one dream." It is this sharing that creates the unity, the change from "I" to "We," the new sense of community through which the people survive. And those who do not share, who continue selfish and distrustful, "the companies, the banks worked at their own doom and they did not know it."

The more one reads *The Grapes of Wrath*, the more thoroughly one knows the many ramifactions of its informing theme, the more perfect and moving seems the novel's ending. Here, in this one real and symbolic act everything is brought together. Rosasharn gives her milk out of biological necessity to do so; she feeds not her own baby but an old man, a stranger. The Rose of Sharon, Christ, offers his body in communion. Biology, sociology, history, and religion become one expression of the community of mankind.

Growth of the Family in
The Grapes of Wrath   Carroll Britch and Cliff Lewis*

> Resistance to innovation indicates, in the eye of nature, senility and senility is doomed to be discarded. . . . That nation thrives best which is most flexible, and which has fewer prejudices to hamper adaption.
> — Brooks Adams

*This essay was written specifically for this volume and is published here for the first time by permission of the authors.

Although it addresses issues of great sociological change, *The Grapes of Wrath*[1] is at its core about the family and the struggle of its members to assert their separate identities without breaking up as a family. In his treatment of the Joads, Steinbeck manages to delineate "kid-wild" Winfield through "growed-up" Tom to "lecherous" Grampa in ways that gain each an individualized life beyond their inherited roles in the family hierarchy as well as beyond the symbolic roles they serve as an "overessence of people"[2] to amplify the argument of the plot. The argument, as Steinbeck writes in his "Journal," is that the Joads and those like them must abandon their felt notions of individualism and move toward an "I to We"[3] relationship with the other migrants if they are to survive the economic and spiritual challenge of their displacement. Hence, the central question of the narrative is whether or not the Joads can act on Casy's principle "to love all people" and still remain as Ma would have it "one thing . . . the fambly . . . whole and clear" (434).

Contrary to some prevailing views,[4] it is our contention that 1) the Joad family does not break up so much as grow up; 2) that its members are less altruistic than self-protective; and 3) that they articulate the argument of the plot precisely because they achieve in the novelistic sense a convincing human reality. In order for the central question to sustain its tension throughout the four odd months of the Joads' wanderings, it is crucial that they as individuals and as a family unit confront the challenge of the transformation from "I to We" in terms of the emotional logic and ethic that characterized their everyday life in Oklahoma. For if the Joads were to embrace Casy's principle just because it seems a nice idea, their being and his idea would pale for lack of credibility.

As Brooks Adams implies in his thoughts about "resistance to innovation," people are slow to change—if at all. And were it not for the intolerable conditions that the Joads encounter on the road, they as a group would likely fall prey to the "senility" that dooms Muley Graves, not to mention Grampa. In a letter to the literary critic Joseph Henry Jackson, Steinbeck argues the motive that leads those like the Joads to growth and change: "The human like any other life form will tolerate an unhealthy condition for some time, and then will either die or will overcome the condition either by mutation or by destroying the unhealthful condition. Since there seems little tendency for the human race to become extinct, and since one cannot through biological mutation overcome the necessity for eating, I judge that the final method will be the one chosen."[5] Most of the Joads survive because they do like to eat, but work to keep on eating because they have a dream. Like the turtle and the seeds it carries on its journey, the Joads take the souls of themselves with them west. Their will to move may have been born of necessity, but their movement is sustained by the down-to-earth hopes of better days that have often seen Americans through to prosperity. For Uncle John especially, the initial "unhealthful condition" is the self-pity that issues from a distorted sense of sin concerning his part in a calamitous childbirth. At times Rosasharn and Pa suffer in just about the same way for similar reasons. Nevertheless, the external unhealthiness of flood, famine, and economic injustice spurs them on to do eventually what, as Ma says of Tom, is "more'n" themselves.

Uprooted, the fundamental dream they share is that of stability and self-respect. On the farm the family enjoyed both. They slide from being land owners to being renters. True. But that slide still afforded them the dignity to serve as hosts. And on the road Ma intends that they do not backslide into the wretchedness that has destroyed the humanity of many in Hooverville. In show of her fundamental spirit she accepts Casy into the family because the Joads just do not refuse "food an' shelter or a lift on the road to anybody that ask[s]" (111). Her dream of "a little white house" and Rosasharn's dream to "live in a town" to make it "nice for the baby" (180) bespeak their ethic to re-establish a home, out from the protection of which they can in the pride of true deed care for themselves as well as for others in need.

All of the blood-Joads, excepting Noah, display a healthy sense of themselves. If Steinbeck had not created them so, they could hardly be used to work out the "I to We" theme either within the family or within the large social unit that the family comes to represent. As proud as it is of its pioneering background, the family is not *a* Joad but a unit—a *we*—made up of several singular "I's" who answer to the name of Joad. At Uncle John's, the staging area and jump-off point of the journey, each family member in his or her own way answers also to the call of pulling together to make the trip happen. Apart from moments of negative self-involvement (which is only human), when it comes to serving the family unit each Joad, with the exception noted, displays a "we" attitude throughout. Even Ruthie and Winfield, who are just too young to consider much other than their own ego-demands, help to pick peaches and do domestic chores. Ma's sense of *we*-ness seems always to have extended beyond the immediate family. And, as evidenced by the famous milk-sharing scene of the final chapter, it is boundless. She exists as the essence of Casy's principle, and is "so great with love," hence fearlessness, that she makes even him feel "afraid an' mean" (253). Her capacity to care marks the measure of her self-respect. As the action progresses, her caring does not change in kind but rather grows in breadth and intensity. But even at that, her family comes first. Steinbeck reveals it as a training ground for an expanded social consciousness. However, with Ma at the head the family harbors no armchair philosophers or bleeding-hearts.

"Citadel" (79) of the family, Ma defines its membership in terms of those who can defend it against disorganization, dishonor, sickness, broken-down transportation, meanness, lack of food, and want of shelter. Well before Tom arrives at Uncle John's to announce his parole and surprise homecoming, the able members of the family have joined in work to prepare for life on the road. Al, the young "tom-catter," has made a good buy on a Hudson that Pa Joad is finishing converting to a truck when Tom does arrive. Uncle John is in town selling off odds and ends to help finance the trip. On the eve of the journey Noah, the first-born, and Tom, the second-born, slaughter the pigs to eat on the way. Casy helps Ma to salt them. His doing "woman's work" foreshadows the reversal of roles the general uprooting engenders, illustrates his personal need to repay his hosts, and demonstrates through actual deed his preachings about love and service to people in need. Rosasharn packs the family clothes and stacks for loading many of the larger household goods. Granma and Grampa and the kids do little but eat and sleep. The narrator does not mention Connie by name as doing anything other than squatting in place with the other men during the family conference, and before that he was off "nestin" (90) with Rosasharn at his folks' place. However, for the Joads work is pride. Al's work with the Hudson earns him not only his "first participation in the conference" (109) but also the compliment from Grampa and big brother Tom that he has "done good" (110). At sixteen, Al may "think of nothin' but girls and engines"; nevertheless, it is that very thinking that helps to get his folks to California, gets him a wife, and will likely make his dream of getting a job in a garage a reality. In essence, Al is a family man. That he leaves his Ma and Pa to make a life of his own with Wainwright is, even in hard times, a good and healthy thing to do — and it in no way hurts his blood-kin or spoils his relationship with them. In reference to the marriage, Ma says "we're glad. We're awful glad" (468).

Given the plain fact that old folks normally fight to stay put and that children struggle to cut the cord to make a life of their own, the Joads as families go are no more split up at the start than at the finish of the novel. Speeding up the normal process is the fact that the highway becomes "their home and movement their medium of expression" (178). Granma and Grampa die en route as casualties of old age, displacement, and exhaustion. Once in the ground they are hardly mentioned by anyone again. Faced with the immediate needs of the living, especially with feeding Ruthie and Winfield and with soothing Rosasharn after Connie leaves, Ma realizes that she must "forget" the dead (264). The ones who depart of their own accord, including Al, do so because they cannot sustain their sense of selfhood if they stay.

Tom's motives for leaving are exceptional. And they are mixed. Wanted for murder and in hiding, he can be of no practical use to the family if he stays. A man of action, Tom exhibits few self-doubts. Near the end of the novel he decides that "long as [he's] a outlaw anyways" (463), he might just as well carry on Casy's work in organizing the strikers, and in that way help the plight of his family from afar. Anyway, as things happen, Ruthie gets into a kid-fight over Cracker Jacks, and to save face she blabs about Tom's having "kil't two fellas" (456), and in light of this brag Tom is forced to leave to save his skin. Unlike Noah and Connie, Tom goes with Ma's blessing and her gift of seven dollars to help him on his way.

By choice Noah is the first to go. He worked all his life on the family farm and helped to ready things for the journey. But as "a stranger to all the world" he has never really dwelt within the bosom of the family. With the words "Listen, you goddamn fool — " Tom is the only one to see Noah off down the Colorado River, and when he is barely out of eyesight Tom lies down to sleep (229). Ma worries a bit about how Noah will eat, but at Weedpatch she dismisses him from her mind, saying, "Maybe he'll have a nice time by the river. Maybe it's better so" (358). Incapable of wrath and amazed by its appearance in others, Noah is Steinbeck's boldest example of the self-involved and self-contained "I." He is the total opposite of his brother Tom, Ma's favorite. He could never find comfort dwelling in Tom's shadow or in the "embarrassed eyes" of his Pa. And he would most certainly shy away from the common cause that Ma supports and that Tom comes to embrace. Marked by a "twisted" birth, and with "no sexual urges" (84), making it on his own is about the most grown-up thing Noah could try.

Connie Rivers is the next to go. He sneaks off without so much as a "so long" to anyone. In chapter 10 the narrator states that he is "a good hard worker and would make a good husband," but that he is "frightened and bewildered" by Rosasharn's pregnancy (103–4). Well, the reader never sees him work. But the reader does see him frightened. The fact of Hooverville is just too much for him. Of a "Texan strain" and not a Joad, Connie brags too much, specifically about how he is going to study radio by mail and get Rosasharn a house and car. Whether he leaves to study up on radios or tractors is anyone's guess. But that he leaves his wife half-way through her pregnancy for the truly illusory dream of making a success of himself through "home study" marks him a failure as a man and husband. He has witnessed Pa Joad lose his place as head of the family because of poverty and Ma's demands, and he no doubt knows that he can in no way live up to Rosasharn's dream of motherhood. He leaves to save face. Aside from Rosasharn, the greater family does not miss him. Pa Joad concludes that "Connie wasn' no good. I seen that a long time. Didn' have no guts, jus' too big for his overalls" (301). Ma agrees, and tells Pa to act as if Connie were "dead" (302).

Now, although Connie and Noah have vanished like deserters from the heat of battle, the essential family structure is still intact, and stronger without them. They were on the fringe at best. And better men have replaced them. Foreshadowing the good luck it has in securing room at Weedpatch and work on the road, the family is strengthened by the chance meeting of Tom and Casy. It will be remembered that, back in Oklahoma, Casy teamed up with Tom on Tom's way "home," and that both arrived at Uncle John's out of the blue and just in time to join the family for the trip West. On behalf of the younger members of her family, Ma would have gone without Tom. Even before the family "shove[d]" off their homestead (48) and their house was "all pushed out a shape" (42),

Tom was all but dead to them. During his four years of imprisonment, he received one Christmas card from Ma and one from Granma, and that is all. Released, Tom brings new life into the family, and in a very material way prefigures the virtual death of his brother Noah, whose knowledge of the outside world and modern machinery is zero. And his gift of Casy to the family, who is an outsider but brother to all, prefigures the demise of Connie, whose behavior as a brother-in-law leaves much to be desired. It may be a bad pun but it is no accident that Steinbeck has Connie *Rivers* and Noah (whose name is associated with the destruction of the world by flood) disappear within a few days of one another along a river and well before the hardship of the flood the family undergoes at the end of the narrative. In short, without Noah and Connie, as without Granma and Grampa, the family as Ma defines it is better equipped to survive the agony ahead, of which Hooverville in all its meanness of spirit is but an initiation.

As a reflection of the sorry spectacle, it is at Hooverville that Uncle John comes face to face with his own lack of self-honor and life-purpose. Having witnessed Casy just go right up to be arrested by a deputy by saying straight out that he clobbered one of them makes Uncle John "feel awful." He knows that he could have stepped in and helped Tom and Floyd, and taken the blame on himself. But he "slipped up," and so goes off by himself to get drunk. Not until the flood and the miscarriage of Rosasharn's baby does Uncle John find himself. He sets the apple box that serves as the baby's coffin afloat in the flood waters and says, "Go down an' tell em. Go down in the street an' rot an' tell 'em that way" (493–94). Given his shy nature, it is fitting that he attacks the system that helped to kill the baby alone and without the need of congratulation from anyone. He does "more'n" himself. Although the gesture may go unheeded, he consciously aligns himself with the struggle of the "We." And he does so in a manner no less creative than, and every bit as shocking as, Rosasharn's baring her breast to nurse a starving man.

If the dead baby were not blood kin, and the stab of injustice personal, he may never have been moved to express his wrath against the general condition. Like John, Pa Joad is moved to action for personal reasons. He wants his family to stay dry. But he needs help. He cannot build a dike alone. Wainwright, Al's future father-in-law, thinks it a waste. But Pa persuades him and others by saying, "Well, we ain't doin' nothin'. . . . We can do her if ever'body helps" (482). The day before the flood Pa feels that his life is "over an' done." Building the dike renews his spirit, and teaches him that there is much to be gained through the "We" attitude. The dike does break, but it holds just long enough for Rosasharn to deliver, and for that Pa is moved to laugh "in triumph" (486).

It will be recalled that when Casy went off to jail at Hooverville he did so with a "smile" and "a curious look of conquest" on his face. Shortly before his arrest he had confessed to Tom that he wanted to "go off alone" because he was "a-eatin" the family food and "doin' nobody no good" in return (276). Hence, like Pa and John, who knowingly or not follow his example, Casy triumphs over his doubts of self-worth by acting in behalf of others in need. For most of the Joads, his spirit does indeed take hold. It shows up in the "smile" of Ma when she gives her blessing to Al to "stay" in the boxcar with Aggie while she leads the rest of the family to higher ground. En route, the spirit even takes hold of Ruthie, who finally realizes that there is little fun in playing alone, and so shares the petals of a wild geranium with her brother Winfield. And it positively radiates from the face of Rosasharn as the "mysterious smile" that concludes the narrative. Finding self-worth through sharing and cooperating with kin and outsiders is what keeps the Joads, with the exceptions noted, from falling apart as a family and failing as migrants.

What probably causes some readers to conclude that the Joads break up is Tom's mission, Al's engagement, and Ma's complaint at the Hooper ranch that "There ain't no fambly now." Yet her family is in fact with her, and those who are able are doing their share of work in the orchard. Her complaint focuses on the "wildness" of the kids to Pa's "lost place" as head of the family. However, it is calculated to persuade Tom to "stay an' help." Tom stays, but he is in no condition to do anything but rest and hide from the vigilantes. In short, Ma at this point is just plain depressed, and so uses every trick of motherhood she knows to delay the inevitable departure of her favorite son, whose spirit she trusts, and whom she has come to lean on as the male leader of the family. Earlier, she told Tom straight out how she felt about him as opposed to the rest of the family: "Them others — they're kinda strangers, all but you. . . . Ever'thing you do is more'n you" (389). And now, at Hooper's, she wants his moral support. They are soul mates. From the strength of that bond she can when the time comes see him off, and say to Pa "I — sent 'im away" (467). During the flood, as mentioned above, she does the same for Al — that is, without emotional blackmail, she releases Al to grow on his own with a new family. And although the narrative is open-ended, Al will likely stay around the boxcar for a few weeks to start the Hudson, for none of the vehicles will dry out until then. Yet, beyond the practical help the Joads lend one another, the basic thing that makes them a family is what George explains to Lennie in chapter 1 in *Of Mice and Men*: "We got somebody to talk to that gives a damn about us."

The Joad who talks the most, and whose thoughts are directed toward putting into action the "I to We" principle, is Tom. He is the one Joad capable of the violence needed to combat the "unhealthful condition" that violates the dignity and very survival of the migrants. The motive source of his tendency to violence is personal. Like Muley Graves, who is ready to kill any of "them sons-a-bitches" that threaten to push him around (49), Tom is quick to protect his pride and person. He admits that prison did not reform him, saying, "if I seen Herb Turnbull comin' for me with a knife right now, I'd squash him down with a shovel again. . . . Do her before I could figure her out. . . . That sort of senselessness kind a worries a man" (58–59). Yet prison taught him how to survive in any environment. He receives an early release for good behavior because he learned how to handle the inmates and the officials without having to use violence to protect his dignity. It is turtlelike willpower and determination to survive that brings Tom back to the family, but it is his ability to change and adapt to a reality even tougher than prison that enables him to view the means by which the Okies will survive. He is capable of picking up on Black Hat's thoughts about the five thousand Akron strikers who "jes' marched through town with their rifles. An' they had their turkey shoot . . . ain't been no trouble sence then" (381).

On the road Tom evolves from just a guy who wanted to enjoy his whiskey, smokes, whores, and home-cooked meals to a figure expansive enough to represent the essence of the American spirit, what Steinbeck later described as the "national character." "I thought," he wrote, "that if we had a national character and national genius, these people, who were beginning to be called Okies, were it. With all the odds against them, their goodness and strength survived."[6] If Tom and his kin had not run out of cash, he would likely not have become Steinbeck's realistic version of the questing knight in search of the lost grail: the American Dream of justice, democracy, and the opportunity to live in dignity.

As illustrated by his angry gesture of crushing the "hard skull-like head" of a grasshopper in response to the nosey truckdriver who pushes him to admit that he is an ex-convict (12–13), Tom is dangerous to anyone who would tarnish his sense of self-dignity. His greatest enemies, of course, are those wanting cheap labor. But with economic individualism doomed, Tom and his like no longer have a power base from which to defend their rights. Hence, to maintain at least the sense of personal power and self-worth, Tom and the others take strength from their subconscious memories or dreams. Steinbeck writes in an editorial chapter that they "seemed to be part of an organization of the unconscious. They obeyed impulses . . ." (108).

However, some of Tom's more violent impulses have to be restrained. His re-education begins with Muley Graves, a former neighbor, and at the very place of his birth where, on a smaller scale, Tom gets a glimpse of the more powerful militant forces that he will face in California. He learns from Muley of Willy Feely, a former cotton farmer, who drives a "cat" for the powerful forces who now own the land. Why hold this demeaning job? Willy remarks: "I got two little kids. . . . What happens to other folks is their look-out" (59). Like his kind in California Willy has become a deputy sheriff, and Tom learns that he can no longer approach the Willys of the land as an equal. Rather than get "pushed around," Tom would "lots rather take a sock at Willy" (62). After Muley explains that Willy may use his gun, Tom realizes his present plight. By challenging Willy and his power structure, "I ain't got a thing in the worl' to win, no matter how it comes out" (63). Later, at the "half a buck" campgrounds in New Mexico, when the proprietor calls Tom a bum, he shows that he has not forgotten Muley's lesson, saying, "It's a hard thing to be named a bum. I ain't afraid . . . I'll go for you an' your deputy with my mitts—here now, or jump Jesus. But there ain't no good in it" (206). However, in California, when stopped on route to Weedpatch, he would have clobbered a whiskey-smelling Legionnaire with a jack handle if Ma had not restrained him. The Legionnaire calls him a "goddamn Okie" but Tom backs down from a fight by assuming a "servile whine" in asking directions to Tulare. Good thing. The Legionnaires are "armed with pick handles and shotguns" (309).

At Weedpatch Tom joins a committee to prevent hooligans from the Cattle and Growers Associations from starting a riot at the Saturday night dance. With but the show of force the committee escorts the trouble-makers out of camp without hurting them. Beyond the obvious lesson that there is strength in a will united, Tom gains also from the experience the good sense that, even outside of prison, there can be dignity in a nonviolent approach to people who would put him down. Happily, he carries that attitude to Hooper Ranch—a false Eden—which the Joads enter for work picking peaches, ignorant that they are strike breakers. The orchard is a virtual prison. Tom wants to get outside to discover what is going on. Neither Pa nor Al will go with him, so he tries alone. An armed guard challenges him. Tom backs away. But he does not whine. In reflection of the Weedpatch strategy, he remains cool, declaring, "If it's gonna cause a mess, I don't give a darn. Sure, I'll go back" (420). He escapes. Unfortunately, he then walks into a real "mess." And, for the second time in his life, he kills a man.

Prone to violence though he is, it is important to see Tom's gentler side. For example, the turtle that some motorists try to hit, Tom treats as a pet and as a worthy gift for Ruthie and Winfield. On his way to Uncle John's, a gopher snake crosses his path. Tom says, "Let him go" (74). Tom is neither instinctively cruel nor destructive. When he drives the Hudson he feels no remorse in running over the dangerous rattlesnake, but his reaction to hitting the frightened jackrabbit is telling: "Gives me a little shakes ever' time" (203). And he confesses to Al that he is sorry he killed young Turnbull " 'cause he was dead" (193). Al, obviously proud of his brother Tom, sums him up at Hooverville in the declaration that he is just "as nice as pie till he's roused, an' then—look out" (281). Tom will not be reduced to the level of a turtle.

Beyond direct threat to his person, what rouses Tom the most is the fact that law has become a tool of the fascistic Association of Farmers. He assures Ma more than once that he is not a "Floyd" who attacks society out of personal bitterness. He explains: "if it was the law they [land owners] was workin' with, why, we could take it. But it *ain't* the law. They're a-workin' away at our spirits. . . . tryin' to break us" (308). The few moments that Tom spends with Casy in the ravine of his bloody murder gives Tom a glimpse of the possibility of organizing the Okies to challenge the power structure. Hence, when the agents of that structure beat Casy down, they in effect attack the new hope in Tom that friend Casy inspired. There is an ugly irony in the fact that the very tool of the laborer, a new pick handle, is used against Casy. Tom is enraged. A man like his brother Noah or brother-in-law Connie would have fled. But Tom wrests the pick handle away from the murderer, and then strikes him not once but five times. The brutality in this overkill demystifies Tom: he is cruel beyond what is necessary to save himself. And now to survive he must run.

With his face looking like the raw meat of a prizefighter's, the last we see of Tom is in chapter 28, what we call the "harvest" chapter. Like Rose of Sharon, he takes counsel with himself in a "cave of vines." There he explains to Ma his new resolve, the harvest of his hard knocks: since he's an "outlaw anyways" he will be present, if not in fact then in spirit, to lead the "fight so hungry people can eat" — this because the struggle for mere self-survival is not enough, for a "fella ain't no good alone" (462–63). He has grown to realize that the rewards of life must be harvested in the here and now, and that hope in the religious hereafter will not cure the present misery. He and the others of his lot must work together to drive back the oppressors who would break their spirit. Tom is not alone in holding this vision. Floyd Knowles at Hooverville and Black Hat at Weedpatch express the same ideas. But Tom's temperament, passion, and particular circumstance make it probable that he will become in word and deed a strike organizer. On the run he has little to lose and much to gain from working underground. Being joined to the just cause of his people will make him a good outlaw.

Al assumes Tom's role as male leader of the family. From the youth who was chastised by Pa for having been away two weeks when preparations for the trip were under way, Al at journey's end is hardly recognizable. He proves Tom's faith in the resurgence of the Okie spirit. He has heeded the big brother who said, "Al, don' keep ya guard up when nobody ain't sparrin' with ya" (200). Hence, when he announces his decision to marry Aggie, his defiant speech is directed not so much against the two families as it is against the outside economic forces that lurk to ambush his dream of a job, a marriage, and a house: "they ain't nobody can stop us" (468). And when a stranger threatens Pa somehow to even the score for having been talked into working on the flood wall that broke, Al's defense of his father is as vigorous as Tom's might have been: "You're gonna fight your way in" (490). Pa restrains Al as Ma restrained Tom and deals in a peaceful manner with the intruder.

After the rains stop it is Al who makes the plans on how to protect both families from the rising flood. Casy or Tom could be speaking: "I been a-thinkin' " (492). While Al and Ma plan on building a platform to shield the families from the water, Ma's eyes open from her sleep and "She crie[s] sharply in warning, 'Tom! Oh, Tom! Tom!' " (492). Then she lapses back into her dream. It is dawn. Whether or not her warning saves her favorite in his travail, it seems to summon Al to take Tom's place of leadership—for upon the instant he sets to work to keep the family high and dry. Finishing the job, Al makes a conscious stand as leader by requesting of Pa that he go buy food for breakfast: "I need some meat" (494).

The Joads and the Wainwrights have a new warrior. As such, Al accepts the responsibility of guarding his family's possessions as well as his wife-to-be. His harvest does not include the larger questions of social justice that feed Tom. For it will be remembered that at the peach orchard "Al looked away" (416). But his passion for an honest piece of the American pie is undeniable, and, in terms of the family ethic, praiseworthy. As Ma says, "I couldn' want for a better boy" (466). And she sallies forth to nurture Winfield and Ruthie, who, as the seedlings of the family, have a way to go in weathering the hazards of Self and the outside world before reaching the height of Al, Tom, and Rosasharn. That Ma ushers them into "the tool shed" at the close of the narrative is telling. For such is the emblem of the migrant family, and the hope of their lot.

Although the narrative is open-ended, the Joads on the whole have demonstrated that their "fears" of the general "unhealthy condition" have in effect evaporated in their dreams of better days, acts of sharing, and gestures of "wrath." Noah, Connie, and the grandparents never grow beyond their old ways of thinking. But the rest have shown themselves as bright innovators and forward thinkers. Dashed hopes and sudden changes have not broken their spirit. A happy and normal change is that Al has become the star figure of two families. A change of mixed feeling is that the older men have come to accept themselves as well as their deflated status in the family hierarchy. Uncle John has ceased complaining about his old "sins" and Pa does the shopping, even if what he buys displeases Ma. Despite the changes, the family has not, as the critics cited in note 4 insist, broken up. Rather, it has restructured itself to meet the challenge of new life in changing times. Ma gives orders to keep "the family unbroke" (186) because the family is her pride and best means of security. And, in another reversal of family habit, she and Rosasharn earn that security by working in the fields and orchards right alongside of the men. Uncle John and Pa take the orders because they no longer have the particular distinction of being the only family members to bring home the bacon. They stay because the family is their friend, and the best they have.

Each, the kids included, has experienced the intentional meanness of landlords, the indiscriminate fury of the flood, the anger of strangers, and the self-doubts of their own worth. But, excepting Ruthie, they have also reached out in kindness to strangers, and as strangers have accepted kindness. Through it all they have come to know or to sense that their plight is not unique, and that some others are far worse off than themselves. That Pa and Uncle John gaze "helplessly" (501) at the sick man Rose of Sharon feeds bespeaks not only their feeling of vulnerability but also their impulse to help. With the only means they have at hand they do help: Pa, especially, puts aside his authority as the male elder and forgoes any word of sarcasm or defeatism; in silence both men acquiesce to the extraordinary thing Ma urges the daughter to do. They, like Ma and Rosasharn, indeed do "more'n" themselves, and in ways that declare their individuality and their role as "essence people," both. Finally, if ever the mettle of the American spirit and family has been tested and found strong, it has been so with the Joads.

Notes

1. John Steinbeck, *The Grapes of Wrath* (New York: Penguin Press, 1976); hereafter cited in the text.

2. John Steinbeck, "*The Grapes of Wrath* Journal," 6 July 1938 (Austin, Texas: Humanities Research Center, 1938–41), 17: "But my people must be more than people. They must be an over-essence of people."

3. Steinbeck, "Journal," 13 July 1938, 24.

4. In *Steinbeck and His Critics: A Record of Twenty-Five Years*, ed. E. W. Tedlock, Jr., and C. V. Wicker (Albuquerque: University of New Mexico Press, 1957), Frederic I. Carpenter states that "the tragedy of *The Grapes of Wrath* consists in the breakup of the family" (246); Claude-Edmond Magny asserts that "if Steinbeck's characters seldom achieve true novelistic reality, it is precisely because they are so little individualized, so little individuals, and finally so little human" (225); and Woodburn O. Ross argues that although Steinbeck introduces "Altruism" into his ethical system, "he does not support his emphasis upon altruism by any scientific reasoning" (209–10). In his article "Tom's Other Trip: Psycho-Physical Questing in *The Grapes of Wrath*," *Steinbeck Quarterly* 16 no. 1–2 (1983): 17–24, Patrick W. Shaw writes that "The dissolution of the family unit is a natural process which forces Tom to confront the larger issues that lead to transcendence" (22).

5. Letter from John Steinbeck to Joseph Henry Jackson, Bancroft Library [undated], 1939.

6. Letter from Steinbeck to Jackson.

The Culpable Joads: Desentimentalizing *The Grapes of Wrath*

Louis Owens*

The Grapes of Wrath is one of John Steinbeck's great experiments, perhaps his greatest, a novel that exploded upon the American conscience in 1939, bringing home to American readers both the intimate reality of

*This essay was written specifically for this volume and is published here for the first time by permission of the author.

the Joads' suffering and the immense panorama of a people's—the Dust Bowl migrants'—suffering. In spite of howls of outrage from opposite ends of the novel's journey—both Oklahoma and California—America took the Joads to heart, forming out of *The Grapes of Wrath* a new American archetype of oppression and endurance, survival if not salvation.[1] So warmly did readers embrace the Dust Bowl Okies, in fact, that critics began almost immediately to accuse Steinbeck again of sentimentality in his portrayal of the downtrodden proletariat. Edmund Wilson was one of the first serious critics to take such a position, declaring that in this novel Steinbeck learned much from films, "and not only from the documentary pictures of Pare Lorentz, but from the sentimental symbolism of Hollywood."[2] Bernard De Voto had anticipated Wilson when he complained that the novel's ending was "symbolism gone sentimental."[3] Still a third major American critic, R. W. B. Lewis, found Steinbeck's fiction "mawkish" and "constitutionally unequipped to deal with the more sombre reality a man must come up against. . . ."[4]

As Steinbeck's most imposing and both popularly and critically successful work, *The Grapes of Wrath* has been studied from a multitude of angles, with critics focusing on its historical, political, philosophical, religious, symbolic, structural, and stylistic aspects. Steinbeck's great formal experiment in this novel—the interchapters—has been often studied and commented upon. What has been little noted in this novel, however, is the care Steinbeck takes to counterbalance the narrative's seemingly inevitable drift in the direction of sentimentalism as the story of the Joads and of the migrants as a whole unfolds in all its pathos. While Steinbeck is undeniably intensely sympathetic in this novel to the suffering of the croppers and to the plight of the seemingly powerless "little people" caught up in the destructive path of corporate America, he is at the same time painstakingly careful *not* to sentimentalize these figures, a fact of utmost importance to a critical understanding of *The Grapes of Wrath*.

A primary means by which Steinbeck attempts to unsentimentalize this story of displacement and suffering is through his use of interchapters. As has been often noted, the most obvious value of the intercalary chapters is to provide the big picture, to ensure the reader's awareness of the panoramic dimensions of this socioeconomic tragedy. At the same time, the narrative chapters focusing on the Joad family stem from Steinbeck's self-professed awareness that "It means very little to know that a million Chinese are starving unless you know one Chinese who is starving."[5] Through the interchapters we feel the scope and dimension of the Dust Bowl drama; through the narrative chapters we experience the tragedy of one family on a personal, intimate level. A second very important function of the interchapters, however, one that has gone largely unnoticed, is that of offsetting the intimacy of the narrative chapters, of creating necessary distance between the reader and Steinbeck's representative family, the Joads. Steinbeck uses the interchapters skillfully as a means of preventing the reader from identifying too closely with the Joads. Again and again, just as we begin to be drawn fully into the pain of the Joads' experience, Steinbeck pulls us away from the intimate picture into the broad scope of one of the interchapters, reminding us that these are merely representative people, that the scale of suffering is so great as to dwarf the anguish of one small group such as Ma Joad's family. Chapter 18 ends, for example, with the Joads about to descend into the promised land of California's Central Valley, weighted with the emotionally charged burden of the dead Granma. The heartbreaking courage of Ma, who has lain beside Granma all night to ensure that the family gets "across," is deeply moving, and as the Joads drive down into the highly stylized Eden of the valley the reader must respond emotionally to the courage and suffering of the family. Immediately, however, with the opening lines of chapter 19, Steinbeck shifts the reader's focus away from the Joads onto a broad, impersonal sweep of California's agricultural history culminating in a view of the Hoovervilles and a generic portrait of the migrants. The Joads' suffering is put into perspective as we realize once again that this family's tragedy is every migrant's, that there must be a thousand Granmas and as many Ma Joads, and that the family is about to descend into a sea of families in precisely the same circumstances and facing their predicament with roughly the same proportion of courage and cowardice. In place of the familiar voices of Tom and Ma Joad the reader now hears the voice of history, and the perspective is readjusted once again. It is more difficult to become sentimental about the fate of the individual when one is simultaneously aware of the fate of the species.

In addition to the depersonalizing distance achieved through the movement from narrative chapter to interchapter, Steinbeck also takes advantage of a more familiar device to desentimentalize his treatment of the downtrodden sharecropper in this novel: the objective authorial stance that he exploited so successfully in the earlier study of oppressed workers, *In Dubious Battle*. In that novel, published just three years before, Steinbeck was careful to underscore the failings of the migrant workers as well as those of the oppressors—both sides are greedy, selfish, lazy, bloodthirsty, and ignorant. These are simply aspects of the human character, says Steinbeck in that strike novel, simply the way it *is*, nonteleologically.[6] In *The Grapes of Wrath*, Steinbeck does not assume the purely objective stance of the narrative voice of *In Dubious Battle*, choosing not to become "merely a recording consciousness, judging nothing" as he claimed to be in the earlier strike novel.[7] In *The Grapes of Wrath*, Steinbeck allows his authorial voice the freedom to intrude in the guise of a modern Jeremiah, judging, condemning. However, once again in spite of his sympathies with the displaced Okies, as he did in *In Dubious Battle* in *Grapes* Steinbeck takes care to similarly undercut the nobility and "goodness" of the migrants.

Tom, for example, is a loner who begins the novel looking out only for number one, as his solitary initial appearance and his aggressive manipulation of the witless truck driver indicate. Only gradually, through the tutoring of Casy, does the unsympathetic Tom grow into his role of proletarian savior. Throughout the novel, Pa Joad is self-centered and weakwilled, too ineffectual to assume the role of leadership demanded of him, a character thoroughly incapable of igniting the reader's sympathy, as Tom makes clear when he tells Casy late in the novel "Think Pa's gonna give up his meat on account a other fellas?"[8] Tom's brother Al is concerned chiefly with his own concupiscence, eager even near the end of the novel to abandon his family and strike out on his own with his wife-to-be. Rose of Sharon's husband, Connie, proves himself to be a selfish and soft-minded believer in the American Dream advertised in comic books and a deserter of his pregnant wife. Rose of Sharon, in turn, forces the reader to suffer through hundreds of pages of whining self-pity before her miraculous conversion near the novel's end. Even Ma, larger-than-life Earth Mother and obvious heroine of this novel, demonstrates her limitations as she rambles on pointlessly about "Purty Boy Floyd," repeating herself tediously the way real people really do as she intones one of the folkmyths of Oklahoma and the Dust Bowl region.

While the trials of the Joads engage us, even excite our admiration and pity, Steinbeck takes pains to deny us the luxury of sentimental attachment. The Joads, including even the ultimately heroic and Christ-like Casy, are no better, no greater, no less human than they should be. Nor are any of the other migrants in the novel.

More important than either Steinbeck's illumination of the human failings of his characters on such limited levels or his use of the interchapters as distancing devices is his care to emphasize the migrants' culpability, their portion of responsibility for what has happened to the land and to themselves. Certainly Steinbeck makes it clear that the sharecroppers are victimized by an inhuman economic monster that tears at the roots of Jeffersonian agrarianism. However, when Steinbeck causes his representative migrant voice to plead with the owners for a chance to remain on the land, he qualifies the celebrated Jeffersonian agrarianism and love-for-the-land by tainting the croppers' wish: "Get enough wars and cotton'll hit the ceiling" (32), the cropper argues. A willingness to accept war and death as the price for further cottoning out of the land is difficult to admire on any level. And Steinbeck goes a step further, to make it clear that the migrants are firmly fixed in a larger, even more damning American pattern. Though the tenants have tried to persuade the owners to let them hang on, hoping for a war to drive up cotton prices, the tenant-voice also warns the owners: "But you'll kill the land with cotton." And the owners reply: "We know. We've got to take cotton quick before the land dies. Then we'll sell the land. Lots of families in the East would like to own a piece of land" (33). With their words the westering pattern of American history is laid bare: we arrive on the Atlantic seaboard seeking Eden only to discover a rocky and dangerous paradise with natives who aggressively resent the "discovery" of their land; the true Eden must therefore lie ever to the west, over the next hill, across the next plain, until finally we reach the Pacific Ocean and, along with Jody's grandfather in *The Red Pony*, we end up shaking our fists at the Pacific because it stopped us, breaking the pattern of displacement, a pattern put into focus in Walt Whitman's poignant query in "Facing West from California's Shores": "But where is what I started for so long ago? / And why is it yet unfound?"

That the croppers are part of this pattern becomes even more evident when the representative tenant voice informs us that their fathers had to "kill the Indians and drive them away." And when the tenants add, "Grampa killed Indians, Pa killed snakes for the land" (34), we should hear a powerful echo of the Puritan forebears who wrested the wilderness from the Satanic serpent and his Indian servants, killing and displacing the original inhabitants of the new Canaan.

It is difficult to feel excessive sorrow for these ignorant men who are quite willing to barter death to maintain their place in the destructive pattern of American expansion, a pattern that has ravaged a continent. That Steinbeck thought long about the American phenomenon of destroying the Garden just discovered in the search for an even better Garden is suggested in his declaration more than a decade later that in *East of Eden*, his great investigation of the myth of America, "people dominate the land, gradually. They strip it and rob it. Then they are forced to try to replace what they have taken out."[9]

The tenant and owner voices are wrong, of course: you cannot "kill the land." The land can be altered, made inhospitable for the sons of Cain who inhabit it, but it will survive. The epic perspective with which the novel begins suggests the enduring nature of this earth, the land which "abideth forever."

The first paragraph of *The Grapes of Wrath* opens with an impressionistic swath of color reminiscent of Stephen Crane as Steinbeck intones, "To the red country and part of the gray country of Oklahoma, the last rains came gently, and they did not cut the scarred earth." He continues:

> The plows crossed and recrossed the rivulet marks. The last rains lifted the corn quickly and scattered weed colonies and grass along the sides of the roads so that the gray country and the dark red country began to disappear under a green cover. In the last part of May the sky grew pale and the clouds that had hung in high puffs for so long in the spring were dissipated. The sun flared down on the growing corn day after day until a line of brown spread along the edge of each green bayonet. The clouds appeared, and went away, and in a while they did not try any more. The weeds grew darker green to protect themselves, and they did not spread any more. The surface of the earth crusted, a thin hard crust, and as the sky became pale, so the earth became pale, pink in the red country and white in the gray country.

A close look at this paragraph shows that following the panoramic, generalized opening, the paragraph begins to focus, to zoom in: "The plows crossed and recrossed the rivulet marks." And finally, from the impressionistic opening image our vision has closed the distance to focus very closely upon not just "the growing corn" but the "line of brown" that spreads "along the edge of each green bayonet." At once the narrative eye begins to pan back to register broader details of clouds and generalized "weeds" until the paragraph ends where it began, with a panoramic image of the earth, which "became pale, pink in the red country and white in the gray country." In the second paragraph, the camera's eye again zooms in for a close-up: "In the water-cut gullies the earth dusted down in dry little streams." And again this paragraph expands to end with a panorama: "The air was thin and the sky more pale, and every day the earth paled."

In these first paragraphs, Steinbeck is introducing the pattern upon which *The Grapes of Wrath* will be structured: a pattern of expansion and contraction, of a generalized panoramic view of the plight of the migrants in the interchapters followed in the narrative chapters by a closeup of the plight of the representative individuals, the Joads. As early as the novel's opening paragraph, the reader is being subliminally programmed for this movement in the novel, and he is being introduced to the idea that beyond the Joads is the pattern made up of the migrants and the Dust Bowl phenomenon as a whole; beyond the seeming tragedy of the drought and the cropped-out land is the pattern made up of the panoramic earth itself. The shifting focus is designed to remind us that the individual tragedies are played out against a backdrop of enduring life. In teleological terms, as defined by Steinbeck and Ed Ricketts in *The Log from the Sea of Cortez*, the drought, the Dust Bowl, and the tragedy of the migrants seem immeasurable disasters for which blame must be assigned; in nonteleological terms, however, we are reminded by the panoramic sweep of the author's brush that we are seeing only part of the picture, partial indices of what the *Log* defined as "all reality, known and unknowable."[10]

Paradoxically, such a nonteleological perspective serves to make the Dust Bowl a tragedy only insofar as it is judged according to transient, human values. From a distance, the drought-wasted land is lovely, a sweeping panorama of pastels; up close, the picture becomes one of horror, but only in human terms. For the sharecroppers this is a tragedy; the larger picture suggests that the tragedy is limited, transient, that the earth abides beyond man's errors and shortsightedness. To believe, as the croppers and landowners in this novel do, that one can "kill the land" is to see only part of the picture, to commit the error Joseph Wayne commits in Steinbeck's early novel *To a God Unknown* of believing that the land can die. The biblical prose style of these opening paragraphs, recalling the incantatory force of Genesis, also underscores the power of primal creation that precedes man and exists beyond man's ability to affect or effect. Like the people who, drawing their strength from the earth, "go on," the earth

cannot be destroyed, and Steinbeck's style and tone in these first paragraphs is designed to reinforce that message.

If Steinbeck's message in the opening paragraphs is that the land
cannot die, he nonetheless begins as early as the second sentence of the
novel to subtly imply human responsibility for the disruption of the
drought. In the second sentence, he tells us that "The plows crossed and
recrossed the rivulet marks," superimposing an ultimately self-destructive
human pattern—the erosion-inducing plow lines—upon the natural wa-
tershed pattern. The rivulet marks are a sign of the earth's flow, cycle,
continuum; their crossing and erasure is a sign of a failure of human
understanding. The wheels that "milled the ground," and the hooves that
"beat the ground" until "the dirt crust broke and the dust formed" further
underscore man's responsibility for the human tragedy depicted in the first
paragraphs and developed throughout the novel. By the novel's end, the
rain will come again in a great, destructive, cleansing flood, erasing in its
turn the pattern of human failure set upon the edenic valleys of California.

Steinbeck also foreshadows in these opening paragraphs the fate of
the migrants. The "weed colonies" that are "scattered . . . along the sides
of the roads" suggest the colonies of migrants that will soon be scattered
the length of Route 66; and the miniscule ant lion trap, a funnel of finely
blown sand from which the ant simply cannot escape, serves as a
naturalistic image to define the situation of the sharecroppers. They have
no future in the cropped-out region of blowing dust and sand; they have
sealed their fates should they stubbornly struggle to remain. Muley
Graves, whose name hints strongly at his character and fate, chooses to
remain in the trap, a "graveyard ghos' " without a future.

Through this burnt country cut the tracks of walking men and
machines, raising dust clouds as signs of their passage. When Tom Joad
appears, he will be the representative walking man, the individual who
must accept responsibility for what man has done to himself and to the
earth. Along with Tom, the Joads and all of the migrants will be sent on
the road on a quest to rethink their relationship with humanity as well as
with the land itself. What Warren French has aptly termed the "education
of the heart"[11] is a journey toward a new national consciousness, one that
may, Steinbeck seems to imply, finally break the grip of the westering
pattern in this country, causing Americans to free themselves from the
delusive quest for a New Eden and thus from the destructive process of
exploitation and removal entailed in such a pattern.

Once the Joads and their fellow migrants have reached California,
they can go no farther. The Joads are the representative migrants, and the
migrants are the representative Americans. The migrants' westward journey is America's, a movement that encapsulates the directionality of the
American experience. The horrors of the California Eden confronting the
migrants have been brought on by all of us, Steinbeck implies; no one is

innocent. When Uncle John releases Rose of Sharon's stillborn baby upon the flood waters with the words, "Go down an' tell 'em" (493), Steinbeck is underscoring the new consciousness. This Moses is stillborn because the people have no further need for a Moses. The Promised Land has long ago been reached, and there is nowhere else to go, no place for a Moses to lead his chosen people. The American myth of the Eden ever to the west is shattered, the dangers of the myth exposed. The new leader will be an everyman, Tom Joad, who crawls into a cave of vines — the womb of the earth — to experience his rebirth and who emerges committed not to leading the people somewhere else but to making this place, this America, the garden it might be. The cleansing, destructive flood that prepares for the novel's concluding tableau rises not merely around the threatened migrants but over the entire land.

The Grapes of Wrath is Steinbeck's jeremiad, his attempt to expose not only the actual, historical suffering of a particular segment of our society, but also the pattern of thought, the mindset, that has led to this one isolated tragedy. In this novel, Steinbeck set out to expose the fatal dangers of the American myth of a new Eden, new Canaan, new Jerusalem, and to illuminate a path toward a new consciousness of commitment in place of removal, engagement instead of displacement. And in making his argument, Steinbeck was careful not to sentimentalize his fictional creations, careful to emphasize the shared guilt and responsibility — there are no innocents; a new sensibility, not sentimentality, is Steinbeck's answer.

Notes

1. For reactions to *The Grapes of Wrath*, see Peter Lisca, "Editor's Introduction: The Pattern of Criticism," in *The Grapes of Wrath: Text and Criticism*, ed. Peter Lisca (New York: Viking Press, 1972).

2. Edmund Wilson, *The Boys in the Back Room: Notes on California Novelists* (San Francisco: Colt Press, 1941), 61.

3. Bernard De Voto, "American Novels: 1939," *Atlantic Monthly* 165 (January 1940): 68.

4. R. W. B. Lewis, "John Steinbeck: The Fitful Daemon," rpt. in *Steinbeck: A Collection of Critical Essays*, ed. Robert Murray Davis, 171 (Englewood Cliffs, N.J.: Prentice-Hall, 1972).

5. John Steinbeck, in the preface to the *The Forgotten Village* (New York: Viking Press, 1941).

6. See my discussion of *In Dubious Battle* in my study *John Steinbeck's Re-Vision of America* (Athens: University of Georgia Press, 1985), 89–100.

7. John Steinbeck, in *Steinbeck: A Life in Letters*, ed. Elaine Steinbeck and Robert Wallsten, 98 (New York: Viking Press, 1975).

8. John Steinbeck, *The Grapes of Wrath* (New York: Viking Press, 1939; rpt. Bantam Pathfinder Editions, 1972), 424; hereafter cited in the text.

9. John Steinbeck, *Journal of a Novel* (New York: Viking Press, 1969), 39.

10. John Steinbeck, *The Log from the Sea of Cortez* (New York: Viking Press, 1951), 217.

11. Warren French, "From Naturalism to the Drama of Consciousness — The Education of the Heart in *The Grapes of Wrath*," in *Twentieth Century Interpretations of "The Grapes of Wrath*," ed. Robert Con Davis, 24–35 (Englewood Cliffs, N.J.: Prentice-Hall, 1982).

The Ending of *The Grapes of Wrath*: A Further Commentary

John Ditsky*

The current revival of interest in Steinbeck, prompted in part by the efforts of the Steinbeck Society, has thus far not included adequate reconsideration of what was — at the time of the book's first appearance — a matter of some controversy: the value and meaning of the final scene in *The Grapes of Wrath*. Perhaps a greater liberty in the presentation of sex is responsible for this neglect of what was once a crucial problem for Steinbeck's critics; at any rate, it is clear enough that the matter remains unsettled, however relatively ignored at present, and as deserving of attention as ever — if not necessarily for the reasons once advanced. With initial sympathy for the author's presumed intentions as a critical approach, therefore, I have made a series of reflections upon the function of that ending scene within the book as a whole, particularly insofar as that scene may be considered the book's culmination: the apotheosis of the concept of the group-man explicated in *The Red Pony*. Furthermore, it is an appropriate time to weigh the general cultural significance of Steinbeck's work as an American novelist, and this scene is central to such a purpose.

I am speaking, then, of that final scene (612–19, current edition[1]) in which, on the third day of their entrapment by flood, the surviving Joads — Ma, Pa, Uncle John, Ruthie, Winfield, and Rose of Sharon — leave their boxcar refuge and, under Ma's direction, move to new quarters in a nearby barn where they find a boy and his starving father — to whom Rose of Sharon, who has just lost her own baby, is seen giving her breast as the novel closes. A number of observations will follow, divided only partially arbitrarily into general topics: the Bible and religion; myth and the ritual moment; the role of woman; the new community.

I

Steinbeck has constructed this final scene as an emergence from the shadow of death: a resurrection of the group-man in an Easter of the human spirit. Thus the biblical quality of the scene is appropriate (one

*Revised with permission from *Agora* 2 (Fall 1973): 41–50.

thinks of both the Eden and Flood narratives), as is the occasionally biblical-sounding prose ("On the morning of the second day . . ." [613]). It is astonishing that Steinbeck manages to control this scene at all—to keep it working within the demands of the conventional novel form while allowing it to ascend into the simultaneously expressionistic.[2] The reduction to simplicities is totally apt; the scene represents a re-Genesis, mankind deliberately recreating itself in the image of God ("manself" divinized).[3]

Joseph Fontenrose comments at length upon the Mosaic and Messianic parallels in *The Grapes of Wrath*, developing the prior work of Peter Lisca, Celeste Wright, and Martin Shockley, all of whom have noted the eucharistic nature of Rose of Sharon's act. Calling the deserter Connie the group's Judas, Fontenrose notes the fact that the new social organism is itself in its infancy at the book's end, and that Rose of Sharon is imitating primitive adoption ceremonials as she foster-mothers mankind. In effect, he concludes of the ending scene, "The Joads' intense feelings of family loyalty have been transcended; they have expanded to embrace all men."[4] More than this, even by her name Rose of Sharon reminds us of biblical imagery of fertility and promise. Song of Solomon 2, which begins "I am the Rose of Sharon, and the lily of the valleys," goes on to guarantee that "the winter is past, the rain is over and gone," and that the vines will soon put forth "the tender grape." The "beloved" who is described there as feeding among the lilies—a figuratively real event in the novel—completes a relationship traditionally interpreted as that of Christ and His Church, God and His people. Add the other possibilities of Mary (addressed as "Mystical rose") and of the soul, and the potential meanings begin to ripple outward in profusion. Rose of Sharon's act accomplishes, through the influx of divine spirit, a kind of virgin birth of anonymous man—a man who, because of the mystical overtones of the moment, becomes representative Man (as standing for all of mankind), and potentially a version of the Son of Man (for the necessity of playing the Christ-role is emphasized throughout the novel).

As water implies baptism, the flood implies a new start—a re-Creation. Just as there was only one "tree" in the original Eden, there can be no "shame" in the discovery of the knowledge of good and evil in the new Eden. Steinbeck's Testament ends with a fusing of the significant actions of the Old and the New: the snake has been run over by a truck, anticipating the woman's heel; now there is only the "stuff people do," as Casy puts it (32), and the need for intellectualization has been obviated by direct experience. Rose of Sharon's action communicates an immediate redemption of a "chosen" people.

In these religious terms, therefore, the scene is almost devoid of sexuality—for all its sexual implications. Prurient interest remains in the eye of the beholder, and shame to him who thinks it evil. Sex exists here in its most abstracted, perfected sense; implicitly, however, it is within the understanding of the women, Ma and Rose of Sharon, who look "deep into each other" (618) before Rose of Sharon assents to Ma's request, unasked with words. What ensues is an almost philosophically justified use of sexual powers: right use of the body's intimate reproductive faculties to promote Life itself. Thus the ingredients for a possible dirty joke become the elements of an almost passive ritual. It is the reversing of, but also the concomitant of, the joyful flowing of life in the earlier scene of zestful copulation on the moving truck — with Connie and Rose of Sharon finding brief joy in their corner of the moving community, while Granma experiences her death struggle in another (306–07). Both the truck scene and the final tableau share a vitality so significant that both are accompanied by meaningful exchanges, of gifts paid for by losses: death (Granma, the baby) for life.

Finally, the final scene completes a turning-outward into society of energies that, in Greek or Faulknerian tragedy, might have turned into unproductive incestual frustrations.[5] In the new familial system, older terminology is replaced by simpler concepts of "male" and "female" roles, and only the presence of external, social demands legitimizes what might otherwise have become sexual anarchy.

II

There is nothing remarkable in that a moral or religious progress, whose Christ-referents are ample, should end in an epiphany of sorts — miracle-plus-vision. The biblical, even medieval, instinct would have been to erect a shrine. Steinbeck constructs a kind of canopy over this final scene by rendering it as a tableau. The supposed improbability of this final act ignores the fact that the Joad family had long since been wrenched out of the conventional, traditional mores of viable family units. This is especially so after the dead child is set adrift without its sex even being determined. At this juncture, there has finally been a complete break with the past; and a transfer from the normal and specifically literal to the extraordinary and symbolic has been made possible. Thus a showing-forth ensues: a mixed action which shepherds and Magi might attend.[6]

Therefore, Rose of Sharon becomes statuary, as worn mother and starving man fuse in a lasting composition. Steinbeck's endowment of the ordinarily human with exceptional qualities on extraordinary occasions is made possible by his exterior presentation during all other times — the result of his deliberately scientific, empirical approach to human nature, itself premised on the belief that humanity can never understand itself until it first understands the animal within the human. It is not, as Edmund Wilson phrased it in his classic missing-of-the-point, that Steinbeck tends "to present human life in animal terms," but that Steinbeck sees humanity as above the animal when it demonstrates the intelligence required to grasp its real situation and act accordingly—or when, driven by an evolutionary process to discover radical methods of survival as a species, it finds the instinctive understanding to make changes for the better. It is not, then, that Rose of Sharon "must offer her milk" to a starving stranger, as Wilson has it, out of an animal "loyalty to life itself." Rather, it is that people like the Joads finally understand what they will have to do for themselves if society should continue to fail to recognize their humanity; and Rose of Sharon's gesture is its admission. To say, as Wilson did, that "Mr. Steinbeck almost always in his fiction is dealing with the lower animals or with humans so rudimentary that they are almost on the animal level . . ." is to display a peculiar distance from reality in the speaker himself.[7]

Of course, Wilson was writing at the end of a decade—the thirties—when writers commonly described human beings out of a preconceived notion of human worth rather than by trying, as Steinbeck did, to decide what was truly human by observation. This approach by Steinbeck, when at his best, shows dehumanized human material straining upward towards its own ideal—precisely what occurs at the ending of *The Grapes of Wrath*. Negative interpretations such as Wilson's should not be allowed to obscure the validity of Steinbeck's ruthlessly honest (not "sentimental") questioning of the human condition: "What am I? What are the limitations inherent in my mode of existence?" Not only are Steinbeck's methods interestingly predictive of logical positivism and structuralism, but his approach to anthropology has become increasingly widespread as well.[8] Rose of Sharon can be said to have pointed the way; extending the Mosaic parallels of the novel, we can say that with her act, mankind has been to the mountain to see the Promised Land—rather than the "mirage" of the Joads' first sight of California. Thus she can be said to have acquired monumentality, the quality of significant statuary, in her final scene.

Again, Theodore Pollock correctly noted that the supposedly sentimental gesture under discussion occurs after the "human sacrifice" of Rose of Sharon's baby. But Rose of Sharon is openly abandoning, however intellectually and temporarily, conventional folk expectations about the attainment of futurity—the bearing of children to "carry on"—in order to establish futurity in societal, or "group," terms. Though Warren French footnotes Pollock's argument by drawing literal parallels of scene ("drought and downpour"—with Eliot's *The Waste Land*, he does not take the argument far enough.[9] Surely this dead infant, prophet of solidarity and "wrath," can also be paralleled with the same year-myth of "human sacrifice" that Eliot exploits, with all its suggestions of Nature-appeasement—and in a similar texture of spring's ironies.[10] The exploration of Steinbeck's awareness and employment of myth has barely begun, in other words.

III

Folk-sensitivity to mythic elements is also central to Steinbeck's consideration of the role of women, particularly in the evolving group-family. Earlier in the novel, Rose of Sharon and Granma are established as linked together, as poles of womanhood on the Ma-axis, when well-meaning Jehovites offer a service for the dying Granma in a nearby tent. The fervor of sympathy causes the men and women of the sect to join in a "feral howling," making "a thudding sound on the earth." Though Ma shivers in testimony to the power of the experience, Granma joins her whining with the whining she hears (like a dog joining a siren's wail), and Rose of Sharon's breath comes in short pants. When the service concludes, Granma sinks into restful sleep, and Rose of Sharon acknowledges that "It done Granma good" (288–89). Like the final rain-dance scene in the earlier *To a God Unknown*, in which the joyful people don animal skins and roll in the mud in an ecstasy of celebration of the land's fecundity, this scene involves the three adult women of *The Grapes of Wrath* in an act of tribute to a power older than organized medicine and a ritual prior to established religions. Out of this power and ritual emerges the final scene, in which Rose of Sharon, once she sees what is wanted of her, similarly reacts with "short and gasping" breaths (618).

Rose of Sharon repeatedly emphasizes the damage being done to her ability to function as wife and mother by the events of the novel. Found nibbling "a piece of slack lime," she wails "Got no husban'! Got no milk!" (483) and predicts "This here baby ain't gonna be no good." Her willingness to perform within woman's conventional biological roles is dealt serious and seemingly permanent damage by the losses of Connie and the baby, both arguably the result of the evils of the social structure whose failure has produced the dramatic tension of the book. Miraculously, both are restored when she encounters a man in specific need of, as his boy puts it, "soup or milk" (618). Gently caressing the hair of the man as she feeds him, she smiles "mysteriously" — having pulled off the splendid trick of mothering an anonymous beloved.

"Women's always tar'd," Tom had said of his mother early in the novel. "That's just the way women is . . ." (147). But when the family is under way, and the possibility of the "folks" being "busted up" arises, Ma revolts, raising a jack handle against Pa and shaming him out of absolute control of the family unit (229–31). It is a successful revolt, one that Ma justifies in a later scene:

> Pa sniffed. "Seems like times is changed," he said sarcastically. "Time was when a man said we'd do. Seems like women is tellin' now. Seems like it's purty near time to get out a stick."
> Ma . . . smiled down at her work. "You get your stick, Pa," she said. "Times when they's food an' a place to set, then maybe you can use your stick an' keep your skin whole. But you ain't a-doin' your job,

either a-thinkin' or a-workin'. If you was, why, you could use your stick,
an' women folks'd sniffle their nose an' creep-mouse aroun'. . . ."

(481)

When the male-dominated society fails, woman asserts her centrality in human affairs, and control is hers to exercise. This latter-day reflection of the effects of the frontier on woman allows Ma the privilege of speaking *for* the group: "Why, we're the people—we go on," she tells Tom in a celebrated passage (383).

Implicit within this final scene, then, is the completion of a sociological change—the development of a sort of Moynihan-syndrome of absent father and ruling mother—that has been seen coming throughout the novel. The stage of menopause becomes a sort of substitute for the distinctions of sex: a masculine authority allows Ma to take the reins of government away from Pa; Rose of Sharon, however, remains a functioning biological woman on her side of the barrier of age. However, the change is not quite this simple, for while woman is assigned new roles *within* the revised familial structure, man is given certain new functions of leadership and strength *outside of* it—that is, within the evolving group structure of the family-at-large. If this is less than clear in the cases of Pa and Uncle John, it is decidedly so for Tom, who inherits the mantle of Casy's philosophical/ethical authority (with Ma's blessings) and his stance as Christ, as divinized manhood.

For Rose of Sharon herself, her final action is also the personal attainment of maturity. The relative lack of full emotional growth in both her and Connie is perhaps most clearly seen when Connie frightens her by putting "Soon's I get on my feet" ahead of thoughts of how her baby is to be born, and she responds by putting "her thumb in her mouth for a gag" and crying silently (344). Yet she is still developing within her role of woman, and when Connie deserts his moral responsibilities for the chance of making money, Rose of Sharon achieves her full womanhood through Other-commitment. The split between Connie and Rose of Sharon mirrors the conflict within society at large, between the materialistic success-ethic and what used to be called the Life-force.

Rose of Sharon had been frightened by the prediction of a woman at the government camp that "hug-dancing" and play-acting (she had been in a "Chris' chile play" at school) would cause her to lose her baby, as had happened to another girl like her. She is consoled by the "white-clad" (and presumably angelic?) camp-manager, who gives a factual answer, and by Ma, who argues that Rose of Sharon isn't big enough to attract God's attention (420–26). Ironically enough, she acquires epic dimension after the predicted loss of her baby occurs—in a final balletic stasis, a frozen hug-dance with a stranger, a second Christ-child play if ever there was one.

The boy whose father Rose of Sharon nurses explains that the father's hunger was aggravated by his having given his own food to his son. When, after this initial sacrificial act, the son took more immediate measures to obtain food — he "stoled some bread" for his father, the most revolutionary action in the final scene (but only in conventional legal terms) — the father had "puked it all up" (618). Neither protective self-sacrifice nor violent seizure are successful, therefore; only the return to woman, to the feminine principle, provides the answer: not inward or outward force, but a balanced exchange. Ironically, this hungry, wet, and "beat" Rose of Sharon still smiles mysteriously as she gives of herself. Is she satisfied? (She is certainly relieved, for it is the anxiety caused by her milk's arrival that has spurred Ma, and thus the family, out of their boxcar coffin and back into movement [612–13].) Thus this sharing of resources involves a simple, if unconventional, realignment of needs and assets. Rose of Sharon's "mysterious" smile is the outward sign of the discovery of a timeless truth: the simplicity and goodness of cycles, the rightness of necessity, the perfectness of circles. "You go to," she says, and the new order leaps into being. She has regained the "self-sufficient smile, the knowing perfection-look," of her early pregnancy (129). Because she is wiser than before, her idea of fulfillment has been altered forever.

IV

Warren French described the ending of the novel in terms of the Joads' initiation: "Their education is completed."[11] This is precisely so. Steinbeck has taken that hackneyed expression of the Depression genera- tion, "The School of Hard Knocks," and its politer antecedent, "The School of Life," and made them a figurative dramatic structure for the whole novel. There are dropouts aplenty, but enough survivors are present for the graduation: the rebirth of Rose of Sharon, swaddled in a dirty blanket, nursing instead of being nursed, giving instead of taking. She is a Louvre of mixed subjects: a Nativity, a *Mona Lisa*, an immense and heroic Delacroix. Most of all, however, she is a tableau of quasi-Christian giving, the paradox of exchange among those with no possessions whose doctrinal source in the New Testament apparently so fascinated Steinbeck.

It is a fundamentally conservative gesture, of course — this rewiring of circuits accomplishing a restoration of power. It is precisely the common man's commonsense answer to the enormity of the Depression and the absurdities of the system that allowed it to happen at all, and then permitted it to go on. It is the perfect refutation of the values inherent in the classic examples of capitalistic unreason: fruit rotting on the vine; crops plowed under; the killing of little pigs.

In Steinbeck, the real is neither inflated nor cosmetically altered, but idealized: the "real" persons simply fade away at the end, and out of identity-consciousness. In the "true" pop-culture version of the same elements, the Playmate of the Month, every mole air-brushed away, descends into the gutter — or the hands of a trembling wino in a 42nd-

Street old-magazine shop. How ironic that in the boob-culture that is America, objections should have been raised on the fittingness of such a scene of wish-fulfillment as this one, in which tableaux of the Nativity and the Pietà are superimposed upon a vision of breast-attainment. Indeed, the scene is in this respect ideal, taking its leap into the transcendental by virtue of its very elemental qualities — satisfying the national craving with a contact as aesthetically electric (hence disquieting, even as it is satisfying) as the touch of God and Adam on the Sistine Chapel ceiling: the perfect stranger finding solace of suck at the breast of the husbandless wife and childless mother. What a forbidden, what a necessary, nourishment!

The new society posited at the close has been in obvious development throughout the book. Its growth as idea has been organic, involving the pruning of the unfit. Its utopian vision is the last and most telling avatar of the "westering" urge so central to Steinbeck's Americanism, the ultimate submersion of the human in the "natural"; it is motion in quest of a dream and harmonic stasis. But in realistic terms, Utopia was the government camp, already glimpsed as the token of what might have been: in strict American literary tradition, it is that experimental unit of agrarian democracy, the land-based model community.

"There the story ends *in medias res*," Fontenrose concludes by way of setting up something of a straw man.[12] For in truth, the narrative of the Joads has nowhere to go after Rose of Sharon draws the camera in to focus upon that mysterious smile, then holds the pose while the camera backs away — by means of a helicopter shot, say — to make it clear that she has become the world's true center. In terms of contemporary American culture, it is Woman picking up the pieces of the American dream and holding the man-caused shards together, the seams invisible. The power to work this miracle is implied in Rose of Sharon's smile. It is an Eastern smile, a smile of understanding, in this ultimate Western book. She has got it all now. All the lines of narrative come to focus in her; like light, they prism in her:

> For he hath regarded the low estate of his handmaiden: for, behold, from henceforth all generations shall call me blessed. . . .
> He hath filled the hungry with good things; and the rich he hath sent empty away. . . .[13]

Notes

1. *The Grapes of Wrath* (New York: Viking Press, 1939). Further page references will be inserted parenthetically within the text.

2. Compare the ending of Pirandello's *Right You Are*.

3. Again, compare Faulkner's *The Wild Palms*: "The Old Man."

4. Joseph Fontenrose, *John Steinbeck: An Introduction and Interpretation* (New York: Holt, Rinehart and Winston, 1963), 67–83.

5. Compare *The Sound and the Fury* and *As I Lay Dying*.

6. This movement is the simple opposite to what Faulkner accomplishes in gradually humanizing Eula Varner, subsequent to her astonishing introduction in *The Hamlet*, throughout the rest of the Snopes trilogy. Rose of Sharon's transfiguration is more nearly paralleled by the assumption of Remedios the Beauty in Gabriel García Márquez's *One Hundred Years of Solitude*.

7. Edmund Wilson's *"John Steinbeck"* is included in his *"The Boys in the Back Room,"* reprinted in *Classics and Commercials* (New York: Farrar, Straus and Giroux, 1950), 35–45.

8. Even in such simplistic accounts as those of Desmond Morris.

9. Theodore Pollock, "On the Ending of *The Grapes of Wrath*," in *A Companion to "The Grapes of Wrath*," ed. Warren French, 224–26 (New York: Viking Press, 1963).

10. Compare *To a God Unknown*, in both this context and that of the following paragraph.

11. Warren French, *John Steinbeck* (New York: Twayne Publishers, 1961), 107.

12. Fontenrose, *John Steinbeck*, 69. A further argument for the artistic integrity of Steinbeck's ending *as a point in the novel* is provided in Jules Chametzky's "The Ambivalent Endings of *The Grapes of Wrath*," *Modern Fiction Studies* 11 (Spring 1965): 34–44. Chametzky reasons that Steinbeck's apparent "evasion" of easier solutions avoids the double traps of simplistic "happy" or Marxist endings.

13. Luke 1:48, 53.

From Heroine to Supporting Player: The Diminution of Ma Joad   Mimi Reisel Gladstein*

John Ford's movie version of *The Grapes of Wrath* is generally considered to be one of the few successful film adaptations of an acclaimed novel. The movie is honored as a classic, firmly ensconced on lists of landmark films.[1] Perhaps that is because there had been so much concern among fans of *The Grapes of Wrath* that the book's grim vision would be softened beyond recognition by the Hollywood dream machine and that concern proved to be only partially well-founded. Or perhaps because the film version of Steinbeck's novel has so many virtues as a work of cinematic art: the commanding but underplayed acting of Henry Fonda; the gemlike performances of Charley Grapewin as Grandpa and John Qualen as Muley Graves; the extraordinary cinematography of Gregg Toland with its sensitive use of light and shadow, memorable particularly in such scenes as the opening shot of a long, long road bordered by telephone poles and in Muley Graves's recounting of his family's dispossession, culminating in a shot of tractor treads traversing their hapless shadows.

Robert Morsberger, speaking at the Second International Steinbeck Congress, noted that *The Grapes of Wrath* was the first film translation of

*This essay was written specifically for this volume and is published here for the first time by permission of the author.

a Steinbeck novel to be both an artistic and a commercial success.[2] *Tortilla Flat*, which attempted to make Spencer Tracy, John Garfield, Hedy Lamarr, and Akim Tamiroff believable as California paisanos, had been a commercial success, but an artistic failure. *Of Mice and Men*, on the other hand, bolstered by the strong performances of Burgess Meredith and Lon Chaney, received high critical praise, but did poorly at the box office. *The Grapes of Wrath* opened to near-universal acclaim. Steinbeck, himself, called the film "hard" and "truthful," and "a harsher thing than the book."[3] In the face of all this approbation, particularly that of the original creator, it is no wonder that negative evaluations have been minimal.

Perhaps the voices of dissatisfaction have been few because the field of criticism that encompasses serious fiction and filmmaking is not a crowded one.[4] This is bound to change in the near future. Films, particularly old ones, have been, until the last few years, generally unavailable. Unless one happened on a late night television rerun, the only other access to the movie version of *The Grapes of Wrath* was through either purchase or rental of the four-reel film, an expensive and cumbersome undertaking for any individual. The advent of videocassettes has changed this situation. Every shopping center video store has copies of *The Grapes of Wrath* on its shelves, where for as little as one dollar, one can take the movie home and there, complete with rewinds and fast-forwards, watch to one's heart's content. Soon, *The Grapes of Wrath* may be watched as often as it is read. The power of visual images is strong. It is not unlikely that many people will substitute watching the film for reading the book. Therefore it seems appropriate, in view of this technological bonanza, to voice some misgivings about a troublesome aspect of the film that, though touched upon by a few critics, has not been thoroughly explored: John Ford's reduction and devitalization of the role of woman in his film version of *The Grapes of Wrath*. This enervation would be evident even if one were viewing the film without reference to the novel, but when the film is compared with the novel, the full dimensions of this diminishment are more clearly revealed.

Why Ford did this is not clear. It might have been a result of studio politics, of Ford's strong patriarchal bent, or of the practical constraints of film time. Whatever the reason, Ford reduced and softened the character of Ma Joad, and thereby diluted Steinbeck's depiction of woman's strength, durability, and significance in the human struggle for survival, a depiction that is distinctly embedded in the many layers, both realistic and mythic, of the book.[5] This diminishment of woman's character is also evident in Ford's version of Rose of Sharon, who in the book matures from a self-centered girl into a woman nearly ready to inherit Ma's mantle.

Steinbeck described Ma as the Joad family "citadel," "the strong place that could not be taken."[6] Her significance in the novel cannot be overemphasized. Tetsumaro Hayashi's perceptive analysis, in "Steinbeck's Women in *The Grapes of Wrath*: A New Perspective," clearly articulates the importance not only of Ma, but also of Rose of Sharon, in conveying

Steinbeck's message: "The men in the novel articulate the theme, but it remains for women like Ma and Rose to provide the continuity of generations by translating the thought into action."[7] Leonard Lutwack, building on Steinbeck's description of Ma as "remote and faultless in judgment as a goddess," envisions Ma as the mother-goddess who inspires and protects her hero-son, much like the goddesses of ancient myth.[8] Warren Motley calls her the "central, cohesive force" in the novel and argues that the movement from patriarchy to matriarchy in the novel is a result of the influence of Robert Briffault's *The Mothers* on Steinbeck's thinking.[9] Motley convincingly argues that Tom, as Ma's chosen child, functions as a means to bring about a matriarchal sense of community.

The Ma of director John Ford, screenwriter Nunnally Johnson, and actress Jane Darwell is a very different creature. Though she maintains a central role in the Joad saga, she is hardly the "citadel," in no way suggests a goddess, and her cohesiveness is a sticky sweet kind, like honey, instead of the fiercely binding kind practiced by Steinbeck's jack handle–wielding woman. She delivers the movie's message, but it, like the woman who speaks it, is a weaker, more conciliatory, Pollyannaish vision than the one posited by Steinbeck's Ma. Whatever plaudits the screen version of Ma has earned, as an interpretation of the novel's heroine she falls short on many counts.

The diminution of Ma begins with her first scene in the movie. In the novel, Tom hears Ma's voice before the reader is introduced to her by the narrator. Her voice is "cool . . . friendly and humble." Her first words reflect her hospitality. Without knowing who the "coupla fellas" are who "wonder if we could spare a bite," she responds with an immediate "Let 'em come." This, although the Joads have just lost their homes and have little to sustain them on their impending journey. Ma's strong sense of sharing with strangers in this scene foreshadows her behavior in inviting Casy along with the family. Neither action is shown in the film. In the novel Casy asks Ma, Grandpa, and Tom if he can go along. When none of the men answers, it is Ma who tells Casy she would be proud to have him along. Later, in the family council, when Pa worries about the extra mouth to feed, it is Ma who firmly pronounces the code of hospitality and neighborliness: "I never heerd tell of no Joads or no Hazletts, neither, ever refusin' food an' shelter or a lift on the road to anybody that asked" (139). A sense of community that reaches beyond the boundaries of kinship is an important aspect of Steinbeck's message, a message that is considerably blunted in the movie. Cutting out Ma's articulation of these values early in the film presages their loss in the rest of the script.

There is high drama in Steinbeck's staging of Ma's and Tom's first encounter. Tom sees Ma before she knows who he is. What he sees is a heavy, "but not fat" woman, a woman who is "thick with child-bearing and work." "Strong, broad, bare feet" move "quickly and deftly over the floor." Ma's arms are described as "strong" and "freckled." Her full face is "not soft," but is "controlled, kindly" (99–100). All of these adjectives suggest a hardy and rugged woman, one who knows that her imperturbability and sure-handedness are counted on by her family. She is shocked and relieved to see Tom and her first words to him are "Thank God." When she runs to him she does so "lithely, soundlessly in her bare feet" (101). She touches him, feeling his arm; then her fingers touch his cheek. The emotion between the two is so intense that Tom bites his lip till it bleeds. Only when Ma sees the blood does she pull back from the intensity of the moment in order to normalize the situation. The recurrent word in her description is "strong"; both feet and arms are described with that word. In her scene with Tom, the reader is shown the powerful feelings generated by their relationship.

The first glimpse of the movie Ma is of Jane Darwell standing by the family table. The commanding presence in the room is not Ma, but Grandpa. Charley Grapewin's Grandpa, whether quarreling with Grandma or imagining himself sitting and "scrooging around" in a tub of grapes, steals this scene, even from such traditional scene-stealers as the children.[10] Darwell's Ma is a soft and dumpy-looking woman. Just in terms of outward appearance, she is a great disappointment. Russell Campbell tells us that John Ford would have preferred Beulah Bondi's "gaunt, stringy resilience" in the role, but had to accept Jane Darwell in return for getting Henry Fonda to play Tom instead of Don Ameche or Tyrone Power, whom the studio had on hand as contract players.[11] John Baxter concedes that Jane Darwell is "perhaps too plump, too matriarchal, too *Irish*, for her role," but he counters that "so effective is Ford's use of the actress that one can no longer imagine anyone else playing it."[12] Baxter's point is a good one, but I think it has more to do with the impact of visual images than with the limits of imagination. It is just such concession to the power of the movie that I am arguing against.

The reunion of Tom and Ma is awkwardly handled in the film. Though Johnson's published script version follows the novel closely, preserving Steinbeck's dialogue, word for word, and includes directions for Ma to touch Tom's arm and cheek and for Tom to bite his lip with emotion, in the film it does not happen that way. Instead, there are two close-ups in which both Fonda and Darwell express the joy of seeing each other. But then, as they are impelled toward each other, for some unfathomable reason, rather than reaching to touch her son, to feel the muscle under the flesh, Darwell's Ma sticks her hand out to shake his hand. The action is awkward and establishes Ma as peculiarly undemonstrative. Later, she does touch Tom's arm and then his lapel, but the initial handshake aborts the intensity of the reunion. If Ford was trying to show that such quaint peasant types maintained certain formal distances between mother and son, then for the sake of consistency he should never have included the dance scene later in the movie. A Ma who will dance with her son, while he sings to her, is not a Ma who shakes hands with him after he has been away in prison for years. Later, when Tom is about to leave, as if to explain the early handshake, the movie Ma asks for a good-bye kiss, although she explains, "We ain't the kissin' kind." This line is in neither the novel nor the published screenplay.

The novel's movement from patriarchy, identified with power relationships and individualism, to matriarchy, associated with coopera-tion and communal feelings, as the family becomes uprooted and dispos-sessed, is carefully traced by Warren Motley. Motley explains that Ma has been receptive to Jim Casy's ideas about community from the beginning.[13] Andrew Sarris, seeing a similar plot structure in the film, describes its movement as "nothing less than the transformation of the Joad family from a patriarchy rooted in the earth to a matriarchy uprooted on the road."[14] Ma's appropriation of the role of head of the family as the story progresses is read by both Motley and Sarris as strong evidence of that movement. What is apparent in the novel and what has not been noted by most critics is that Ma has been the de facto head of the family all along. Her power does not grow; only the overt expression of it does. That Ma is the real head of the family is strongly suggested in the panegyrical first description of her, a description that equates her position in the family not only to citadel and goddess, but also to healer and arbiter. She is the locus of the family's will, and she knows that "if she swayed the family shook, and if she ever really deeply wavered or despaired the family would fall" (100).

Ma is not unaware of her power in the family, but her sense of tradition prevents her overt expression of it except when necessary. When the family council meets before setting out for California, she takes her place with the women and children, outside the circle of squatting men. Ritual is observed; Grandpa as titular head of the family is given right of first comment. The men all speak, giving their reports. During this process, Ma works on the periphery of the group, and even leaves to go into the house. However, when the question of whether or not Jim Casy can accompany the family to California comes up, after all the figuring by Pa and comment by Grandpa, it is Ma who makes the decision, one based not on practicalities but on a sense of sharing and community. Pa is shamed by Ma for what she sees as his meanness. After she has had her say in front of the whole group, he turns away, and "his spirit was raw from the whipping." Once that decision is made and Casy is asked to join the group, Ma goes into the house again. This time the council waits for her return, "for Ma was powerful in the group" (140).

The family council scene is deleted from the screenplay, and with it both incident and indication of Ma's eminent position in the family and her sympathy with the kind of communal values that Jim Casy comes to represent. Instead there is a scene where Grandpa is lifted onto the loaded truck, in a semi-conscious state, and when the truck starts to move, Casy is asked by Pa, "Ain't you goin' with us?" (345). When Casy voices his desire to accompany them, it is the men who pull him onto the truck, expressing the sentiment that there is always room for one more.

One of the most touching scenes in both the novel and film is the scene in which Ma must dispose of her mementos, something she does in private where the family members cannot see the toll it takes on her. Steinbeck's Ma, barefoot and haggard from packing and food preparation, is seen by Casy at this moment as looking "real tar'd, like she's sick-tar'd" (147). Ma, hearing these words, tightens her face, straightens her shoulders, and goes into the stripped room for her lonely task. It is this barefoot and tired woman who must waken her family, deal with Grandpa's sudden refusal to go, and then get in the truck whose load prevents her looking back. While the scene is still touching in the movie, certain costuming decisions greatly reduce the magnitude of Ma's task and the audience response to it. For reasons that will probably never be unearthed, the costumer in the film decided to put Jane Darwell in a silly-looking hat for this and many other scenes. Not only is she burdened with a hat that gives her face a decidedly porcine cast as she puts the earrings to her ears and looks at her reflection, but an apron and a sweater are chosen to complete her outfit. Perhaps this costuming decision came from the same impulse that saw Ma as a woman who would shake hands with her favorite son. The hat makes Ma look ridiculous in the context of the family situation. It is also emblematic of the very different kind of woman the film Ma is from the novel Ma. Steinbeck's Ma is taut and muscular, her feet bare and her hands encrusted with salt. The movie Ma not only wears shoes, but bedecks her head with a hat. The result is a quaint country woman, whose strength is softly muted, rather than a tough pioneer who can work all night and leave her home behind with nary a whimper. To be sure, Darwell speaks Steinbeck's words about the change brought about in her by having her house pushed over and her family stuck out in the road. But because she has had time to dress for the occasion in such droll finery, the words do not hit with the same impact.

The filmmakers wisely decided to leave out the Wilsons; there is not time in a two-hour film for too many subplots. This choice also dictated the deletion of one of the most significant scenes in the revelation of Ma's iron will and family domination. When the Wilson touring car breaks down on the road, Pa and Tom decide it would be best if all but Tom and Casy go on to California so that the rest of the group can start earning money and not lose the extra time it will take Tom and Casy to fix the car. The men consider the idea, gathering together: "Uncle John dropped to his hams beside Pa" (228). But when Pa tells the group to "get a-shovin'," Ma revolts. She challenges his authority openly and violently, threatening to hit him with a jack handle or knock him "belly-up with a bucket" (230). Ma does this to prevent the separation of the family. "The eyes of the whole family shifted back to Ma. She was the power. She had taken control" (231). Tom's good-natured suggestion that no more than two or three of them would be killed if they tried to rush her, only serves to underline the completeness of her takeover. With her authority thus established, Ma reverts back to her traditional role as the angel of the hearth, sending bread and meat to Tom and Casy as they work on the Wilson car.

The importance of the jack handle scene was not entirely lost on Nunnally Johnson. His published screenplay retains it in altered form, though he has had to create a new rationale for it because of the deletion of the Wilsons. In the Johnson version, Ma challenges Pa when it appears as if Al is about to run off and thus break up the family. Johnson's scene retains much of Steinbeck's dialogue. Ma challenges Pa to "whup" her; she brandishes the jack handle and insists that the family must stay together. Her concern is for the "fambly unbroke" (360). This scene is interrupted by Tom's return with the information that the Hooverville they are in is going to be burned down by some pool-room boys. Tom takes the jack handle from Ma with the admonition that she and Pa can fight it out later. Ma then tells him that Connie has "lit out," and Tom goes in the tent to comfort Rose of Sharon. Ford's movie omits most of this scene. All that is left is Tom's interruption of a squabble between Ma and Pa. Neither why they are fussing nor why Ma has the jack handle is established. It might be any family quarrel and it certainly does not show Ma in control. Perhaps the scene, as handled by Jane Darwell, was not convincing. Perhaps John Ford, who was to make so many pictures with John Wayne, could not convincingly direct a woman beating a man in a challenge to combat. For whatever reason, since the scene is not in the movie, Ma's overt ascension to the position of head of the family is not accomplished.

As Ma never does take over, there is little motivation for the last scene in the movie when Pa tells Ma: "You're the one who keeps us goin' Ma. I ain't no good anymore, an' I know it." This statement launches Ma into her "Woman can change better'n a man" speech, a recitation often cited as the embodiment of Steinbeck's message about the nature of womanly endurance, of the flexibility and timelessness of matriarchal values. However, since there are few scenes in the movie to illustrate that Pa or any of the men have lost any stature in the family, this speech has little context. It is not well-motivated and certainly is not foreshadowed. The men seem fine. In the beginning of this last part of the movie Pa, Al, and Uncle John are shown loading up the truck. Pa is described as "beaming" when he hollers to everybody, "All aboard for Fresno." He expresses confidence when he says, "Be glad to get my han' on some cotton. That's the kin' a pickin' I understand" (377). Al is chipper enough to be "grinning" when he asks Ma if she is "Gettin' scared?" (377). The only one who is unable to stand on her own two feet and seems thoroughly beaten in this scene is Rose of Sharon.

In the novel the family's experiences with the Wilsons, their working together in times of need, illustrate the already strong sense of hospitality and sharing among these country people. Sairy Wilson responds to Ma's offer to repay the Wilsons for the quilt Granpa died on: "We're proud to help. People needs — to help" (192). When the Joads can return the favor by repairing the Wilson car and caravanning with them, Ma speaks the formula of the need to work together. "Each'll help each, an' we'll all git to California" (202).

Steinbeck's interchapter following this scene clearly underscores the implications of the Wilson/Joad scenes. In it he explains the power of peoples banding together, the danger to those who own things, of "I" becoming "we," for revolutionary thinkers such as Paine, Marx, and Jefferson, are results, not causes, according to John Steinbeck. So Casy first, and then Tom, are results of the terrible treatment of the dispossessed. They learn that the only way for the migrant workers to be paid a living wage is by transcending the "I" and working together as "we." This whole idea of the larger family of humanity is also greatly diminished in the movie.

Ma's conversations with Sairy Wilson give her the opportunity to articulate her family pride in "holdin' in." Ma quotes her father's dictum that anybody can break down, but it takes a man not to. It is significant that the "men" who do not break down in this scene are women: Sairy, Grandma, and Ma. The deletion of the Wilsons, though practical in terms of cinematic necessities, removes the opportunity to express in word and action the values of hospitality and holding in, values that Ma exemplifies.

Furthermore, it is in the scenes with the Wilsons that Rose of Sharon is shown both helping Ma and learning from her. Rose of Sharon peels the potatoes and does the cooking while Sairy and Ma prepare Grandpa for burial. After dinner, Rose of Sharon goes and lies with her Grandma, comforting her and whispering with her in the night.

Perhaps there was no need for the movie's Rose to be shown doing anything to contribute to the family's sustenance since her role in the screenplay is essentially truncated. Rather than a Rose of Sharon who drags herself out of bed though she is sick, pregnant, and undernourished, in order to pick cotton or try to help her mother with the cooking and cleaning chores, the film gives us a whiney, helpless creature who is last seen being loaded, half-dead, onto the truck by the able-bodied men in the family (377). There is no preparation for this. In the scene that takes place the night before at the dance, Rose of Sharon is pictured sitting prettily beside Ma. Tom even comments on how good she looks and Ma responds that a girl with a baby always gets prettier (374).

Dorris Bowdon plays Rose of Sharon in the movie. She later became the wife of Nunnally Johnson. Acting was obviously not her métier. Whereas most of the other members of the family have good approximations of Oklahoma accents, Bowdon's initial "Hi Tom! How 'ya doin'?" sounds like a sophomore rendition of Scarlett O'Hara. In most of the other scenes that are left to her, she is portrayed as either petulant or passive. Since the pregnancy is never completed in the movie, and the controversial final scene is never played, Rose has no role in the survival of either the Joad or the whole human family. Though we see her at the dance, wearing the earrings Ma salvaged in the memento scene, there is no scene that shows Ma giving them to her. Nunnally Johnson includes such a scene in the screenplay, though it is quite different from the scene in the novel (372). But it was obviously edited out. In the novel, in order to coax Rose of Sharon out of her depression, Ma gives her the earrings and entices her to go to the dance. But before Rose of Sharon can wear the earrings, she must have her ears pierced. Symbolically, Rose must learn to bear pain in order to inherit Ma's role. Ma comments to Rose of Sharon that she "very near let you have a baby without your ears pierced" (484). The statement suggests that having the ears pierced is an initiation rite, indicating readiness to assume the womanly role. Now that she will be a mother also, Rose of Sharon must not only learn to behave like Ma, but she also is ready to wear Ma's jewelry. Rose asks Ma, "Does it mean sompin'?" And Ma responds, "Why, 'course it does. 'Course it does." Rose's contributions to Steinbeck's themes in the novel are significant. Learning from Ma and acting with her, Rose is an agent of survival of the species.[15] In the film, not only does she contribute little, but Bowdon's acting is so poor that one is grateful her scenes are so few.

Ford's Ma is a pacifier, whereas Steinbeck's Ma is a fierce woman who faces people down and speaks her mind. The difference in the two Ma's is patently illustrated in the scene where, after their first day of picking peaches, Ma tries to purchase enough food to feed her family. In the novel, Steinbeck shows us Ma at the company store. This scene clearly demonstrates how the migrant workers are exploited at every turn. The prices at the company store are outrageously high, and the quality of the food poor. Ma does not react kindly to this situation. She looks at the clerk "fiercely," she moves "menacingly toward him" (511). His treatment of her is cavalier; whenever she complains about the high prices, he reminds her sarcastically that she can always go to town, which is too far away, to get better prices. But Ma will not be whipped. She confronts the clerk about his nasty behavior, which she realizes is a defense against the anger of those he must help exploit. "Doin' a dirty thing like this. Shames ya, don't it? Got to act flip, huh?" (512). Her tone at this point is gentle and she wins the clerk's respect. Ma shows her psychological astuteness and she inspires the clerk to a gesture of charity and defiance. Though Ma does not have enough credit to pay for sugar after buying meat, potatoes, bread, and coffee, the clerk takes ten cents out of his own pocket in order to give her credit until the next day. The scene is germinal for Steinbeck's "we the people" theme, for in this encounter with the clerk, Ma reminds him that he is one of them. When she asks him why he does this nasty job, he replies "a fella got to eat." Ma responds, "What fella?," thus allying all of the hungry and dispossessed. After the clerk has taken money from his own pocket so Ma can have sugar, she articulates the lesson of group interdependentness: "If you're in trouble or hurt or need—go to poor people. They're the only ones that'll help—the only ones" (514).

The store scene is left out of the film. All we see is the eating scene that follows it. The dialogue, though chronologically rearranged, is straight from the novel. Tom expresses his desire for more hamburgers. Ma explains that the prices at the company store are high and that what they have is all a dollar will buy. Her tone is conciliatory. She suggests that tomorrow there will be more food since they can get in a full day's work, thus earning more money. Because the store scene has been deleted, Ma's fierceness and perceptive manipulation of the clerk are also omitted and all that is left is a Pollyannish woman emitting empty optimistic reassurances. There is no indication that Ma understands the exploitative system and its toll on individuals. All the film Ma knows is that if they work more, there will be more money and more to eat.

Steinbeck's Ma is not a soother; she cajoles, prods, pricks, and angers her family into action. In the novel Ma insists that the family must leave the comfort and relative safety of the Weedpatch camp because of the scarcity of work in that area. Their food is running out. She tells Pa, "You ain't got the right to get discouraged. This here fambly's goin' under. You just ain't got the right" (479). When the men in the family don't react swiftly enough for Ma, she decides "We'll go in the mornin'." Pa's pride is hurt by her assertion of authority and he sniffs, "Time was when a man said what we'd do. Seems like women is tellin' now. Seems like it's purty near time to get out a stick" (481). Ma's response is immediate and challenging. She tells him that when he returns to fulfilling his responsibilities as head of the household, then he can use his stick. However, since he is not, she defies him with the information that she has a stick all laid out too. This is the second scene in the novel where Ma challenges Pa to some kind of physical combat and he backs away. As in the jack handle scene, Ma's reason is not a selfish grab for power, but concern for the welfare of the family. She explains to Tom that if you can make a man mad he will react better than if he just worries and "eats out his liver." Ma's perspicacious handling of Pa is not unlike her astute maneuvering of the company store clerk.

In the novel there are many occasions where Steinbeck shows us Ma's assertive strength and sagacity. The aggressive nature of Ma's strength even becomes an occasion for jokes. Tom teases Al that he better have the truck ready or "I'll turn Ma on ya" (481). The stick scene is in neither screenplay nor film. Its loss is not crucial in and of itself, except when added to the loss of other scenes that illustrate Ma's assertiveness, natural wisdom, and family authority. The combined losses significantly affect the nature of Ma's character. Ford's Ma is sweet, good, and reassuring, but there is little evidence that she understands their situation, nor is she assertive about her beliefs. She does not *act* to effect her values.

Her lack of action helps account for much of the devitalization of the image of woman in the movie. The movie Ma does not determine the judgment of the family council about Casy's accompanying them, she does not face down the company store clerk, she does not wield a jack handle to keep the family together, and she does not threaten Pa with a stick to anger him lest he become too dispirited. All such scenes in which Ma acts assertively are absent from the movie.

Not only is the movie Ma less active than Steinbeck's Ma, but she also understands less. In the film, one of Ma's major speeches comes after Tom has killed the deputy who killed Casy. Tom wants to run away, but Ma wants him to stay and help her with the family. She begins the speech with the statement "They's a whole lot I don't understan' " and then bemoans the loss of land and traditions that bound the family together. Darwell's Ma is both nostalgic, her eyes cast on faraway sights, and pleading, she needs Tom to stay and help her.[16] Her pleas are effective. Tom does stay, and they go on to a better situation, the Weedpatch camp. The same speech in the novel has a different context. First of all, Ma is questioning Tom about Casy's death. She wants to know how and why it happened and what Casy said. The significance of Casy's Christ-like final words, "You don' know what you're a-doin'," is not lost on Ma. She repeats the words and exclaims, "I wisht Granma could a heard" (535).

In the novel, after Ma delivers the speech about the family "crackin' up," she is shown acting decisively to assure both Tom's safety and to protect, as best she can, the health of the other members of the family. Ma has a clear sense of priorities. She makes Pa buy milk for Winfield, though the rest of the family must eat mush for dinner. Winfield has collapsed, suffering from an acute case of the "skitters." When Rose of Sharon complains that she needs milk, Ma responds, "I know, but you're still on your feet. This here little fella's down." Nonetheless, she manages to sneak a little of the milk to Rose of Sharon later. Again, when the group has a family council about what to do about Tom, it is Ma who decides they will leave the camp they are in, sneaking Tom out between the mattresses. Pa complains, "Seems like the man ain't got no say no more. She's jus' a heller. Come time we get settled down, I'm a-gonna smack her" (546). Ma barely acknowledges his challenge, responding "Come that time, you can," as she orders Al to get the truck ready and Pa and Uncle John to put the mattresses in.

They accomplish their goal of hiding Tom, but rather than going to a better place, the Joads end up sharing a boxcar with another family. Tom is hidden in a cave and it is Ma who, fearing for his safety after Ruthie's indiscreet remarks about him, tells him he must go away. Rather than the movie's passive and plaintive "Ain't you gonna tell me goodbye, Tommy?," the novel presents Ma moving "majestically" through the camp, down the stream, and up an embankment to deliver Tom some food and tell him he must go. This Ma is anything but resigned and passive. She tells Tom to come close so she can feel his face to know how his scars are healing. She tells him, "I wanta touch ya again, Tom. I wanta remember, even if it's on'y my fingers that remember. You got to go away, Tom." She then gives him some money that she has been "squirrelin' " away. When he demurs, her response is a good illustration of how effectively Ma can manipulate people. She tells Tom that he has no right to cause her pain. Tom knows he is beaten and tells her, "You ain't playin' fair" (570).

In the film, although much of Tom's speech about being part of a great big soul and following Casy's lead in the separation scene follows Steinbeck's dialogue exactly, the differences in context and in Ma's dialogue effectively diminish her character. No longer is she the actor; she is responding to Tom's decisions. Her astuteness is not evidenced. And the intensity of her feelings for Tom are changed from a desire to memorize the feel of him with her fingers to asking for a good-bye kiss with the feeble excuse, "We ain't the kissin' kind, but. . . ." The end of the scene finds her weeping softly, an appropriate behavior for Ford's stereotyped mother. Steinbeck's Ma responds in an opposite manner. Her eyes are wet and burning, "but she did not cry." Instead she returns to the boxcar to face still more adversity.

There follows yet another scene in which Ma articulates her authority. Mr. Wainwright asks Pa to speak to Al so as to forestall any shame that might come on their family by Aggie becoming pregnant. Ma speaks up, assuring Mr. Wainwright not only that Pa will talk to Al, but that if he will not, she will. When she realizes how she has embarrassed Pa, she apologizes. Pa's response indicates how deeply disheartened he has become. No longer able to manage even an impotent threat to get out a stick, he says, "Funny! Women takin' over the fambly. Woman sayin' we'll do this here, an we'll go there. An I don' even care" (377–78). This is then followed by Ma's "woman is all one flow like a river" speech in which she assures Pa that though people are changing a little, they will go right on.

In the novel Ma's encouragement is not buttressed by subsequent scenes. The engagement between Al and Aggie Wainwright means that Al will be lost to the family group. Rose of Sharon's baby is born dead. And to cap off their troubles, the family is flooded out of their boxcar home. Steinbeck's closing scene is only faintly reassuring. That reassurance is embodied in the behavior of mother and daughter, particularly in Rose of Sharon's nurturing gesture. Though she is weak, wet, and undernourished, Rose of Sharon inherits her mother's mantle and acts as an agent for the preservation of life.

The film Joads are not nearly so beaten. When, in the last scene, they head out to find work, they are leaving a situation in which the people have shown that they can take care of themselves. The clean and orderly government camp is a haven where even the powerful hand of the law is not allowed entrance. Using their own resources, the men in camp preserve the peace and prevent a riot. Though Tom must leave, the family situation is not as dire as in the novel. Pa, Uncle John, and Al all seem fit and raring to go. The only one down is Rose of Sharon. There is no occasion for her to rise to and therefore Ma's thematic sentiment that "Woman can change better'n a man" is not borne out by the behavior of the women in the film. Rose of Sharon does not change, nor does she bear up to the hardships as well as the men. Ma changes very little. She is nurturing and optimistic from beginning to end.

If at one level the Joads represent the human family, then Ma and Rose of Sharon embody the role of women in that context. They are Mother and Daughter, Demeter and Persephone, the eternal feminine that duplicates itself and thus provides continuity and promise for the future. The truncation of Rose of Sharon's role in the movie removes this aspect of the significance of feminine renewal. While the film Ma remains a figure of hope, her passivity and lack of assertion leave the film's audience with a reinforcement of the traditional stereotype of the sweet, but long-suffering mother, a woman very unlike Steinbeck's strong, forceful, invincible Ma Joad.

Steinbeck's early novels, with their terse, dramatically developed plots, lend themselves well to the film medium. His scenes can often be lifted directly from the page to the screen. And the best screenwriters did just that. It is possible that an actress such as Beulah Bondi could have translated both the physical and spiritual strength of Steinbeck's Ma Joad. With her in the role, the jack handle scene might have been retained. But production decisions prevented this possibility and we are left with a fine, but flawed, film. John Ford's *The Grapes of Wrath* has many excellences. Still, as the story of humanity, the story of family, it grossly underplays the role of half the human race. One is left disappointed by the devitalization and diminishment of Ma Joad, one of the American novel's most admirable and engaging heroines. The women in the film are soft, sweet, passive, and long-suffering — nurturers, but not leaders in the struggle for survival. Steinbeck's women, though few in number, are strong in significance. They are tough as well as tender, feisty, and assertive. Though often helpless against overwhelming odds, they do more than mouth platitudes. At the end of Steinbeck's *The Grapes of Wrath* it is Ma Joad and Rose of Sharon who serve as both the symbols and the actors in human survival.

Notes

1. Besides the Academy Award *The Grapes of Wrath* won for its director and for Jane Darwell as best supporting actress, the movie appears on various other "best" lists. The American Film Institute voted it one of the ten best American films of all time. John Gassner includes it in his *Twenty Best Film Plays*.

2. Robert E. Morsberger, "Steinbeck's Films," Second International Steinbeck Congress, 3 August 1984.

3. Letter to Elizabeth Otis, 15 December 1939, in *Steinbeck: A Life in Letters*, ed. Elaine Steinbeck and Robert Wallsten, 195 (New York, Viking Press, 1975).

4. Joseph R. Millichap calls *Of Mice and Men* and *The Grapes of Wrath* the best film

adaptations of Steinbeck's works although he acknowledges "the ultimate failure to translate the full meaning of Steinbeck's novel to the screen." About Ma Joad, his understatement is that Jane Darwell is "a bit less fierce than Steinbeck's Ma," noting that if Ford had not chosen to excise the jack handle scene it might have provided a nice balance to the "sentimentalizing of Jane Darwell's film role" (*Steinbeck and Film* [New York: Frederick Ungar Publishing Co., 1983], 45). Russell Campbell thinks that Ma's sentimental idealization is a result of Ford's view of the Okies as "simple folk" and that by excising the jack handle scene Darwell's character is consistently presented as passively resigned to the vagaries of fate rather than fiercely resistant ("Tramping Out the Vintage: Sour Grapes," in *The Modern American Novel and the Movies*, ed. Gerald Peary and Roger Shatzkin, 114–15 [New York: Frederick Ungar Publishing Co., 1978]). Andrew Sarris argues that "Ford's own feelings are so powerfully patriarchal that when Grandpa dies, something in the movie seems to die with him." The inference, then, is that perhaps Ford's strong patriarchal feelings may account for the softening of Ma's part (*The John Ford Movie Mystery* [Bloomington: Indiana University Press, 1975], 98). Peter Roffman and Jim Purdy think that in keeping with Johnson's and Ford's highlighting of "Steinbeck's optimistic belief in the indestructibility of mankind" as opposed to "his many references to the need for mass action," Ma's role in the film is to counter Tom's radicalism. In the novel, Ma shares some of Tom's political sense; in the movie she just calls for all to sit back and wait for the good times to come back (*The Hollywood Social Problem Film* [Bloomington: Indiana University Press, 1981], 126).

5. Steinbeck says that there are five layers to the book and that the reader can participate to the level of his or her depth or hollowness. Letter to Pascal Covici, 16 January 1939, in *Steinbeck: A Life in Letters*, 178.

6. John Steinbeck, *The Grapes of Wrath* (New York: The Viking Press, 1939). All references to the novel will be in the text and refer to this edition. All references to the movie will also be in the text and are taken from the film script as published in *Twenty Best Film Plays*, ed. John Gassner and Dudley Nichols, 333–78 (New York: Crown Publishers, 1943).

7. Tetsumaro Hayashi, "Steinbeck's Women in *The Grapes of Wrath*: A New Perspective," *Kyushu American Literature* 18 (October 1977):4.

8. Leonard Lutwack, *Heroic Fiction: The Epic Tradition and American Novels of the Twentieth Century* (Carbondale and Edwardsville: Southern Illinois University Press, 1971), 54.

9. Warren Motley, "From Patriarchy to Matriarchy: Ma Joad's Role in *The Grapes of Wrath*," *American Literature* 54 (October, 1982): 397–98.

10. Andrew Sarris says it is no accident that this scene is dominated by Charley Grapewin's Grandpa while scenes between Jane Darwell's Ma and Russell Simpson's Pa are dominated by Darwell (*John Ford Movie Mystery*, 97).

11. Campbell, *Modern American Novel and the Movies*, 109.

12. John Baxter, "The Grapes of Wrath," in *The International Dictionary of Films and Filmmakers: Volume 1*, ed. Christopher Lyon, 185 (Chicago: St. James Press, 1985).

13. Motley, "From Patriarchy to Matriarchy," 397.

14. Sarris, *John Ford Movie Mystery*, 97.

15. See my *The Indestructible Woman in Faulkner, Hemingway, and Steinbeck* (Ann Arbor: UMI Research Press, 1986), for a fuller explication of Rose of Sharon's role in the novel.

16. Warren French is so unsympathetic and out of patience with Jane Darwell's Ma that his description of this scene reads, "the camera jumps nervously about as Ma *rattles* [emphasis mine] on about her need for help" (*Filmguide to "The Grapes of Wrath"* [Bloomington: Indiana University Press, 1973], 51).

John Steinbeck's *The Grapes of Wrath* as a Primer for Cultural Geography

Christopher L. Salter*

There is no need to write additional textbooks in cultural geography. All the messages of the profession are already committed to ink. The motivations, processes, patterns, and consequences of human interaction with the landscape have all been discovered and chronicled with grace and clarity. Authors dedicated to the comprehension and elucidation of order within the overtly haphazard flow of human events have given academics the materials needed to profess the patterns that illustrate this order. We fail, however, as scholars to make adequate use of these data for the simple reason that this material is labelled "fiction."[1]

Fiction in its primary meaning denotes invention. Ironically, the process of invention in the human species is one of the most consistently lauded acts that we can be associated with. Invention in professional fields is celebrated as creativity and insight. Invention in the commercial world often generates considerable cash. And even greater commendation is heaped on the inventor if the product of his or her imagination can be used in fields other than the inventor's own. That becomes the product of genius.

Yet, invention in the field of creative writing — the fiction of imaginative observation — is too often held to be nontransferable. It is in this domain that — for academics — fiction can assume its pejorative connotation. Constrained by a narrowly conceived framework of objectivity, the inventions of a good literary mind may indeed be unsuitable source material for research or teaching. The nature of human experience, however, whether that between fellow humans or in their relationship with place, cannot be captured in a rigidly objective framework. Imaginative literature articulates the kaleidoscope of human experience. Thus, the teacher of cultural geography who adopts an alternative artistic or humanistic stance to such material may himself be deemed inventive. The arguments in favor of such a literary teaching program for cultural geography may be briefly enumerated.

Consider first the learning atmosphere engendered by the use of a novel in addition to, or in lieu of, an orthodox text in cultural geography. Largely because a novel is a work of fiction, a reader slips into the narrative with a curious mind. The interest in understanding the author's work derives from an informal competition between the reader and the author. "What is the message here?," asks the student. "Can the author make me concerned enough about it to give of my mind, wit, and time?"

In the same situation, a traditional textbook would be anticipated as

*Revised with permission from *Humanistic Geography and Literature: Essays on the Experience of Place*, ed. Douglas C. D. Pocock (London: Croom Helm, 1981), 142–58.

a collection of facts strung together much like beads on a time line. The ambition of the reader would most probably be focused upon retention rather than upon understanding, thus diminishing creative speculation regarding the implications of the material presented. A novel gains strength because it may fire one's imagination through subtle allusion and illusion. A textbook, on the other hand, damps down the same fire through demands for inclusion and conclusion.

Literary fiction works well with cultural geography because the substance of both endeavors is life itself. The capacity for attitudes that shape environmental manipulation are present in all people, whether their perspectives emerge from an author's pen or a social scientist's interview data. The task of the cultural geographer is the same regardless of the data base: to mold individual specifics into understandable, reliable predictabilities. If the target audience of such an intellectual effort becomes involved in and concerned with the specifics of the human process, it will be easier for the teacher to instruct in the larger realities. These mundane specifics are exactly the material the novelist employs to create his fiction.

The Grapes of Wrath as Example

Because so many works of fiction are fundamentally genuine in their descriptions of people and places, the range of works available to a class is large. When selecting a novel for such an experiment, therefore, the teacher's best guide is his or her own personal preference in authors and settings.[2] The re-reading of a classic, with an eye focused upon the themes of cultural geography, may well produce new insights and new analysis.

For this chapter, I have chosen to use the major work by the American author John Steinbeck. His 1939 The Grapes of Wrath[3] meets several significant criteria. First, the novel is the product of vital and personal fieldwork conducted by the author. He was writing of a world that he knew very intimately.[4] Second, he makes his characters move through a variety of distinct physical and cultural regions. Such movement adds variety to the geographic observations that are potential in a novel. Third, Steinbeck employs a useful literary convention in the book in his use of inner chapters. These short episodes that break up the specific narrative of the Joad family provide the reader with an overview of the cultural landscape during the time the fiction of the novel takes place. By interrupting the flow of the personal narrative of the primary family, Steinbeck effectively causes the reader to back away from the specific incidents of his main family and, instead, to view the difficulties of these people as part of a larger social fabric. While such a technique is far from unique to Steinbeck, the structure of The Grapes of Wrath is particularly well suited to developing societal themes alongside personal themes.

The final reason for the selection of The Grapes of Wrath concerns related readings. If members of a class become interested in Steinbeck's style and concerns, they can be directed towards the large corpus of work about the Dust Bowl migrations or the more general topic of migration itself. Once a student begins to read fiction with part of his mind searching out distinctive landscapes and culture systems, education has essentially reached a new and higher level. It is fitting that a cultural geographer should play some role in that attainment.

In *The Grapes of Wrath* three major theme areas in cultural geography are particularly evident for elaboration. Human mobility—the kinetic energy of so much landscape transformation—plays a dominant role in Steinbeck's narrative. Tensions between competing modes of land use spark much of the drama in the novel, and also illustrate the social consequences of such variant decisions in economic patterns. Finally, the specific social and spatial configurations encountered by the Joads during their epic move from Oklahoma to California serve as vignettes around which a geographer can structure expanded explanations of human transformation of the land. In this paper, my concern is focused upon the themes of human mobility.

Human Mobility as a Dominant Force in Cultural Geography and in *The Grapes of Wrath*

Systems of belief as well as spatial order are constantly subject to change. The intrusion of competing systems—through the processes of migration and expanded communications—is a key force in such change. To the cultural geographer human mobility affords a thematic domain that embraces environmental perception, regional, cultural, and economic variation, problem landscapes that impede migration and mobility, as well as contesting systems of custom, government, and settlement. Steinbeck weaves all of these elements into his novel of America in the 1930s. By sorting out several of the most significant subthemes in this universe of movement, an orderly analysis of both the novel and this aspect of cultural geography becomes possible.

Information Fields and the Selection of a Goal Area

Axial to any model of decision-making in a migration scenario is the process of deciding where one is to go when the hearth area no longer accommodates a person or a people. The information available in that selection of a goal area derives from hearsay, media messages, feedback from earlier migrants, reading, and current folklore. This initial consideration of the choice of goal area is appropriate in our analysis of *The Grapes of Wrath* because so great a part of the novel is concerned with the search for a haven. During this process, the Joads and their fellow travellers are continually confronted with the riddle of "where to go." The image of California that was known in Oklahoma was one of a tarnished

Eden. Although news of the fields, the fruit, the opportunity for land, and the generalized abundance of everything in California was widespread, there were also increasing rumors of the existence of an ugly, dark side to this vision. In the two passages below, members of the Joad family touch on the emotional extremes of the images that came to the Okies as they were forced to pack up their few belongings and set out for new lands. Grampa speaks first, representing the popular image of an abundant reward awaiting those who chose California for a goal area in the departure from the drought-stricken Great Plains:

> The old man thrust out his bristly chin, and he regarded Ma with his shrewd, mean, merry eyes. "Well, sir," he said, "we'll be a-startin' 'fore long now. An', by God, they's grapes out there, just a-hangin' over inta the road. Know what I'm a-gonna do? I'm gonna pick me a wash tub full a grapes, an' I'm gonna set in 'em, an' scrooge aroun', an' let the juice run down my pants."
>
> (126)

Just before this passage, Ma Joad speculated on some of those same images when she allowed herself to think of "how nice it's gonna be, maybe, in California. Never cold. An' fruit ever'place, an' people just bein' in the nicest places, little white houses in among the orange trees. . . . An' the little fellas go out an' pick oranges right off the tree. They ain't gonna be able to stand it, they'll get to yellin' so." (124)

But a parallel ambivalence the family felt about California and the decision to uproot and head west is evident in this turn of the conversation between Ma and her son, Tom, who has just been paroled from prison:

> ". . . I knowed a fella from California. He didn't talk like us. You'd of knowed he come from some far-off place jus' the way he talked. But he says they's too many folks lookin' for work right there now. An' he says the folks that pick the fruit live in dirty ol' camps an' don't hardly get enough to eat. He says wages is low an' hard to get any."
>
> A shadow crossed her face. "Oh, that ain't so," she said. "Your father got a han'bill on yella paper, tellin' how they need folks to work. They wouldn't go to that trouble if they wasn't plenty work. Costs 'em good money to get them han'bills out. What'd they want ta lie for, an' costin' 'em money to lie?"
>
> (124)

Ma's refusal to accept the information that Tom brought from prison — from one who had witnessed a different image of the state — is significant, for it illustrates the manner by which the migrant begins to exclude information that threatens the positive image of the goal area. Once plans for a migration have been made, blinkers are put on in an attempt to disallow any dilution of that resolution. As one ponders the trauma of an uprooting from the hearth and place that has served as home for a family for decades, such a response becomes increasingly understandable. The psychological costs of such a move provide the second theme for consideration.

The Psychological Costs of Mobility

The whole tone of movement in *The Grapes of Wrath* is one of regretful departure. Except for occasional, if powerful, allusions to a better life in California voiced by the young Joads and Grampa, the family leaves its Oklahoma sharecropping past with great reluctance.[5] This emotional wrenching is not limited to the Joads. Steinbeck creates one of his strongest characters in the person of Muley, one of the few people the reader meets who has decided not to move to California. The combination of Ma Joad and Muley — although they never share the same stage — is effective in making an observer realize that this process of uprooting at a time of crisis has deep and profound psychological costs far beyond the economic dislocation associated with such a migration.

In the one case — that of Ma Joad — a buffer is created by the fact that she is taking her family with her. She will at least be able to maintain basic associations with the people who are most important to her. In the case of Muley, however, Steinbeck creates a character who is cast adrift entirely. In his attempts to maintain his attachment to the past and his personal tradition, Muley reverts to a near-primitive state, taking solace in his attempts to make trouble for the agents of change sent by the banks and the police.[6]

This trauma of movement derives also from the sheer financial burdens of relocation. For the Okies, to whom Steinbeck gives his novel, there were few resources available to lighten the burden of the move. Human resources were the greatest riches these farmers had, and it was these very family members who found themselves at odds with each other because of decisions about where to go or how to travel or what to drive. Details in the inner chapters as well as the Joad narrative itself point out to the reader the complexity of human mobility, a complexity that involves both the emotions and the finances of individuals and families. Such an understanding helps an observer to realize the gravity of the decision to uproot and move on.

Passages that demonstrate the power of these themes of dislocation come from conversations between Tom and Muley, and Ma and Tom, and from descriptions of the car lots in the inner chapters. In the first excerpt below, Muley, Tom, and Casy are talking around a small fire on the nearly deserted farmlands of the town where Tom and Muley were raised. Muley is getting increasingly excited as he explains how he felt as he saw his house emptied, his parents leave, and his farmland all reduced to a sameness under the power of the new tractors on the land:

". . . I wanta talk. I ain't talked to nobody. If I'm touched, I'm touched, an' that's the end of it. Like a ol' graveyard ghos' goin' to neighbors' houses in the night. Peters', Jacobs', Rance's, Joad's; an' the houses all dark, standin' like miser'ble ratty boxes, but they was good parties an' dancin'. An' there was meetin's and shoutin' glory. They was weddin's, all in them houses. An' then I'd want to go in town an' kill folks. 'Cause what'd they take when they tractored the folks off the lan'? What'd they get so their 'margin a profit' was safe? They got Pa dyin' on the groun', an' Joe yellin' his first breath, an' me jerkin' like a billy goat under a bush in the night. What'd they get? God knows the lan' ain't no good. Nobody been able to make a crop for years. But them sons-a-bitches at their desks, they jus' chopped folks in two for their margin a profit. They jus' cut 'em in two. Place where folks live is them folks. They ain't whole, out lonely on the road in a piled-up car. They ain't alive no more. Them sons-a-bitches killed 'em." And he was silent, his thin lips still moving, his chest still panting. He sat and looked down at his hands in the firelight. "I—I ain't talked to nobody for a long time," he apologized softly. "I been sneakin' aroun' like a ol' graveyard ghos' "

(70–71)

Ma shows some of the same unprecedented irritation as she attempts to organize her family's goods for the uncertain trip west:

". . . Ma," [Tom] said, "you never was like this before!"

Her face hardened and her eyes grew cold. "I never had my house pushed over," she said. "I never had my fambly stuck out on the road. I never had to sell — ever'thing — "

(104)

This typical mother looks at the pile of household goods that her family cannot carry with them and asks two critical questions: "How can we live without our lives? How will we know it's us without our past? No. Leave it. Burn it" (120).

The economic difficulties of the sharecroppers' moves are compounded by the size of the multitude that is taking to the road. In one of the novel's most effective inner chapters, Steinbeck gives the reader a close-up of a used car lot. In the excerpt below, the reader gains a strong sense of how migrants can be victimized when some environmental or social catastrophe forces so many people to move simultaneously that individuals lose any economic leverage they might otherwise have had:

What you want is transportation, ain't it? No baloney for you. Sure the upholstery is shot. Seat cushions ain't turning no wheels over.

Cars lined up, noses forward, rusty noses, flat tires. Parked close together.

Like to get in to see that one? Sure, no trouble. I'll pull her out of the line.

Get 'em under obligation. Make 'em take up your time. Don't let 'em forget they're takin' your time. People are nice, mostly. They hate to put you out. Make 'em put you out, and then sock it to 'em.

Cars lined up, Model T's, high and snotty, creaking wheel, worn bands. Buicks, Nashes, De Sotos.

> Yes, sir. '22 Dodge. Best goddamn car Dodge ever made. Never
> wear out. Low compression. High compression got lots a sap for a
> while, but the metal ain't made that'll hold it for long. Plymouths,
> Rocknes, Stars.
>
> (84)

This reality is further exploited in scenes from town when the Joads
attempt to sell their household goods. A lifetime of accumulation provides
little economic return when the entire farm community is trying to sell its
untransportable furniture and farm implements at the same time.[7]

Notwithstanding the agonies associated with the move, the people do
uproot and leave. Not only is that departure essential to the novel, but it is
a reality in consideration of human mobility. Even in the face of the
hardships narrated in *The Grapes of Wrath*, as well as in the myriad others
that exist in all migration, people do carry through with the plan to try
some other place, hoping that the change will bring them more benefit
than cost. In that movement, the people and the landscape are changed.
Such change introduces a third major theme area in the study of human
mobility from the perspective of cultural geography.

Personal and Landscape Changes Associated with the
Process of Human Mobility

It is not the migrants alone who are changed by the process of
migration. Demographic shifts modify the complexion of the hearth area
as well as the goal area. If the process or the novel that we are studying is
based on an individual's experience, then the scale of such impact is
probably small. However, as the size of the population in motion grows,
the magnitude of the influence created by the migration increases propor-
tionately. Additionally, the corridor through which the movement takes
place is bombarded with new demands, demands that are seldom met
with warm welcomes.

The nature of this intermediate response is captured in a number of
episodes by Steinbeck, but perhaps most powerfully in his scenes from a
Highway 66 diner. The excerpt below shows the pensive nature of a
waitress, for example, who has had her entire universe confused by all of
the people and families moving west:

> Flies struck the screen with little bumps and droned away. The
> compressor chugged for a time and then stopped. On 66 the traffic
> whizzed by, trucks and fine streamlined cars and jalopies; and they went
> by with a vicious whiz. Mae took down the plates and scraped the pie
> crusts into a bucket. She found her damp cloth and wiped the counter
> with circular sweeps. And her eyes were on the highway, where life
> whizzed by.
>
> (220)

This life that whizzed by in Mae's eyes brought changes all along Highway 66. Traditionally free services such as water and air at the roadside gas stations became so overused that dealers began to charge for these services. Used tires, fan belts, and engine repair all became more expensive as service-station owners' reactions went from irritation and suspicion to entrepreneurial opportunism, creating an image of their services through roadside junk:

> The truck drove to the service-station belt, and there on the right-hand side of the road was a wrecking yard—an acre lot surrounded by a high barbed-wire fence, a corrugated iron shed in front with used tires piled up by the doors, and price-marked. Behind the shed there was a little shack built of scrap, scrap lumber and pieces of tin. The windows were windshields built into the walls. In the grassy lot the wrecks lay, cars with twisted, stove-in noses, wounded cars lying on their sides with the wheels gone. Engines rusting on the ground and against the shed. A great pile of junk; fenders and truck sides, wheels and axles; over the whole lot a spirit of decay, of mold and rust; twisted iron, half-gutted engines, a mass of derelicts.

> (242)

The images of the migration process—whether in the novel or in a teacher's reality—are frequently tied to this very problem of transportation. Just as the covered wagon of a century earlier became metonymy for the entire process of American westward expansion and settlement, the jalopy with its load of children, inverted chairs, wooden barrels filled with dishes, pans, and rags became the visual signature of the migration depicted by Steinbeck in *The Grapes of Wrath*. Keeping these rigs going required impressive levels of self-reliance and inventiveness, qualities that begin to emerge in any migration as the movers are forced to deal with the landscapes and the people they encounter in their flight from the past:

> Thus they changed their social life—changed as in the whole universe only man can change. They were not farm men any more, but migrant men. And the thought, the planning, the long staring silence that had gone out to the fields, went now to the roads, to the distance, to the West. That man whose mind had been bound with acres lived with narrow concrete miles. And his thought and his worry were not any more with rainfall, with wind and dust, with the thrust of the crops. Eyes watched the tires, ears listened to the clattering motors, and minds struggled with oil, with gasoline, with the thinning rubber between air and road. Then a broken gear was tragedy. Then water in the evening was the yearning, and food over the fire. Then health to go on was the need and strength to go on, and spirit to go on. The wills thrust westward ahead of them, and fears that had once apprehended drought or flood now lingered with anything that might stop the westward crawling.
> The camp became fixed—each a short day's journey from the last.
> (267–68)

To accompany this psychological change in attitude came an associated change in setting. Finding a few physical elements deemed necessary for a nighttime haven — water, a little firewood, and perhaps a nearby dump for scavenging — these people began a pattern of creation anew each night. As some of these "Hoovervilles" became established, they took on a geography of their own. Such settlements are a bona fide segment of the landscape of change in this human movement:

> There was no order in the camp; little gray tents, shacks, cars were scattered about at random. The first house was nondescript. The south wall was made of three sheets of rusty corrugated iron, the east wall a square of moldy carpet tacked between two boards, the north wall a strip of roofing paper and a strip of tattered canvas, and the west wall six pieces of gunny sacking. Over the square frame, on untrimmed willow limbs, grass had been piled, not thatched, but heaped up in a low mound. The entrance, on the gunnysack side, was cluttered with equipment. A five-gallon kerosene can served for a stove. It was laid on its side, with a section of rusty stovepipe thrust in one end. A wash boiler rested on its side against the wall; and a collection of boxes lay about, boxes to sit on, to eat on. A Model T Ford sedan and a two-wheel trailer were parked beside the shack, and about the camp there hung a slovenly despair.
>
> Next to the shack there was a little tent, gray with weathering, but neatly, properly set up; and the boxes in front of it were placed against the tent wall. A stovepipe stuck out of the door flap, and the dirt in front of the tent had been swept and sprinkled. A bucketful of soaking clothes stood on a box. The camp was neat and sturdy. A Model A roadster and a little home-made bed trailer stood beside the tent.
>
> And next there was a huge tent, ragged, torn in strips and the tears mended with pieces of wire. The flaps were up, and inside four wide mattresses lay on the ground. A clothes line strung along the side bore pink cotton dresses and several pairs of overalls. There were forty tents and shacks, and beside each habitation some kind of automobile. Far down the line a few children stood and stared at the newly arrived truck, and they moved toward it, little boys in overalls and bare feet, their hair gray with dust.
>
> (328–29)

Every choice humankind makes for the manipulation of an environment sets in motion a tension. The prior state of development at any given point was either natural (increasingly unlikely) or represented some other human wish or design. Cultural geography finds much of its meaning from the process of analysis and evaluation of such a change process, and resultant environments. Questions of natural conditions, technology, economic systems, social attitudes, demography, custom, and, finally, special forces of the moment all must be factored into any equation that attempts to explain change. The creation of the Hoovervilles — noted above — was one of the most explicit signals to the Californians that their state was destined to undergo marked social and spatial change in response to this migration stream that had been initiated more than a thousand miles away. These response patterns in the goal area introduce us to our final theme in the cultural analysis of mobility in the novel.

Cultural Response Patterns in the Goal Area

Although public response to the 1939 publication of *The Grapes of Wrath* was vastly supportive in terms of book purchases, Steinbeck found himself very uncomfortable in his native California.[8] His portrayal of his state's citizens as being unsympathetic, avaricious, even malicious towards this stream of poor migrants from Oklahoma and other states of the Dust Bowl, sorely wounded the pride of the folk with whom Steinbeck had grown up.[9] Criticism was focused upon his inability to acknowledge the impact this immigration of penniless, rural, and distraught folk would have on the social order of California. The Great Depression, although not damaging this western state as profoundly as it had states in other parts of the country, had already taxed municipal and state agencies to the margin of their abilities to cope with unemployed, angry people. The specter of additional hundreds of thousands of like souls, but souls new to the state, making similar demands on modest resources excited no small anxiety in the minds of nearly all Californians.

Steinbeck establishes the potentially explosive mood of this tension between the migrants and Californian patterns of farming in one of his strongest inner chapters. He describes the capital-intensive nature of local farming, pointing out the fixed expenses for chemical fertilizers, spraying, and irrigation technology. The depressed prices of the late 1930s, however, drove prices below a level that generated essential income for the strictly managed farms. Instead of selling at such a level, owners decided to destroy fruit in order

> to keep up the price, and this is the saddest, bitterest thing of all. Carloads of oranges dumped on the ground. The people came for miles to take the fruit, but this could not be. How would they buy oranges at twenty cents a dozen if they could drive out and pick them up? And men with hoses squirt kerosene on the oranges, and they are angry at the crime, angry at the people who have come to take the fruit. A million people hungry, needing the fruit — and kerosene sprayed over the golden mountains. . . .
>
> There is a crime here that goes beyond denunciation. There is a sorrow here that weeping cannot symbolize. There is a failure here that topples all our success. The fertile earth, the straight tree rows, the sturdy trunks, and the ripe fruit. And children dying of pellagra must die because a profit cannot be taken from an orange. And coroners must fill in the certificates — died of malnutrition — because the food must rot,

must be forced to rot. . . . In the souls of the people the grapes of wrath are filling and growing heavy, growing heavy for the vintage.

(476–47)

One of the classic confrontations of the new migrants with the old order in California came in the hiring of pickers for the ripening fruits up and down the Central Valley. Contractors would go to the Hoovervilles, offer work at thirty cents an hour at some distant farm, and give families directions about how to get there. Arriving at the place, having exhausted their resources and already given up their space at the government camp, people would be told that the rate was only fifteen cents an hour — and that there would be a surplus of workers even at that rate. Occasionally, migrants who had been caught up in this painful misrepresentation several times would attempt to dissuade the Okies from falling into the trap. The scene below illustrates one such happening:

> The man said, "You men want to work?" . . . men from all over the camp moved near.
> One of the squatting men spoke at last. "Sure we wanta work. Where's at's work?"
> "Tulare County. Fruit's opening up. Need a lot of pickers."
> Floyd spoke up. "You doin' the hiring?"
> "Well, I'm contracting the land."
> The men were in a compact group now. An overalled man took off his black hat and combed back his long black hair with his fingers. "What you payin'?" he asked.
> "Well, can't tell exactly, yet. 'Bout thirty cents, I guess."
> "Why can't you tell? You took the contract, didn' you?"
> "That's true," the khaki man said. "But it's keyed to the price. Might be a little more, might be a little less."
> Floyd stepped out ahead. He said quietly, "I'll go, mister. You're a contractor, an' you got a license. You jus' show your license, an' then you give us an order to go to work, an' where, an' when, an' how much we'll get, an' you sign that, an' we'll all go."
> The contractor turned, scowling. "You telling me how to run my own business?"
> Floyd said, " 'F we're workin' for you, it's our business too. . . ."
> Floyd turned to the crowd of men. They were standing up now, looking quietly from one speaker to the other. Floyd said, "Twicet now I've fell for that. Maybe he needs a thousan' men. He'll get five thousan' there, an' he'll pay fifteen cents an hour. An' you poor bastards'll have to take it 'cause you'll be hungry. 'F he wants to hire men, let him hire 'em and write out an' say what he's gonna pay. Ast ta see his license. He ain't allowed to contract men without a license."

(357–59)

Clandestine farming was another point of contention between the uprooted farmers of the Dust Bowl and the California residents who became increasingly uneasy about the threat to their patterns of agriculture:

> Now and then a man tried; crept on the land and cleared a piece, trying like a thief to steal a little richness from the earth. Secret gardens hidden in the weeds. A package of carrot seeds and a few turnips. Planted potato skins, crept out in the evening secretly to hoe in the stolen earth. . . .
> Secret gardening in the evenings, and water carried in a rusty can.
> And then one day a deputy sheriff: Well, what you think you're doin'?
> I aint' doin' no harm.
> I had my eye on you. This ain't your land. You're trespassing.
> The land ain't plowed, an' I ain't hurtin' it none.
> You goddamned squatters. Pretty soon you'd think you owned it. . . . Get off now.
> And the little green carrot tops were kicked off and the turnip greens trampled. . . .
> Did ya see his face when we kicked them turnips out? Why, he'd kill a fella soon's he'd look at him. We got to keep these here people down or they'll take the country . . .
> Outlanders, foreigners.
> Sure, they talk the same language, but they ain't the same. Look how they live. Think any of us folks'd live like that? Hell, no!
> (321–22)

In *The Grapes of Wrath* — and even more so in the reality of the migration — there were instances of a more welcoming response to the migrants. People were able to see these families as fundamentally hardworking farm people who had been set in motion by the extraordinary combination of the natural forces of the drought and dust conditions of the Great Plains and the economic chaos of the Depression. Steinbeck portrays one such sympathetic farmer in the person of a Mr. Thomas who hires men from the government camp of Weedpatch. He is a small farmer, deeply dependent upon a credit line from his bank, even though he appears to be an efficient farmer. In this excerpt Mr. Thomas has just told his small work crew that the thirty cents an hour they had been getting was being reduced to twenty-five cents that morning:

> Timothy said, "We've give you good work. You said so yourself."
> "I know it. But it seems like I ain't hiring my own men any more." He swallowed. "Look," he said, "I got sixty-five acres here. Did you ever hear of the Farmers' Association?"
> "Why, sure."
> "Well, I belong to it. We had a meeting last night. Now, do you know who runs the Farmers' Association? I'll tell you. The Bank of the West. That bank owns most of this valley, and it's got paper on everything it don't own. So last night the member from the bank told me, he said, 'You're paying thirty cents an hour. You'd better cut it

down to twenty-five.' I said, 'I've got good men. They're worth thirty.' And he says, 'It isn't that,' he says. 'The wage is twenty-five now. If you pay thirty, it'll only cause unrest. And by the way,' he says, 'You going to need the usual amount for a crop loan next year?' " Thomas stopped. His breath was panting through his lips. "You see? The rate is twenty-five cents — and like it."

(402)

Conditions, then, at the place of arrival paralleled the set of conditions that drove the farmers off the land and onto Highway 66 at the place of departure. The banks that had been seeking the "margin of profit" that Muley spoke of in Oklahoma also appear to be in charge of farming decisions on small and large landholders alike in California. The vagaries of nature that brought drought and made sharecropping counterproductive also produce the prolonged rains and floods that end the book with the remnants of the Joad family stranded in a desolate boxcar, still out of touch with the land that they had set out for. Although the migration had been fulfilled, the same paucity of options that faced these families at the outset seems to characterize their future as the novel concludes.

That, perhaps, is the fiction that cultural geographers should do battle with in their instruction on human mobility. Even with the specifics broadly varying from case to case, the fact of migration *does* open new options. People change in the process of movement; places change as the migrants grow more familiar with the setting and cultural fabrics of these new locales. In a harsher sense, the least adaptive of initial migrants have probably left the migration stream, diminishing the competition in the search for support at the final destination.

New skills are learned by the migrant farmers as they leave the land to their past and find outlets for their ambition in the cities. New settlement features grow up around the migrants who finally do create a marginal haven for themselves and their families, and bring their music, foods, clothes, and language into the society of the new setting. Almost nothing escapes some modification in the face of a migration stream as robust and intense as this particular American flight from the Great Plains in the mid-1930s. The event in itself is a dramatic exercise in the elements of cultural geography.

Conclusion

To the cultural geographer, then, lessons from the landscape and human movement in *The Grapes of Wrath* provide focus for instruction in migration, settlement forms, economic systems, cultural dualism, agricultural land use patterns, transportation technology, and social change. To the reader of creative fiction, these same realities generally lie scattered within the pages of this epic of one family's unsuccessful search for a new beginning. But to the reader of fiction who is also attempting to comprehend something of the underlying systems in this chaos of conflict and flight, the study of this novel provides a window on geographic phenomena broadly ranging from mental maps to economic infrastructures.

In the face of such complexity, effective thinking—let alone instructing—calls for the use of all the human resources available. Evocative fiction in creative literature is one of these resources. Such work, when read first with a searching mind, and then re-read with a disciplined perspective, is capable of illustrating patterns, preferences, and problems of humankind. And it conveys all of these dynamics with vitality. Cultural geographers—in their ambitious quest for the understanding of human society and cultural landscapes—would do well to capture and utilize such dynamics and such vitality. John Steinbeck's *The Grapes of Wrath* is one volume that possesses both qualities in such abundance that it serves provocatively as a primer for cultural geography.

Notes

1. There is a broad literature discussing the use of fiction in both teaching and research. Some of the items of interest in the literature of fiction include A. J. Lamme III, "The Use of Novels in Geography Classrooms," *Journal of Geography* 76, no. 2 (February 1977): 66–68; D. W. Meinig, "Environmental Appreciation: Localities as a Humane Art," *Western Humanities Review*, 25 (Winter 1971): 1–11; C. L. Salter and W. J. Lloyd, "Landscape in Literature," *Resource Papers for College Geography* 76, no. 3 (Washington: Association of American Geographers, 1977); Sherman E. Silverman, "The Use of Novels in Teaching Cultural Geography of the United States," *Journal of Geography* 76, no. 4 (April–May 1977): 140–46; C. L. Salter, "Signatures and Settings: One Approach to Landscape in Literature," in *Dimensions of Human Geography*, ed. Karl W. Butzer, 69–83 (Chicago: University of Chicago Press, 1978); John Conron, *The American Landscape* (Chicago: Oxford University Press, 1973).

2. Salter and Lloyd, "Landscape in Literature," 29–30, includes a number of useful references for searching out fiction to coincide with the region and, sometimes, theme of a teacher or researcher.

3. John Steinbeck, *The Grapes of Wrath* (New York: Viking Press, 1939); hereafter cited in the text.

4. Elaine Steinbeck and Robert Wallsten, eds., *Steinbeck: A Life in Letters* (New York: Viking Press, 1976). This collection has two sections that deal with the period of preparation for *The Grapes of Wrath* (57–189). These Steinbeck letters and their associated discussion provide the reader with a strong sense of how immediate the Oklahoma sharecropper migration was to Steinbeck during the 1930s. See also John Steinbeck, *Their Blood Is Strong* (San Francisco: Simon J. Lubin Society, 1938); Peter Lisca, "The Grapes of Wrath", 75–101, and George Bluestone, "The Grapes of Wrath", 102–21, in Robert Murray Davis, ed., *Steinbeck: A Collection of Critical Essays* (Englewood Cliffs, N.J.: Prentice-Hall, 1972).

5. Grampa fills the role of a particularly tragic character in the early part of the novel because of the naivete of his vision of California, as well as his difficulty in comprehending the magnitude of the family move. The Joad children and their friends become caught up in the adventure of moving and exploration, also failing to sense the impending rupture in the family's situation. See chapter 10 (122–56).

6. In chapter 6 (54–82) Muley shows Tom and Casy how thorough his adaptation to his new life has been. He anticipates the arrival and search behavior of the sheriff; he produces

rabbits that he has caught with a fierce efficiency, and he rants on and on about the bank and its determination to ruin the sharecroppers of the region for its "margin a profit." Steinbeck uses his character to illustrate the consequences of making a decision *not* to move away from this drought-plagued region.

7. Chapter 9 (117–21) is a short inner chapter that dramatizes the deep frustration that the sharecroppers felt as they tried to sell the goods that they could not transport west. The intensity of this sorrow and anger is shown as families pile household goods in their front yards, set fire to them, and watch them burn as they climb into their overloaded trucks and head for their uncertain future. Peter Lisca discusses these inner chapters and their accuracy, while pointing out that Steinbeck's novel launched numerous volumes supporting and disputing the images created by this characterization of the migration (Lisca, "The Grapes," 78–93).

8. The Viking Press issued the first edition of *Grapes* in April 1939 and the book went through ten printings before the end of the year.

9. Steinbeck once revealed that an undersheriff of Santa Clara County in California — a prime agricultural county at the time — warned him to be careful because local people had plans to set up a fake rape case in order to discredit him (Steinbeck and Wallsten, *Letters*, 187). In a conversation with a librarian in Salinas, California, in the summer of 1979, I was told that only "in the last few years have the townspeople taken any pride at all that John Steinbeck was born here. Before that he was seen as a disgrace."

John Steinbeck and Modernism (A Speculation on His Contribution to the Development of the Twentieth-Century American Sensibility)

Warren French*

Although we members of what might be called the "Steinbeck Community" quibble over details, there is general agreement that John Steinbeck's work arches over the American landscape in a giant parabola, rising suddenly like the Spring sun to the glories of *The Red Pony, Tortilla Flat,* and *Of Mice and Men,* reaching noon's zenith between 1939 and 1945 with *The Grapes of Wrath, The Forgotten Village,* and *Cannery Row,* and then diminishing into the twilight asperities of *The Winter of Our Discontent,* "Letters to Alicia," and *America and Americans.*

In my recent revision of *John Steinbeck* (1975), I offered one theory accounting for Steinbeck's rise and decline by presenting a contrast in his fiction between "Naturalism" and the "Drama of Consciousness." I am not satisfied, however, that the matter can be settled by one such simplistic scheme; we must continue to explore the phenomenon of his genius in the light of other theories that may provide useful and new perspectives and

*Reprinted with permission from *Steinbeck's Prophetic Vision of America*, ed. Tetsumaro Hayashi and Kenneth D. Swan (Upland, Ind.: Taylor University for John Steinbeck Society of America, 1976), 35–55.

appease those not content with earlier speculations. I find one such theory that I think provides an equally valid and perhaps even more important explanation in the concept of Modernism, which has lately become a central concern in literary criticism.

What is "Modernism"? Although critics rarely achieve consensus, they agree that we have reached the end of that period during which the present generation has grown up and been trained and that has come to be known as "Modernist." The term rose to the threshold of attention through a lecture that Harvard's distinguished comparativist, Harry Levin, delivered in 1959 to Stanley Burnshaw's Seminar in Modern Literature at New York University. Subsequently it was published in Burnshaw's *Varieties of Literary Experiences* (1962). The rapid and wide adoption of the term that Levin used to ask "What Was Modernism?" indicates that it provided a useful label for something that it was generally felt needed to be named.

Levin's essay, however, goes only a little way toward answering the question its title poses. Concerned principally with an international style of life and architecture, Levin equated Modernism especially with the expatriate writers of the 1920s and provided less an essay in definition than a nostalgic reminiscence by an erudite cosmopolitan whose own sensibilities were too deeply steeped in nineteenth-century "pre-Modernist" traditions to view dispassionately the fragmentations of the "Modernist" years.

More useful than Levin's essay is another also first presented to the same Burnshaw seminar and printed in *Varieties of Literary Experiences* by that middle-class metropolitan who until his recent, much-lamented death used his remarkable gifts as an undergraduate teacher and critic to speak to the public in an age of obscurantism and to preside for years as one of the principal shapers and judges of "Modernist" writing. Lionel Trilling's "The 'Modern Element' in Literature" deliberately appropriates from Matthew Arnold the title of a precedent-shattering talk at Oxford at the end of another age—just at the time that the study of modern languages and literatures was beginning to supplant the classical as the business of our academies. Thus Trilling casts himself also in the role of a figure straddling two eras. After explaining faculty uneasiness early in this century about offering the courses that students had begun to demand in modern literature, Trilling points out that "resistance to the idea of the course had never been based on an adverse judgment of the literature itself," which is "difficult" and the equal "in power and magnificence" of any of the past, but to misgivings arising from the narcissistic and solipsistic dangers of a preoccupation with the problems and productions of one's own time to the exclusion of a broadening tradition.

In the most important part of the essay, however, after observing that Thomas Mann had "once said that all his work could be understood as an effort to free himself from the middle class," Trilling proposes that this effort describes "the chief intention of all modern literature." "I venture to say," he concludes, "that the idea of losing oneself up to the point of self-destruction, of surrendering oneself to experience without regard to self interest or conventional morality, of escaping wholly from societal bonds, is an 'element' somewhere in the mind of every modern person who dares to think of what Arnold in his unaffected Victorian way called 'the fullness of spiritual perfection.' "

"Escaping wholly from societal bonds," which Trilling sees as the characteristic effort of the "Modernist," recalls surely the conclusion of that fiction often cited as both the progenitor and exemplar of the "Modernist" sensibility — James Joyce's *A Portrait of the Artist as a Young Man*, in which Stephen Dedalus vows, "I will not serve that in which I no longer believe, whether it call itself my home, my fatherland, or my church: and I will try to express myself in some mode of life and art as freely as I can and as wholly as I can, using for my defense the only arms I allow myself — silence, exile, and cunning."

Trying further to pin down the characteristics of Modernism with a precision that befits the founder/editor of a *Journal of Modern Literature*, Maurice Beebe launches the July 1974 issue devoted to the theme "From Modernism to Post-Modernism" by turning Levin's question into an assertion, "What Modernism Was." Quoting from his own earlier "*Ulysses* and the Age of Modernism," Beebe lists "four features in particular," which enable us to differentiate Modernist literature "from that of the earlier nineteenth century and that of today" — its formalism (that is, its insistence on the esthetic autonomy of the work), its attitude of detachment and non-commitment, its use of myth as an arbitrary means of ordering art, and its great concern with its own creation and composition. This catalogue, however, strikes me as just a little too much like those lengthy and highly exceptionable lists of differences between Classicism and Romanticism, which eminent scholars of another era used to bore classes by shifting attention from the experience of the literature itself to its pickling. Even Beebe feels compelled to admit after compiling his list that he "would not attempt to argue that these four characteristics are uniquely the property of the Age of Modernism."

Can we focus on some more simply stated characteristic that is? Beebe comes closest to doing so, I feel, when abandoning his categorical approach to the Modernist sensibility, he observes that he finds Philip Stevick's essay, "Sentimentality and Classic Fiction," correct in pointing out that "one could almost define modernism by its irony, its implicit admiration for verbal precision and understatement." Certainly *irony* has been the quality in literature most sought by the most prominent school of critics — those so-called "New Critics," now generally considered somewhat old-hat — to rise during the Modernist years to establish the canon of its great.

Irony, however, has been used in so many ways and has come to mean so many things that it has become almost as vague and useless a term as A. O. Lovejoy in *The Great Chain of Being* found "nature," unless we specify precisely what kind of "irony" we have in mind when we speak of this quality as defining Modernism. I would argue that this irony is most exactly specified by a definition taken from Kierkegaard's *Concluding Unscientific Postscript* by Marston LaFrance to provide the focus in his *A Reading of Stephen Crane* (1971): "Irony is a synthesis of ethical passion which infinitely accentuates inwardly the person of the individual in relation to the ethical requirement—and of culture, which infinitely abstracts externally from the personal ego, as one finitude among all other finitudes and particularities." I believe it is possible to make this concept more comprehensible without distorting it by stating that Kierkegaard defines *irony* as a synthesis of ethical passion, which infinitely stresses within the mind, the personal integrity of the individual, and of culture, which as one of the finite external forces operating upon the individual, infinitely abstracts externally from the personal ego. I agree, in any event, with LaFrance when he goes on to take Kierkegaard's statement to mean that the individual endowed with this "ironic vision" has "a perception or awareness of a double realm of values where a different sort of mind [LaFrance suggests Hamlin Garland in contrast to Stephen Crane] perceives only a single realm." He conceives of this "ironic vision," in short, as a quality that might be most memorably emblemized by Wallace Stevens's "Blue Guitar," upon which "things as they are"—inescapably to the literal-minded—"are changed."

Now this kind of "ironic vision" did not suddenly spring into being in the dying days of the pre-Modernist, Victorian period; some writers have always possessed it. Certainly Melville did; but his contemporaries deplored and ignored those of his works like *Moby-Dick* and *The Confidence Man* that have been elevated to pre-eminent rank during the Modernist years. What distinguishes, I would argue, the Modernist period from others is the special, exalted value that was placed then upon this particular ironic vision. What in an earlier period of "faith" might have been a serious liability cutting the possessor off from "societal bonds" to his detriment became during the first two-thirds of the twentieth century a characteristic so highly prized that those lacking it fell into critical disrepute.

I have had to defer the introduction of my announced subject until this point because there is still so little agreement about the nature of Modernism—despite general agreement about its coming and going—that I have had to place my remarks about John Steinbeck against a background of what I must remind you is purely my personal conception of what the Modernist sensibility "is" or "was." Clearly this concept must have some relationship to John Steinbeck, because his whole career is contained within this period; but what was this relationship? In my tribute to Marston LaFrance in the *Steinbeck Quarterly*, Winter 1976, I outlined my answer to this question: "Certainly there would [be a place in a study of the Modernist period] for attention to John Steinbeck, because the 'ironic vision' that LaFrance attributes to Crane is fundamentally what Steinbeck was attempting to describe through his long preoccupation with 'non-teleological thinking' and Steinbeck's fiction was marked by this intrinsically ironic outlook from the earliest known specimens (like "Saint Katy the Virgin") to *Of Mice and Men*. The quality disappeared only after whatever Pauline vision occurred on Steinbeck's private road to Damascus caused him to re-draft the work that became *The Grapes of Wrath*." I do hope that readers may have found this pronouncement intriguingly or infuriatingly inadequate; surely it needs development, and I think that this bicentennial seminar provides the opportunity that I have wanted to expand my perception of Steinbeck's relationship to our national literature and the dominant literary trend of his age.

Asked to exemplify the presentation in fiction of this "double realm of values" that characterizes the "ironic vision," one would tend to turn first to Nick Carraway's paradoxical opening comment about the title character in F. Scott Fitzgerald's *The Great Gatsby*: "When I came back from the East last autumn I felt that I wanted the world to be in uniform and at a sort of moral attention forever. . . . Only Gatsby . . . was exempt from my reaction — Gatsby, who represented everything for which I have an unaffected scorn." Because Nick Carraway is *able to perceive* that Gatsby embodies the extreme opposites of complete innocence and complete corruption rather than merely look at him and the world in terms of some "uniform" set of values, Fitzgerald's novel has come to be recognized and will probably remain unchallenged as the supreme fictional embodiment of its age; yet I am increasingly tempted, perhaps as I turn myself from the anxious impatience of youth to the resignation of middle age, to find the most poignant expression of this ironic vision in Willa Cather's final description of the protagonist of that neglected novel of our own time that is finally winning proper respect as the age it castigatingly depicts passes, *The Professor's House* (1925), "He had never learned to live without delight. And he would have to learn to, just as, in a Prohibition country, he supposed he would have to learn to live without sherry. Theoretically he knew that life is possible, may be even pleasant, without joy, without passionate griefs. But it had never occurred to him that he might have to live like that."

Yet one can only do just as well in Steinbeck. In the framework around *The Pastures of Heaven*, he presents a vision that is in every way the match of Fitzgerald's and Willa Cather's and that justifies our placing him beside these luminaries as among those artists gifted with the power not just to look at their times, but to see *through* them: a sightseeing bus has brought a group of tourists to an eminence from which it may view the beautiful valley called "The Pastures of Heaven." As they express their admiration, the bus driver meditates, "I always like to look down there and think how quiet and easy a man could live on a little place." But before we hear this speech, we have been "down there" in a series of episodes that reveal how the troubled lives of the inhabitants perceived close up belie the distant promise of their valley.

I have also already summarized the relationship of Steinbeck to his age in a message celebrating the tenth anniversary of the John Steinbeck Society in the *Steinbeck Quarterly* (Summer–Fall 1976), in which I point out that from *Cup of Gold* to *Of Mice and Men*, "He presented an outraged but defeatist picture of man as victim of an established world he never made — of man whose only escape apart from death lies in forging a solipsistic world from his private fantasies." It would require papers as long as this to explore thoroughly the Modernist elements in each of these early Steinbeck works; but here I would like to try to suggest how all of these works that were originally praised for their differences present aspects of a single vision. I do this to show how they connect Steinbeck to the characteristic sensibility of this time and how each contributed to the development of this relationship.

I have spoken so often in my earlier writings of Henry Morgan's key speech late in *Cup of Gold* that those who have read them may become restive; yet I cannot enough emphasize the importance of his remark when, having become a West Indian government official, he condemns to death some of his former pirate associates — "Civilization will split up a character, and he who refuses to split goes under." His cynical resignation sums up not only the dilemma of Steinbeck's own characters of this period, but what I have tried to indicate is the characteristic plight of man during the Modernist period: he longs to be one thing, but our reductivist culture condemns him to be only a fragment of himself of the kind most trenchantly realized in Elmer Rice's play *The Adding Machine* and Fritz Lang's film *Metropolis*. The correctly depreciated *Cup of Gold* — for it is not a strong work — is a rare thing, a swashbuckling tragedy. When Henry Morgan leaves his native England, he promises he will return, when he becomes "whole again," but he never does, because he can never reconcile the Romantic and the practical aspects of himself. The climax of the book occurs when, after successfully sacking the city of Panama, "the cup of gold," he is told by a woman that he has taken prisoner that he is "no realist at all, but a bungling romancer." Infuriated, he exacts his revenge by returning her to her husband for a ransom; but she tells him that he has "pricked the dream on which my heavy spirit floated" and that he "will turn no more vain dreams into unsatisfactory conquests." Morgan has realized that he cannot both fulfill his dreams and have wealth and security, so that he does "split." A pre-Modernist would have either sacrificed himself for his single vision of Romantic glory or smugly accepted his wealth and security like Rockefeller and Carnegie and other American "robber barons." Steinbeck's Henry Morgan, like Willa Cather's

Professor St. Peter and Fitzgerald's Nick Carraway, reconciles himself to the life that is "pleasant" without joy, but Steinbeck reads this as a defeat for the spirit, which in the end simply fades away.

Steinbeck's other early works all repeat this same pattern: either the unreconciled Romantic with a single vision is destroyed, or else a cynical "Realist" is willing to "split" and accept life without joy; sometimes both. I have already commented upon the framework surrounding the stories that make up the cycle of *The Pastures of Heaven*. As I have explained at length in *John Steinbeck*, the Romantic dreamers in the nine stories are all defeated at last by the "curse" of the Bert Munroe family — and this "curse" is that the Munroes with the pre-Modernist kind of single vision never "know the right thing to say or do," yet continually push themselves into positions in which they influence the lives of others. A key episode occurs in the story of Junius Maltby and his son, which Steinbeck valued sufficiently to publish separately under the title "Nothing So Monstrous," when Mrs. Munroe pushes unwanted charity on the Maltbys, because she thinks that the son's "health is more important than his feelings." Again, we see Kierkegaard's point perfectly dramatized: the representative of narrow, imperceptive establishment values, the "infinitely abstracting" Mrs. Munro sees the boy only in terms of his "health," but Junius Maltby, dedicated to the inward "ethical requirements," placed the integrity of individual "feeling" before such societal bonds. (We might recall here another Modernist satirist's observation — e. e. cummings's in a poem in which he observes that "Since feeling is first / Who pays any attention / to the syntax of things / Will never wholly kiss you.")

In *To a God Unknown*, Joseph Wayne remains faithful to his vision, but only to die for it. The "Modernism" of the work is apparent from the priest's final verdict on Wayne, "Thank God he has no will to be remembered, to be believed in, else there might be a new Christ here in the West." But there are no new Christs in this declining West; and he who will not "split" must go under. Exactly the same thing happens in *Tortilla Flat*. Comic as the work may appear on the surface, it is written in the valedictory spirit of its inspiration *Morte d'Arthur*; and after Danny pronounces, "I will find the Enemy who is worthy of Danny!" and stalks out, his friends "heard his roaring challenge. . . . And then, behind the house in the gulch, they heard an answering challenge so fearful and chill that their spines wilted like nasturtium stems under frost. . . . They heard Danny charge to the fray. They heard his last shrill cry of defiance, and then a thump. And then silence."

The Red Pony cycle seems a reversal, because Jody challenges his grandfather's defeat with the speculation that the boy may someday himself become a "leader of the people." Yet he is reduced at the end of the stories to the ambiguous gestures of mouse-hunting and offering the small compensation of a lemonade to his disgruntled elder. Looked at from the viewpoint of Modernism, the grandfather's famous injunction about "westering" takes on a new, painful significance. "It wasn't getting here that mattered, it was movement and westering," he tells Jody; but he feels that "westering" has died out among the people. The single vision is dead, and the old man is defeated. Steinbeck shares his despair, but not his defeat, for with this ironic authorial vision he sees that while the possibility of realizing the dream no longer exists as it did in the nineteenth century, the dream itself lives on in Jody. The grandfather cannot separate internal vision and external action; but the grandson sees that we no longer live in such simple, active times and that we may have to retreat into our heads to retain the integrity of our dreams.

Two marvelous fables that have already proved capable of many readings, *In Dubious Battle* and *Of Mice and Men*, assume new significance when viewed in the light of Modernist theorizing. Both confront with a tough-mindedness rare in American fiction the painful defeat of dream, what Kierkegaard would call the overwhelming of "the infinite accentuation inwardly of the individual in relation to the ethical requirement" by gross materialistic pressures, which "infinitely abstract externally from the personal ego." In both fictions, the conditions of modern society destroy the dreamer. In *In Dubious Battle* not only is the naively idealistic Jim Nolan exploitatively destroyed by the very radical cause to which he is attracted to find meaning in his life, but even more depressing is the portrayal of Doc Burton, "dreamer, mystic, metaphysician,"—distrustful of all simplistic schemes and striving for complete self-consciousness—simply disappearing as a result of his selfless effort to help the strikers despite his distrust of their simplistic goals. Steinbeck's use of "dubious" in his title indicates his distrust of the merits of both battling contenders; and he writes not in hope of partisan victory, but to lament the tragic loss in such battle of even the man of good will who has transcended partisanship. Similarly in *Of Mice and Men*, the dreamer is doomed to defeat. The key to the novel, however, is not the black stableman Crooks' cynical observation that "Nobody never gets to heaven; and nobody gets no land"; but the serene moment after the harrowing killing, in which Steinbeck describes Curley's wife lying "with a half-covering of yellow hay. And the meanness and the plannings and the discontent and the ache for attention were all gone from her face."

"The meanness and the plannings and the discontent and the ache for attention": these are the visible symbols of the characteristic alienation of the Modernist period. When shall they be gone from our faces and by what magic removed? For the characters in Steinbeck's blackest work, only in death! Every evidence indicates that Steinbeck intended the book once called *L'Affaire Lettuceberg*, then retitled *The Grapes of Wrath*, to follow up and confirm the example of *In Dubious Battle* and *Of Mice and Men*; but about halfway through the project he wrote to his publishers that although the book was finished, "it is a bad book and I must get rid of it," because "My whole work drive has been aimed at making people understand each other and then I deliberately write this book, the aim of which is to cause hatred through partial understanding" (Lisca, *The Wide World of John Steinbeck*, p. 147). Interestingly, he objected to writing satire, because it "restricted" the picture, what Kierkegaard described as "abstracting" from the personal ego. Steinbeck had rejected the Modernist double vision with its defeatist implications. He was never to return to this vision, although his early novels, which established his reputation, are almost models of the alienated Modernist sensibility, displaying (to take just one example, in *Tortilla Flat*) all the characteristics that Maurice Beebe lists — the formalistic structure and mythological order borrowed from the *Morte d'Arthur* and the detachment and concern with composition exemplified by his self-conscious explanations of the structuring of the work, as well as — surely as powerfully as possible — the effort to free one's self from the middle class that Lionel Trilling had found "the chief intention of all modern literature." Although this Modernist sensibility was to continue to dominate our literature until the early 1970s, Steinbeck had abandoned it by 1938 before the publication of what remains his most monumental work.

There is not time on this occasion to describe fully what came afterwards, where Steinbeck moved from Modernism; but the question is of such large importance to the development of our literature that I feel obliged to add to this discussion of Steinbeck and Modernism a postscript outlining the viewpoints that dominated his subsequent works and especially my concept of an important cause for the decline in the power of his work that it is widely agreed occurred after World War II.

What Steinbeck did in reshaping *L'Affaire Lettuceberg* into *The Grapes of Wrath* was to transcend the ironic detachment of Modernism with a new affirmative conception of individual regeneration. Elsewhere I have argued that the Joad story in the novel portrays "the education of the heart." The Joads have failed to achieve full self-realization, not because of their persecution by a soulless society, but because they themselves have had the expansion of their consciousness limited by the reductivist concept of "family": "Use'ta be the fambly was fust," Ma Joad tells a neighbor at the final turning-point of the story, "It ain't so now. It's anybody." Under the power of preacher Casy's example, the Joads have come to realize that "it's all men an' all women we love." Although the term would not have been used then, *The Grapes of Wrath* is a fiction of consciousness-raising.

Nor is it Steinbeck's only one. The later *Cannery Row* (1945) presents through Steinbeck's portrayal of Doc, modeled on his friend Ed Ricketts, a living example of heightened consciousness. As I explain at the end of my chapter on *Cannery Row* in *John Steinbeck* (1975), "the novel is about the man who has learned with the assistance of art to triumph over his immediate sensations and surroundings, to move from Monterey to 'the cosmic Monterey.' . . . He has learned to find compensation for the frailties of human nature and other aspects of a physically imperfect universe in what William Butler Yeats calls 'monuments of unaging intellect.' "

Although literary critics have conceded that we have entered a "Post-Modernist" period and there are even journals exploring its literature, there is even less agreement about the nature of this writing than the Modernist and most literary historians are likely to go along with Maurice Beebe's judgment that "it is difficult to point to successful works of literature" which embody the new sensibility. There is a widespread feeling, however that whatever direction Post-Modernism takes, the growing emphasis will be — as it has been during the past few years — on consciousness-raising techniques and the implications for a bankrupt industrial culture of transcendentalist philosophies, especially of Eastern origin. Should this speculation indeed prove true, John Steinbeck may be seen on the strength of *The Grapes of Wrath* and *Cannery Row* as one of the significant prophets of Post-Modernism, as Edgar Allen Poe, for example, was a remarkable precursor of Modernism. Yet, Steinbeck did not persist in developing this new vision in his own work; instead he went, after World War II, into what almost all critics have recognized as a marked decline in his artistic power.

What happened? Actually, I think that there were foreshadowings of this decline even in the short works between *The Grapes of Wrath* and *Cannery Row — The Forgotten Village, Bombs Away,* and *The Moon Is Down* — all of which emphasize, among other things, the strengthening of traditional societal bonds through technological know-how in medicine and munitions. The pivotal example is, however, I believe, the work that I have at other times argued really marks the turnabout in Steinbeck's career, *The Pearl*. While, on the one hand, Kino and Juana do transcend materialistic obsessions by discarding the great pearl and the worldly ambitions it fostered, they, on the other hand, also do not continue their flight from the past but turn back to try to resume their old roles in their traditional community. They do not — like the Joads and Doc in *Cannery Row* — aspire to transcend the Modernist waste land, but rather seek to compromise with the past.

The same thing happens in all of Steinbeck's succeeding works except the relatively frivolous *Short Reign of Pippin IV* (1957). In *The Wayward Bus* (1947), the bus-driver with the suspicious initials J. C. gives up his dream of flight and returns to his passengers and his troubled wife; the whole lumbering structure of *East of Eden* (1952) turns at last upon the extension of an enlightened patriarchal blessing to an errant son; and in Steinbeck's last novel, *The Winter of Our Discontent* (1961), Ethan Allen Hawley finally overcomes the temptation to commit suicide that would have turned this work into a late reversion to the alienation of the Modernist sensibility by accepting the very primary obligation to "fambly" that the Joads rejected in *The Grapes of Wrath*. Most distressingly, in

Sweet Thursday (1954), Steinbeck takes the very character of Doc, who embodied a transcendent consciousness in *Cannery Row*, and reduces him to a two-dimensional harlequin who needs the consolation of a stereotyped love affair to rescue him from the vapors.

I choose that last term quite deliberately to emphasize the "nineteenth-century quality" of these late Steinbeck fictions. What they represent is a complete swing of the pendulum from his foreshadowing of Post-Modernism to his embracing of a Pre-Modernist, Victorian compromise with traditional establishments, a tendency that reaches an almost self-parodying extreme in the strident defenses of law and order in the uncollected "Letters to Alicia" (who turns out to be a dead woman). Like Nick Carraway in Fitzgerald's *The Great Gatsby*, the final vision expressed through Steinbeck's writing was a wish for "the world to be in uniform and at a sort of moral attention forever."

Now, our sentiments in this matter are bound to vary, and it is not my intention to condemn Steinbeck for his aging desire to return to what he may have begun to fancy a better past. But I must say that such an effort to turn the clock back has simply never worked. I do think that Thomas Wolfe was right when he observed that "You can't go home again"; and I do think also that a turning from the prospects of the future to the consolations of an imagined past means artistic death. Steinbeck's artistry declined when he ceased — in William Blake's term — to "build Jerusalem"; yet, as I have argued on other occasions and for different reasons, his early triumphs cannot be written off because of the disappointment of his later work. In any study of Literary Modernism — now that the Modernist era has itself become part of history rather than one in which we are immersed — he must be recognized as an artist who gave this alienated sensibility some of its most powerful and tough-minded embodiments; and I think, too, that he will continue to be honored as the writer who in the two works that crown his career experienced flickeringly a sensibility prophetic of a different future, though he could not sustain this light.

INDEX

Aaron, Daniel: "The Radical Humanism of John Steinbeck," 9
Adams, Brooks, 97, 98
Adams, J. Donald: *The Shape of Books to Come*, 5
"L'Affaire Lettuceberg," 63, 69, 70
Agrarianism. *See* Jeffersonian agarianism
Allegory, 10, 13, 28, 41, 51, 63
Allen, Mary: *Animals in American Literature*, 14
Allen, Walter, 8
Ambivalence, 8–9, 141
American Dream, 4, 104, 111
American Literary Scholarship, 3
Angoff, Charles: "In the Great Tradition," 33–35
Animal imagery, 2, 8, 14, 118, 119
Arvin Sanitary Camp. *See* Weedpatch
Associated Farmers, 36, 55
Astro, Richard, 11

Balogun, F. Odun, 14
"Battle Hymn of the Republic, The," 26, 70–71, 92
Beach, Joseph Warren, 4
Beatty, Sandra, 12
Benson, Jackson J., 12, 13, 14, 15; "The Background to the Composition of *The Grapes of Wrath*," 51–74
Bernanos, Georges: *Diary of My Times*, 37
Berry, J. Wilkes, 10
Bible: language of, 36, 37, 84, 113–14, 117; motifs, 7–8, 9, 12, 13, 116–17; structure of, and *Grapes of Wrath*, 34
Biological realism, 2
Biology, 6, 9, 14, 89, 90, 91
Birney, Earle: "A Must Book," 29–30
Bluefarb, Sam, 10
Bluestone, George: *Novels into Film*, 6–7

Boren, Lyle H., 4
Bowden, Edwin T.: *The Dungen of the Heart*, 7
Bowdon, Dorris, 131
Bowron, Bernard, 6
Boynton, Percy H.: *America in Contemporary Fiction*, 4
Bracher, Frederick: "Steinbeck and the Biological View of Man," 6
Brasch, James D., 12
Bredahl, A. Carl, 11
Britch, Carroll, 15
Britch, Carroll and Cliff Lewis: "Growth of the Family in *The Grapes of Wrath*," 97–108
Brown, Joyce Compton, 14
Browning, Chris: "Grape Symbolism in *The Grapes of Wrath*," 9
Burgum, Edwin Berry: "The Sensibility of John Steinbeck," 5
Burns, Stuart L., 11

Caldwell, Mary Ellen, 11
Calverton, V. F., 4
Canaan, 112, 115
Cannon, Gerald, 7
Carlson, Eric W., 7
Carpenter, Frederic I.: "The Philosophical Joads," 4, 5
Carr, Duane R., 11
Casy, Jim, 2, 6, 29, 35, 38, 39, 88, 89, 142; as Christ figure 9, 12, 14, 28, 33, 92; and community, 91, 98, 99, 100, 101, 102, 103, 128, 131; in film, 126, 129, 130, 134, 135; and martyrdom, 8; source for, 53; and Tom, 106, 111
Chametzky, Jules: "The Ambivalent Endings of *The Grapes of Wrath*," 8–9, 124n12

163

Champney, Freeman: "John Steinbeck, Californian," 6
Christ, 8, 34, 40, 92
Christ figure, 8, 9, 12, 28, 33, 34, 92, 111, 134
Christianity, 4, 33; and community, 92–93
Christian perspective, 7, 10, 33, 39
Clarke, Mary Washington, 9
Collins, Tom: autobiography, 67–68; and camps, 57–58, 61, 71–72; and dedication, 55–56, 72–73; and film, 71; and *Grapes*, 59, 60, 61; and Steinbeck, 56–57, 58, 64, 65, 66, 67
Communism, 40–41
Community, 72, 87–88, 89, 93, 126, 128; biological, 90, 91, 93–94, 97; historical, 91, 92, 97; religious, 91, 92, 93, 96, 97; social, 94–95, 96, 97
Comte, Auguste, 5, 6
Consciousness, 6, 9, 13, 14, 99, 110, 114–15, 221–22, 224
Cook, Sylvia Jenkins, 13–14; *From Tobacco Road to Route 66: The Southern Poor White in Fiction*, 12
Covici, Pascal: *The Portable Steinbeck*, 5
Covici, Pascal, Jr., 10; "John Steinbeck and the Language of Awareness," 9; *Portable Steinbeck*, 10
Cowie, Alexander, 6
Cowley, Malcolm: "American Tragedy," 27–29
Cox, Martha Heasley, 11–12, 12–13
Creation, 113, 146
Crockett, H. Kelly, 7–8

Darwell, Jane, 126, 127, 129, 130, 134, 136n1, 136–37n4, 137n16
Davis, Robert Murray, 10–11
Davis, Robert Con, 14
Death Comes for the Archbishop (Cather), 74
Degnan, James P., 10
Delisle, Arnold F., 9
De Schweinitz, George, 7
Detweiler, Robert: "Christ and the Christ Figure in American Fiction," 8
Dewey, John, 4
Dialect. *See* Language
Ditsky, John, 13, 15; "The Ending of *The Grapes of Wrath*: A Further Commentary," 116–24
Documentary interest, 1, 2
Donald, Miles: *The American Novel in the Twentieth Century*, 13

Donohue, Agnes McNeill: Crowell Casebook, 9
Don Quixote, 34
Dos Passos, John, 23, 29, 30, 43
Dostoievsky, Fyodor, 78
Dougherty, Charles T., 8
Downs, Robert B., 10
Dunn, T. F., 8
Dust Bowl, 32, 33, 52, 53–54, 61, 62, 63, 109, 111, 113, 147, 148–49; illustr., 47

East of Eden, 3, 112, 161
Eastom, Sherm, 58
Eden, 14–15, 105, 110, 111, 112, 114–15, 117, 140–41
Education, 7, 61, 104, 114, 140
Eisinger, Chester E.: "Jeffersonian Agrarianism in *The Grapes of Wrath*," 5
Elliott, Kathleen Farr, 11
Emerson, 4
Ending, 7, 8, 9, 10, 11, 29, 75, 109
Exodus, 8, 33, 43, 81, 92
Experimental works, 9, 81

Fairley, Barker, 5
Family, 10, 24, 27, 97, 109, 110, 139; and Modernism, 160; unity of, 98, 99, 100, 101, 102, 103, 108n4
Farm, 27, 60
Farmers, 23, 27, 28, 32–33, 51, 52; and Steinbeck's articles, 53–54
Farm Security Administration, 11, 54, 55, 57, 59, 72; and aid to migrants, 66
Faulkner, William, 37
Film, 6–7, 16n1, 84, 124–36
"Fingers of Cloud," 51
Fonda, Henry, 56, 124, 125, 126, 127, 132
Fontenrose, Joseph, 123; *John Steinbeck: An Introduction and Interpretation*, 8
Ford, John, 16n1, 84, 125, 130, 136, 136n1, 136–37n4
Fossey, W. Richard, 11
Freedman, William A., 8
French, Warren, 6, 11, 12, 15, 122, 137n16; "The Education of the Heart," 7; *A Companion to "The Grapes of Wrath*," 8; *John Steinbeck*, 7; "John Steinbeck and Modernism (A Speculation on His Contribution to the Development of the Twentieth-Century American Sensibility)," 152–62; *Sixteen Modern American Authors*, 3, 4; *The Social Novel at the End of an Era*, 9
Frohock, W. M.: "John Steinbeck's Men of

Wrath," 5; *The Novel of Violence in America*, 5

Gannett, Lewis, 5; *John Steinbeck: Personal and Biographical Notes*, 3
Garcia, Reloy, 10, 13
Geismar, Maxwell, 4
Genesis, 113, 117
Geography, cultural, 146; and *The Grapes of Wrath*, 139; and literature, 138–39; and migration, 140, 143; and mobility, 140, 141, 150; reluctance of, 142
Gibbs, Lincoln R.: "John Steinbeck: Moralist," 5
Gladstein, Mimi, 13, 15; "From Heroine to Supporting Player: The Diminution of Ma Joad," 124–37
Grandma, 28, 42, 131
Grandpa, 24, 28, 29, 32, 38, 42, 88, 98, 100; as Okie, 141; as migrant, 151n5; in film, 127, 128
Grapes of Wrath, The: and animal imagery, 2; and agrarianism 5–6; barred, 25–36; Bible in, 12, 34; camp in, 54, 55; characters in, 38–39; Christ figures in, 8, 9; Christianity in, 4, 7; community, 87; and Dos Passos, 23, 29, 30, 43; ending of 7, 8–9, 10, 11, 29, 116, 118, 119; as epic, 4, 24, 31, 81, 82, 112; and Exodus, 8, 81; family in, 10, 24, 27, 97, 98, 99, 101, 102, 103, 108, 109, 110, 139; and Faulkner, 29; film of, 6–7, 16n1, 84; film, 125; first version of, 63, 69, 70; first vs. second half, 24, 28; and *Gone With the Wind*, 83, 84; and Hemingway, 23, 29; house in, 9, 10; naturalism, 6; Nobel, 71; and Nobel Prize, 8; as novel, 36; opening, 112–13; and photography, 4; and Post-Modernism, 12; and Pre-Modernism, 12; as proletarian fiction, 30, 31; as propaganda, 39–40; publication of, 1, 2, 26, 35, 71, 152n8; Pulitzer Prize for, 71; reception in Britain, 74–85; reception of, 109, 147; religion, 6; reviews of, 3–15, 23–43; second, 70; as social protest, 23, 29, 31; source for, 40; Steinbeck's view of, 159–60; structure, 113; symbols, 109; theme of, 4, 7, 8, 32, 76, 97; title, 26, 70–71; turtle, 9, 11, 41, 89, 90, 98, 104, 105; and *Uncle Tom's Cabin*, 23, 29; voices in, 2; women in, 12; writing of, 12
Grapewin, Charley, 124, 127, 137n10

Graves, Muley, 27, 87–88, 98, 103, 104, 114, 124, 142–43, 151–52n6
Gray, James: *On Second Thought*, 5
Great Depression, 1, 147
Great Gatsby, The, 156
Griffin, Robert J., 8
Groene, Horst, 12
Gurko, Leo: *The Angry Decade*, 6

Harvest Gypsies, The, 62
Hauck, Richard B., 9
Hayashi, Tetsumaro, 9, 125–26, "The Function of the Joad Clan in *The Grapes of Wrath*," 9; *A New Steinbeck Bibliography*, 3; *Study Guide*, 11
Hedrick, Joan, 14
Hemingway, 29, 37, 83
Highway 66, 28, 65, 144, 145; illustr., 49
Hoffman, Frederick, 6
Hopfe, Lewis Moore, 12
House image, 9, 10, 88, 89, 90, 99, 129, 142–43, 146
Hugo, Victor, 78
Hunter, J. Paul, 8

Individualism, 2, 29, 32, 40–41, 75, 77, 78, 98, 108, 110, 114, 128; economic, 104
In Dubious Battle, 1, 6, 26, 30, 42, 63, 81; and *Grapes of Wrath*, 30, 51–53, 110; and Modernism, 159
Intercalary chapters, 28, 31, 32–33, 40, 81; and biology, 90; and community, 89, 91; community in, 95–96, 97; and desentimentalization, 109–10; and destruction of fruit, 147–48; as epic, 4; migration in, 79, 152n7; and Old Testament, 92; truck stop in, 11; turtle in, 89; Wilson, 131; and cultural geography, 139, 142, 143
Irony, 3, 106
"Is" — Thinking. *See* Non-teleological thinking

Jackson, Frank H.: "Economics in Literature," 7
Jackson, Joseph Henry, 98
James, William, 4
Jeffersonian agrarianism, 5–6, 12, 111
Jerusalem, 14, 115
Joad, Al, 12, 42, 105; character of, 24, 111; role in family, 100, 103, 106–7, 130, 135
Joad family, 24, 31, 32, 34, 42, 77; ances-

166   Index

try of, 91–92; at ending, 122; in film, 135; identity of, 98; as migrants, 110, 111, 114–15; model for, 58; unity of, 99–101, 107–8

Joad, Ma, 24, 29, 34, 35, 38, 42, 89; assertion of, 120–21; character of, 111, 132, 133, 134, 135; as "citadel", 99, 103, 125, 127–30; in film, 125, 126, 127, 130, 132, 133, 134, 135, 136; as Okie, 141; and Tom, 126–27

Joad, Noah, 102

Joad, Rivers, Connie, 101, 107

Joad, Tom, 14, 27, 93, 121; as picaresque saint, 7; as walking man, 114; source for, 52–53; and community, 90–91

Johnson, Nunnally, 130, 131, 132

Jones, Lawrence William, 11

Journalistic fidelity, 3

Jude the Obscure, 34

Kazin, Alfred: *On Native Grounds*, 4

Kehl, D. G., 11

Kierkegaard, 155, 158, 159, 160

Kiernan, Thomas, 13

Klammer, Enno, 8

Kronenberger, Louis: "Hungry Caravan," 23–25

Kuhl, Art: "Mostly of *The Grapes of Wrath*," 36–42

Kunitz, Stanley: "Wine Out of These Grapes," 35–36

Lange, Dorothea, 11

Language, 5, 29–30, 31, 35–36, 36–38, 78–79, 81, 89; biblical, 84, 113, 117

Leaves of Grass, 74, 76

Levant, Howard, 11

Levenson, Samuel: "The Compassion of John Steinbeck," 4

Lewis, Cliff, 15

Lewis, R. W. B.: "The Picaresque Saint," 7

Life on the Mississippi, 74

Lisca, Peter, 9, 10, 15; "The Dynamics of Community in *The Grapes of Wrath*," 87–97; "*The Grapes of Wrath* as Fiction," 7; *John Steinbeck: Nature and Myth*, 13

Lojek, Helen, 14

Long Valley, The, 26

Lutwack, Leonard, 10, 126

Machine/animal motifs, 5–6, 8, 94, 95, 114

MacLeish, Archibald: "Land of the Free," 27

Manself, 4, 40–41, 89, 91, 93, 96, 97, 98, 99, 102, 131

Marks, Lester J.: *Thematic Design in the Novels of John Steinbeck*, 9

Marshall, Margaret, 4

Martin, Stoddard, 14

Matriarchy, 14, 121, 125–26, 128, 131; and film, 125, 126, 127, 128, 130

Matton, Collin G., 10

McCarthy, Paul, 9, 10, 13

McElderry, B. R., Jr.: "*The Grapes of Wrath*: In the Light of Modern Critical Theory," 5

McKiddy, Cicil, 52, 68

McWilliams, Carey, 65–66; *Factories in the Fields*, 4–5, 36

Migrants, 23–24, 29, 33, 111; culpability of, 111–12; fate of, 114; in film, 132; government aid for, 66; and Israelites, 92–93; Joads as, 110, 111; Steinbeck's view of, 2, 51–55, 60–62

Migration, 23–24, 27, 28, 112, 114, 123; and Californians, 147, 148, 149, 150; and European refugees, 76; goal of 140–41; hardship of, 142–44; illustr., 48; camps, 146; and Modernism, 158–59; and Steinbeck, 64; transportation in, 145

Les Misérables, 30, 75

Mizener, Arthur: "Does a Moral Vision of the Thirties Deserve a Nobel Prize?", 8

Mobility, 140, 142, 144, 147, 150

Moby-Dick, 34, 74, 76

Modernism: definition of, 153–54; irony in, 154–55; and Steinbeck, 155–56, 157, 160; in works, 157, 158, 159, 160, 161

Moloney, Michael F., 6

Monroe, N. Elizabeth: *The Novel and Society*, 4

Moore, Harry Thornton, 3–4

Morte d'Arthur, 51, 158, 160

Moseley, Edwin M., 8

Mother, 126, 127, 132, 135, 136; earth, 14, 111

Motion picture. See Film

Motley, Warren, 14, 126, 128

Mullen, Patrick B., 13

Myth, 12, 14, 51, 112, 115, 126

Naturalism, 6

Nevius, Blake, 6

Nimitz, Jack, 9–10

Nobel Prize, 8, 71
Non-teleological thinking, 5, 110, 113, 156

O'Connor, Richard, 10
Of Mice and Men, 26, 30, 31, 42; family
in, 103; film, 125; irony in, 156; lan-
guage in, 37–38; publication of, 63–64
Okies, 2, 5, 28, 42, 52, 54, 55, 56; and
national character, 104
Otis, Elizabeth, 66, 68, 69, 70
Oversoul. *See* Manself
Owens, Louis, 15; "The Culpable Joads:
Desentimentalizing *The Grapes of
Wrath*," 108–16; *John Steinbeck's Re-
vision of America*, 14–15

Panorama, 77, 109, 112, 113
Pastures of Heaven, The, 51, 156–67
Patriarchy, 14, 88–89, 121, 125–26, 128; in
film, 125, 126, 127, 128, 130, 136
Perez, Betty, 10
Philosophy, 2, 8, 39, 82
Photography, 4, 11, 14
Picaresque, 7, 40
Pollock, Theodore, 119; "On the Ending
of *The Grapes of Wrath*," 7
Post-Modernism, 12, 161
Pratt, John Clark, 10
Pratt, Linda Ray, 12
Pre-Modernism, 12, 162
Pressman, Richard S., 14
Professor's House, The (Cather), 156
Proletarian fiction, 4, 13–14, 24, 30, 31,
41, 43
Promised Land, 28, 110, 115
Propaganda, 7, 39–40, 76, 79, 82, 84; and
In Dubious Battle, 53
Propaganda novel, 4
Pulitzer Prize, 71

Qualen, John, 124

Rahv, Philip: [Review of *The Grapes of
Wrath*], 30–31
Rascoe, Burton, "But . . . Not . . . Fer-
dinand," 25–26
Realism, 2, 4, 13, 32, 79, 82
Reamer, Sis, 52, 68
Red Pony, The, 26, 112, 116
Reed, John R., 10
Religion, 6, 89, 93
Resettlement Administration. *See* Farm
Security Administration
Revolutionary, 4, 30, 31, 70

Ricketts, Edward F., 6, 160; *The Log
from the Sea of Cortez*, 113
Rose of Sharon, 28, 35, 42, 93, 117; char-
acter of, 111; and ending, 121, 122,
123; in film, 125, 131–32; as statuary,
118, 119
Ross, Woodburn O., 5, 6; "John Steinbeck:
Naturalism's Priest," 6
Route 66. *See* Highway 66
Rundell, Walter, Jr.: "*The Grapes of
Wrath*: Steinbeck's Image of the West,"
8
Ruthie, 29, 99, 100, 103, 105, 107

St. Pierre, Brian, 14
Salinas Lettuce Strike, 62–63
Salter, Christopher L., 13, 15; "John
Steinbeck's *The Grapes of Wrath* as a
Primer for Cultural Geography," 138–52
Sarris, Andrew, 128
Schramm, Wilbur L.: "Careers at Cross-
road," 42–43
Sentimentality, 5, 6, 61, 79, 80, 109, 115
Shaw, Patrick W., 14
Shloss, Carol, 14
Shockley, Martin, 5, 7
Simmonds, Roy S., 15; *Steinbeck's Liter-
ary Achievement*, 12; "The Reception of
The Grapes of Wrath in Britain: A
Chronological Survey of Contemporary
Reviews," 74–86
Slade, Leonard A., Jr., 9
Slochower, Harry: *No Voice is Wholly
Lost*, 5
Steinbeck, Carol (author's first wife), 52,
53, 63, 69; and title, 70, 71
Steinbeck, John: and Agee, 12; and
Bernanos, 37; and Comte, 5, 6; and
Crane, 34; and *In Dubious Battle*, 26,
51–53; and Faulkner, 37; and *To a God
Unknown*, 51; and *The Grapes of
Wrath*, 1, 152; and Hawthorne, 34; and
Hemingway, 25, 37; and Lawrence, 10;
and *The Long Valley*, 26; and Melville,
34; and migrants, 53, 54, 58, 59, 62;
and *Of Mice and Men*, 26; and Natha-
nael West, 12; and Norris, 34; and *The
Pastures of Heaven*, 51; and *The Red
Pony*, 26; and Ricketts, 11; and Sa-
royan, 37; and *Tortilla Flat*, 26; and
Wolfe, 42
Steinbeck Quarterly, 3
Steinbeck Society, 116, 157
Stovall, Floyd: *American Idealism*, 5

Structure, 14, 32, 70, 71, 128, 139
Stuckey, W. J., 9
Swan, Kenneth D., 12
Symbolism, 41–42, 109

Taylor, Walter Fuller: "*The Grapes of Wrath* Reconsidered," 7
Tedlock, E. W., and C. V. Wicker: *Steinbeck and His Critics: A Record of Twenty-Five Years*, 6, 16n2
Their Blood is Strong, 3
Timmerman, John H., 15
To a God Unknown, 51, 113
Toland, Gregg, 124
Tortilla Flat, 26, 38, 42, 125
Trachtenberg, Stanley, 12
Travels with Charley, 3
Trilling, Lionel, 298–99
Tristram Shandy, 36
Turtle, 9, 11, 41, 89, 90, 98; and Tom, 104, 105
Tuttleton, James W., 9

Uncle John, 24, 27, 30, 35, 89, 115
Uncle Tom's Cabin, 29, 30
U.S. Route 66. *See* Highway 66

Valjean, Nelson, 12
Vassilowitch, John, Jr., 13
Vaughan, James N.: [Review of *The Grapes of Wrath*], 32–33

Walcutt, Charles Child: *American Literary Naturalism: A Divided Stream*, 6
Watkins, Floyd C.: "Flat Wine from *The Grapes of Wrath*," 12
Watt, F. W.: *John Steinbeck*, 7, 8
Weedpatch, 54, 55, 56, 93; Steinbeck's visit to, 56–57, 62; illustr., 50
Weeks, Donald: "Steinbeck Against Steinbeck," 6
Wells, H. G., 75, 76
Westering. *See* Migration
Whicher, George F.: *The Literature of the American People*, 6
Whitman, Walt, 4
Williams, William Appleman: "Steinbeck in Perspective," 12
Wilson, Edmund, 109, 118, 119; "The Boys in the Back Room," 2, 4, 5
Wilsons, The, 129, 130–31
Winfield, 29, 98, 99, 100, 103, 105, 107, 134
Winter of Our Discontent, 161
Women, 12, 13, 14, 88–89, 126; biology, 118, 120; in film, 125, 133–34, 136; reversal of, 100, 107, 120–21
Woodress, James: "John Steinbeck: Hostage to Fortune," 8
Woollcott, Alexander, 74–75, 76
Wyatt, Bryant N., 9
Wyatt, David, 14

Zola, Émile, 35, 77, 78, 82
Zollman, Sol, 10